Fodor's InFocus

NAPA AND SONOMA

1st Edition

Fodor's Travel Publications   New York, Toronto, London, Sydney, Auckland
www.fodors.com

Be a Fodor's Correspondent

Your opinion matters. It matters to us. It matters to your fellow Fodor's travelers, too. And we'd like to hear it. In fact, we *need* to hear it. When you share your experiences and opinions, you become an active member of the Fodor's community. Here's how you can help improve Fodor's for all of us.

Tell us when we're right. We rely on local writers to give you an insider's perspective. But our writers and staff editors also depend on you. Your positive feedback is a vote to renew our recommendations for the next edition.

Tell us when we're wrong. We update most of our guides every year. But things change. If any of our descriptions are inaccurate or inadequate, we'll incorporate your changes in the next edition and will correct factual errors at fodors.com *immediately*.

Tell us what to include. You probably have had fantastic travel experiences that aren't yet in Fodor's. Why not share them with a community of like-minded travelers? Share your discoveries and experiences with everyone directly at fodors.com. Your input may lead us to add a new listing or a higher recommendation.

Give us your opinion instantly at our feedback center at www.fodors.com/feedback. You may also e-mail editors@fodors.com with the subject line "Napa and Sonoma Editor." Or send your nominations, comments, and complaints by mail to Napa and Sonoma Editor, Fodor's, 1745 Broadway, New York, NY 10019.

Happy Traveling!

Tim Jarrell, Publisher

FODOR'S IN FOCUS NAPA AND SONOMA

Editors: Doug Stallings, *series editor*; John Rambow

Editorial Contributor: Sharron Wood

Production Editor: Carrie Parker

Maps & Illustrations: David Lindroth and Mark Stroud, *cartographers*; Bob Blake and Rebecca Baer, *map editors;* William Wu, *information graphics*

Design: Fabrizio La Rocca, *creative director*; Guido Caroti, *art director*; Tina Malaney, Nora Rosansky, Chie Ushio, Jessica Walsh, Ann McBride, *designers*; Melanie Marin, *senior picture editor*

Cover Photo: (Vineyard near Hopland, Mendocino County) Gary Crabbe/ Enlightened Images Photography

Production Manager: Angela L. McLean

COPYRIGHT

1st Edition

ISBN 978-1-4000-0493-5

SPECIAL SALES

This book is available for special discounts for bulk purchases for sales promotions or premiums. Special editions, including personalized covers, excerpts of existing books, and corporate imprints, can be created in large quantities for special needs. For more information, write to Special Markets/ Premium Sales, 1745 Broadway, MD 6-2, New York, NY 10019, or e-mail specialmarkets@randomhouse.com.

AN IMPORTANT TIP & AN INVITATION

Although all prices, opening times, and other details in this book are based on information supplied to us at press time, changes occur all the time in the travel world, and Fodor's cannot accept responsibility for facts that become outdated or for inadvertent errors or omissions. **So always confirm information when it matters,** especially if you're making a detour to visit a specific place. Your experiences—positive and negative—matter to us. If we have missed or misstated something, **please write to us.** We follow up on all suggestions. Contact the Napa and Sonoma editor at editors@fodors. com or c/o Fodor's at 1745 Broadway, New York, NY 10019.

PRINTED IN CHINA

10 9 8 7 6 5 4 3 2 1

CONTENTS

ABOUT THIS BOOK

Our Ratings

We wouldn't recommend a place that wasn't worth your time, but sometimes a place is so experiential that superlatives don't do it justice: you just have to be there to know. These sights, properties, and experiences get our highest rating, **Fodor's Choice**, indicated by orange stars throughout this book. Black stars highlight sights and properties we deem **Highly Recommended**, places that our writers, editors, and readers praise again and again for consistency and excellence.

Credit Cards

Want to pay with plastic? **AE, D, DC, MC, V** after restaurant and hotel listings indicate whether American Express, Discover, Diners Club, MasterCard, and Visa are accepted.

Restaurants

Unless we state otherwise, restaurants are open for lunch and dinner daily. We mention dress only when there's a specific requirement and reservations only when they're essential or not accepted—it's always best to book ahead.

Hotels

Unless we tell you otherwise, you can assume that the hotels have private bath, phone, TV, and air-conditioning. We always list facilities but not whether you'll be charged an extra fee to use them, so when pricing accommodations, find out what's included.

Many Listings
- ★ Fodor's Choice
- ★ Highly recommended
- ⊠ Physical address
- ✛ Directions
- ⌂ Mailing address
- ☎ Telephone
- 🖷 Fax
- ⊕ On the Web
- ✉ E-mail
- 🎟 Admission fee
- ☉ Open/closed times
- Ⓜ Metro stations
- ⊟ Credit cards

Hotels & Restaurants
- 🏨 Hotel
- ⇔ Number of rooms
- ⚘ Facilities
- ¶◎¶ Meal plans
- ✕ Restaurant
- ⇧ Reservations
- ⌿ Smoking
- 🄱🄿 BYOB
- ✕🏨 Hotel with restaurant that warrants a visit

Outdoors
- ⛳ Golf
- ⛺ Camping

Other
- ♨ Family-friendly
- ⇨ See also
- ⊠ Branch address
- ☞ Take note

Experience
Napa and
Sonoma

WHAT'S WHERE

1 Napa Valley. By far the best-known of the California wine regions, Napa is home to many of the biggest names in wine. Densely populated with winery after winery, especially along Highway 29 and the Silverado Trail, it's also home to many luxury accommodations and some of the country's best restaurants.

2 Carneros Region. Many visitors quickly pass through this compact region, which spans southern Napa and Sonoma counties, on their way north from San Francisco. Those who take the time to stop will discover wineries that specialize in pinot noir and chardonnay. Both grapes thrive in its comparatively cool climate.

3 Sonoma Valley. Centered on the historic town of Sonoma, the Sonoma Valley is slightly less developed and glitzy than Napa. Still, in addition to a plethora of winery tasting rooms, there's no shortage of inns, bed-and-breakfasts, and fairly casual restaurants serving hearty California cuisine.

4 Northern Sonoma County. Ritzy little Healdsburg, called "Beverly Healdsburg" by locals who remember when it wasn't much more than a small farming town, is a popular home base for exploring the winding roads that follow the Russian River, as well as the delightfully rural Dry Creek and Alexander valleys.

NAPA AND SONOMA PLANNER

Getting Around	Timing
Driving your own car is by far the best way to explore the Wine Country. Well-maintained roads zip through the centers of the Napa and Sonoma valleys, and scenic routes thread through the backcountry. Distances between towns are fairly short, and you can sometimes drive from one end of the Napa or Sonoma valleys to the other in less than an hour—if there's no significant traffic. (However, it's not quite as easy as you might think to get between the two valleys, since they're divided by the Maya-camas Mountains.) This may be a relatively rural area, but the usual rush hours still apply, and high-season weekend traffic can be excruciatingly slow, especially on Route 29. ■TIP→ If you're wine tasting, either select a designated driver or be very careful of your wine intake. Local cops are quick with DUIs.	"Crush," the term used to indicate the season when grapes are picked and crushed, usually takes place in September or October, depending on the weather. From September until November the entire Wine Country celebrates its bounty with street fairs and festivals. The Sonoma County Harvest Fair, with its famous grape stomp, is held the first weekend in October. Golf tournaments, wine auctions, and art and food fairs occur throughout the fall.
	In season (April through November), Napa Valley draws crowds of tourists, and traffic along Route 29 from St. Helena to Calistoga is often backed up on weekends. The Sonoma Valley, Santa Rosa, and Healdsburg are less crowded. In season and over holiday weekends it's best to book lodging, restaurant, and winery reservations at least a month in advance. Many wineries give tours at specified times and require appointments.
	To avoid crowds, visit the Wine Country during the week and get an early start (most wineries open around 10). Because many wineries close as early as 4 or 4:30—and almost none are open past 5—you'll need to get a reasonably early start if you want to fit in more than one or two, especially if you're going to enjoy the leisurely lunch customary in the Wine Country. Summer is usually hot and dry, and autumn can be even hotter, so dress appropriately if you go during these times.

1

About the Hotels

Napa and Sonoma know the tourism ropes well; their inns and hotels range from low-key to utterly luxurious, and generally maintain high standards. Most of the bed-and-breakfasts are in historic Victorian and Spanish buildings, and the breakfast part of the equation often involves fresh local produce. The newer hotels tend to have a more modern, streamlined aesthetic and elaborate, spalike bathrooms. Many hotels and B&Bs have excellent restaurants on their grounds, and those that don't are still just a short car ride away from gastronomic bliss.

However, all of this comes with a hefty price tag. As the cost of vineyards and grapes has risen, so have lodging rates. Santa Rosa, the largest population center in the area, has the widest selection of moderately priced rooms. Try there if you've failed to reserve in advance or have a limited budget. In general, all accommodations in the area often have lower rates on weeknights, and prices are about 20% lower in winter.

On weekends, two- or even three-night minimum stays are commonly required, especially at smaller inns and B&Bs. If you'd prefer to stay a single night, though, innkeepers are usually more flexible in winter. Many B&Bs book up long in advance of the summer and fall seasons, and many of them aren't suitable for children.

About the Restaurants

Star chefs have come into the Wine Country's orbit, drawn by the area's phenomenal produce, artisanal foods, and wines. Although excellent meals can be found virtually everywhere in the region, the small town of Yountville has become a culinary crossroads under the influence of chef Thomas Keller. Keep in mind that Keller is also behind a number of more modest restaurants in town in addition to the French Laundry. Such high quality (and hype) often means high prices, but you can also find appealing, inexpensive eateries. With few exceptions (which are noted in individual restaurant listings), dress is informal. Where reservations are indicated as essential, you may need to make them several weeks in advance.

What it Costs

	¢	$	$$	$$$	$$$$
Restaurants	Under $10	$11–$14	$15–$22	$23–$30	over $30
Hotels	Under $200	$201–$250	$251–$300	$301–$400	over $400

Restaurant prices are per person for a main course at dinner, or for a prix fixe if a set menu is the only option. Hotel prices are for two people in a standard double room in high season.

TOP WINERIES

Far Niente

(A) Visitors take a tour of the 1885 stone winery and the founder's collection of gleaming classic cars before sitting down to a tasting of their famed cabernet blend and chardonnay. Although a visit here is a bit pricier than it is at most other wineries, the small size of the tour groups, the beauty of the grounds, and the quality of their wines make it worth a stop, especially if you're a fan of dessert wines (their sister property produces Dolce, one of the world's most highly regarded dessert wines).

Frog's Leap

(B) The rare winery that doesn't seem to take itself too seriously, Frog's Leap is known for its entertaining, lighthearted tours. While you learn about the winery's history and get a glimpse of the organic gardens and deluxe chicken coop, the guides aren't afraid to tell a few jokes or tell you about all the whimsically named wines they've produced. Even better, the tour is free.

Hess Collection Winery and Vineyards

(C) Before heading to the tasting room to try the excellent cabernets and chardonnays, take an hour or so to wander through owner Donald Hess's personal art collection, full of large-scale canvases and other modern artwork by important 20th-century artists such as Robert Motherwell and Frank Stella.

Iron Horse Vineyards

(D) Proving that tasting sparkling wine doesn't have to be stuffy, Iron Horse pours its bubblies (and a few still wines) at an outdoor tasting bar, where tremendous views

over the vine-covered hills make the top-notch sparklers taste even better. Especially on fair days, it's well worth the drive down a winding one-lane road near rural Forestville.

Matanzas Creek Winery

(E) The sprawling field of lavender plants next to the winery makes this winery especially beautiful in May and June, when the plants are in bloom. But the winery's lovely Asian-inspired aesthetic—a far cry from all the French châteaus and Tuscan villas you'll see everywhere else—make it delightful year-round, especially if you're a fan of sauvignon blanc, chardonnay, or merlot.

Ridge Vineyards

(F) Serious oenophiles will be familiar with Ridge, which produces some of the best cabernet sauvignon, chardonnay, and zinfandel in California. Although some of their most highly regarded wines are produced in the Santa Cruz Mountains, their tasting room in the Dry Creek Valley is a great place to learn about their wines from a friendly staff, buy a bottle, and have a picnic on their gorgeous patio.

Schramsberg

(G) One of the most entertaining tours in Napa is at sparkling wine producer Schramsberg, where a tour of their 19th-century cellars reveals millions of bottles stacked in ceiling-high piles. After you learn about how their bubblies are made using the laborious *méthode champenoise* process, and how their bottles are "riddled" (turned every few days) by hand, you can try generous samples of several during a seated tasting.

TOP EXPERIENCES

Eat at French Laundry

Reserve two months in advance to the day (or call to put your name on the waiting list and hope for the best) if you want to eat in one of the country's most celebrated restaurants, Thomas Keller's darling of the foodie world. The tab is undoubtedly steep ($250 for the fixed-price menu), but many swear it's worth it for a once-in-a-lifetime culinary experience with unparalleled service.

Visit the Culinary Institute of America

Although much of the Greystone Winery, the imposing stone building that houses the Culinary Institute of America, is limited to students and instructors, visitors with culinary aspirations can still enjoy themselves by browsing the well-stocked store (especially strong in cookbooks), eating at the restaurant, or attending one of the frequent one-hour cooking demos in the cooking theater. If you're serious about improving your kitchen skills, check their Web site for information about day- and weekend-long hands-on classes.

Stay at Meadowood Resort

For a serious dose of pampering, check into the Meadowood Resort. The service is superlative, the rooms are luxurious, and the extensive list of amenities includes a highly rated restaurant, a spa, a golf course, croquet, tennis, swimming pools, and a hiking trail. The only challenge will be leaving the grounds long enough to go wine tasting—or having enough money to pay the hefty tab.

Pack a Picnic

If the weather is even remotely cooperative, it would be a shame to pass up the chance to have a picnic. Whether you pick up a simple sandwich at a deli or assemble a lavish spread by visiting Dean & Deluca in St. Helena or Napa's Oxbow Public Market, many wineries will allow you to use their picnic tables. We note which wineries have particularly pretty facilities, but many others have them, too. Call to ask, and don't forget that it's considered good form to buy at least a bottle from the winery you're visiting.

Pamper Yourself

The Wine Country has more than its fair share of spas, from slightly rustic, peaty-smelling spots in Calistoga (known for mud baths and soaking pools filled with local mineral water) to sybaritic spas attached to luxury hotels (the Fairmont Sonoma Mission Inn & Spa has the largest). In addition to the usual menu of massages and facials, you can sometimes find body treatments that incorporate grape seeds, skins, or vines, giving your treatment a Wine Country spin.

View the Art at di Rosa

Thousands of 20th-century artworks by Northern California artists are scattered around the sprawling property at this little-known art preserve, about 5 mi from downtown Napa. Although you can see a handful of works in the gatehouse for free whenever it's open, you can also sign up for a tour (from 1 to 2½ hours) that includes a tram trip throughout the property and access to the former di Rosa residence and main gallery.

Walk Around Sonoma's Plaza

The oldest town in the Wine Country, Sonoma was founded in the early 1800s, and in 1846 it was the site of an uprising declaring independence from Mexico. Sonoma's central plaza, where children romp on the playground and their parents rest on benches in the shade, is surrounded by 19th-century adobes, some of which have been converted to shops and restaurants, others of which are small museums displaying relics from the town's past.

Drinks or Dinner at Cyrus

Healdsburg's poshest restaurant has racked up accolades in recent years. Not only is it one of Sonoma County's most elegant choices for a special dinner out, but its bar is easily the best in the Wine Country (and worth a trip even if you don't want to splurge on the restaurant). When you're ready for an expertly prepared cocktail made from fresh local produce, or a flight of spirits served by a knowledgeable bartender, make this your first stop.

Explore the Anderson Valley

If the crowds in the Wine Country ever seem oppressive, or you simply want a glimpse of the more rural side of the region, take the time to drive out to the Anderson Valley (its main town, Boonville, is about an hour from Healdsburg). After a twisting but beautiful drive along Highway 128 you'll be rewarded with winery tasting rooms that are less packed and more rustic than those elsewhere, as well as some great wines, especially chardonnay, pinot noir, and gewürztraminer, which thrive in this generally cool region.

Shop Around Healdsburg's Plaza

Healdsburg's picture-perfect main plaza is surrounded by boutiques and tasting rooms, making it a pleasant spot for a spin on a sunny afternoon. You can stock up on everything from clothing and kitchenware to gifty items at the ritzy little shops, and should hunger or thirst strike, there are plenty of restaurants, bakeries, coffee shops, and winery tasting rooms in which to fortify yourself for the rest of the afternoon.

WHEN TO GO

In high season (April through October), and on weekends and holidays during much of the year, Wine Country roads can be busy and tasting rooms can be crowded. If you prefer less hustle and bustle, tour on a weekday.

Winter

Though many visitors avoid traveling from December to March, in part because they are the wettest months in California, winter is still a good time to visit the state's wineries. In December and January, naked, spindly grapevines huddle in rows, and bright yellow mustard plants start to sprout in the vineyards. The hills turn green with velvety grass in February, and the first wildflowers spread beneath the oaks. While the vineyards lie dormant, you're more likely to meet winemakers in their tasting rooms, since they have some time to discuss their work with visitors. The tasting rooms, wineries, and inns tend to be much less busy in winter than at other times of the year, although the pace picks up a bit between Christmas and New Year's Day.

Spring

Spring is another great time to visit the wine regions because it brings even more wildflowers: golden poppies, buttercups, blue and cream irises, and red, white, blue, and yellow lupines. Wine-makers stick close to their work, because this is not only the season when they are bottling last year's vintages, but also a time of dubious weather, when late frosts can descend on the vineyards and kill the tender leaf buds. The crowds of visitors start to grow in late April, but you can still enjoy quiet moments.

Summer

If you travel between July and September, expect the days to be hot and dry. The wineries get mobbed with visitors, and so do the hotel swimming pools. If the weather is favorable, the first of the grapes, those destined for crisp white wines and sparklers, will be harvested as early as August.

Fall

Fall is both the busiest and most exciting season to watch the wineries at work. This is the time when field hands and machinery comb the vineyards for ripe clusters, trucks groan with loaded fruit bins as they lumber along the roads, and winery workers dash about, seeing to massive vats of fermenting juice. The air is heavy with the aroma of grapes. As October wears into November, the vineyards turn flaming red and burnished gold.

MAKING THE MOST OF YOUR TIME

Many first-time visitors to the Wine Country are tempted to zip from one spot to another, trying to jam as many wineries as possible into a short vacation. It's a far better strategy, however, to slow down and smell the rosés, so to speak. Still, if you're expected back at work in a couple of days, no one can blame you for wanting to maximize your wine-tasting fun. Here are some ways to do just that.

Visit on a weekday, especially if you're here May to November, to avoid traffic-clogged roads and crowded tasting rooms. (Tasting rooms are usually least crowded on Tuesday and Wednesday.)

Call ahead. If you have your heart set on visiting a specific place, double-check their hours and tour times to avoid disappointment. Better yet, choose a winery that requires reservations for a tour or tasting. Most such wineries are more efficient at scheduling visitors.

Get an early start. Tasting rooms are often deserted before 11 AM or so, when most visitors are still lingering over a second cup of coffee. On the flip side, wineries are usually most crowded between 3:30 and closing.

Get off the beaten track. In the Napa Valley, when tasting rooms along Highway 29 and the Silverado Trail are jammed, those just over the ridge, in the neighboring Pope and Chile valleys, might be nearly deserted. If you're based in Healdsburg, you might find the wineries in the nearby Russian River Valley packed to the brim, whereas the equally close ones in the Alexander Valley are comparatively quiet.

Avoid driving during rush hour. From roughly 4 to 6 PM on weekdays the cars of tourists are joined by those of commuters, resulting in traffic jams in certain areas. The worst bottlenecks are usually on Highway 29 around St. Helena and along U.S. 101 near Santa Rosa.

Make lunch and dinner reservations. Calling ahead (or having your hotel and B&B do it for you) can save you considerable time waiting for a walk-in table to open up.

Choose your hotel carefully. If you stay in ritzy St. Helena, for example, you'll have easy access to tasting rooms pouring Rutherford's famous cabernets, but you'll be at least an hour away from the bucolic Russian River Valley. Conversely, staying at an inn in rural Forestville is great for romantics exploring the Russian River, but you'll have to drive half an hour to get to the shops and restaurants of Healdsburg. If you have only a few days, limit yourself to either Napa or Sonoma, or you'll risk spending half your time on the road.

KIDS AND FAMILIES

By its very nature, the Wine Country is not a particularly child-friendly destination. Don't expect to see many other children, or to find a plethora of activities organized with them in mind. That said, you'll find plenty of playgrounds (there's one at Sonoma's Plaza, for instance), as well as other kid-friendly attractions here and there, most notably the Charles M. Schulz Museum in Santa Rosa.

Choosing a Place to Stay

If you're traveling with kids, always mention it when making your reservations. Most of the smaller, more romantic inns and B&Bs discourage or prohibit children, though a few like the Glenelly Inn are welcoming to kids. Those places that do allow guests with children may prefer to put such families in a particular cottage or room, so that any noise is less disruptive to other guests. Larger hotels are a mixed bag. Some actively discourage children, whereas others are more welcoming. Of the large, luxurious hotels, Meadowood tends to be the most child-friendly.

Eating Out

Unless your kid is a budding Thomas Keller, it's best to call ahead to see if a restaurant can accommodate those under 12 with a special menu. You will find inexpensive cafés in almost every town, and places like Taylor's Automatic Refresher, a retro burger stand in St. Helena, are big hits with kids of all ages. However, many of the Wine Country's better restaurants are virtual child-free zones, and meals at such places can stretch for two or more hours.

At the Wineries

Children are few and far between at most wineries, but well-behaved children will generally be greeted with a smile. Some wineries offer a small treat—grape juice or another beverage or sometimes crayons and coloring books or another distraction. When taking reservations for a tour, a winery should be able to tell you if it's appropriate for kids, how long it takes, and whether there's another tour option that would be more suitable.

A few particularly kid-friendly wineries include Sterling Vineyards, where a short aerial tram ride takes visitors from the parking lot to the tasting room, and Arrowood Vineyards and Winery, whose tasting room has a small toy box. Arrowood will also offer your child a flight of nonalcoholic drinks if given advance notice. At Benziger, a tractor-pulled tram is used for the vineyard tours. For more information on wineries with perks for the kids, check out ⊕ www.napavintners.com, which lists about 50 self-described family-friendly wineries.

Visiting the Wineries

WORD OF MOUTH

"Save money wine-tasting at wineries with free wine-tasting coupons. You can find and print them online before you leave home. Do an online web search for free wine-tasting coupons."

—Howfortunate

LIFE IS LIVED WELL in the California Wine Country, where eating and, above all, drinking are cultivated as high arts. And if all those magazines, epicurean memoirs, and gorgeously shot movies saturated with lush, romantic images of the area have made you pine for a visit, the good news is that you likely won't be disappointed when you get here. The meandering back roads, vineyard-blanketed hills, and ivy-draped wineries—not to mention the luxurious restaurants, hotels, and spas—really *are* that beautiful.

Whether you're a serious wine collector making your annual pilgrimage to the Napa Valley or a wine newbie who doesn't know the difference between a merlot and mourvèdre but is eager to learn, you can have a great time touring California. Your gateway to the wine world is the tasting room, where the staff (and occasionally even the actual winemaker) are almost always happy to chat with curious guests. Tasting rooms range from the grand to the humble, offering everything from a few sips of wine to in-depth tours of the wine-making facilities and vineyards. The one constant, however, is a deep, shared pleasure in the experience of wine tasting.

WINE TASTING 101

Wine tasting has the reputation of an occult art that's usually practiced by snooty French sommeliers who toss around esoteric adjectives as they swirl their glasses. Don't be intimidated. At its core, wine tasting is simply about determining which wines you like best. However, knowing a few basic tasting steps and a few key quality guidelines can make your winery visit much more enjoyable, and help you remember which wines you liked and why long after you return home. ∎TIP→ **Above all, however, follow your instincts at the tasting bar: there is no right or wrong way to describe wine.**

If you watch the pros, you'll probably notice that they take time to inspect, swirl, and sniff the wine before they get around to sipping it. Follow their lead and take your time, going through each of the following steps for each wine. Starting with the pop of the cork and the splashing of wine into a glass, all of your senses play a part in wine tasting.

Before tasting, wine should be clear and free of sediment.

USE YOUR EYES

Before you taste it, take a good look at the wine in your glass. Holding the glass by the stem, raise it to the light. Whether it's white, rosé, or red, your wine should be clear, without cloudiness or sediments, when you drink it. Some unfiltered wines may seem cloudy at first, but they will clear as the sediments settle.

In the natural light, place the glass in front of a white background such as a blank sheet of paper or a tablecloth. **Check the color.** Is it right for the wine? A California white should be golden: straw, medium, or deep, depending on the type. Rich, sweet, dessert wine will have more intense color, but chardonnay and sauvignon blanc will be paler. A rosé should be a clear pink, from pale to deep, without too much red or any orange. Reds may lean toward ruby or garnet coloring; some have a purple tinge. They shouldn't be pale (the exception is pinot noir, which can be quite pale yet still have character). In any color wine, a brownish tinge is a flaw that indicates the wine is too old, has been incorrectly stored, or has gone bad. If you see brown, try another bottle.

BREATHE DEEP

You might notice that experienced wine tasters spend more time sniffing the wine than drinking it. This is because this step is where the magic happens: aroma plays a huge role in wine's flavor. After you have looked at the wine's color, **sniff the wine once or twice** to see if you can identify any aromas. Then gently move your glass in a circular motion to swirl the wine around. Aerating the wine this way releases more of its aromas. (It's called "volatilizing the esters," if you're trying to impress someone.) Stick your nose into the glass and take another long sniff.

Wine should smell good to you. You might pick up the scent of apricots, peaches, ripe melon, honey, and wildflowers in a white wine; black pepper, cherry, violets, and cedar in a red. Rosés (which are made from red wine grapes) smell something like red wine, but in a scaled-back way, with hints of raspberry, strawberry, and sometimes a touch of rose petal. You might encounter surprising smells, such as tar—which some people actually appreciate in certain (generally expensive, red) wines.

For the most part, though, wine's aroma should be clean and pleasing to you, not "off." If you find a wine's odor odd or unpleasant, there's probably something wrong. Watch out for hints of wet dog or skunk, or for moldy, horsey, mousy, or sweaty smells. Sniff for chemical faults such as sulfur, or excessive vanilla scents (picked up from oak barrels) that overwhelm the other aromas. A vinegar smell indicates that the wine has started to spoil. A rotten wood or soggy cardboard smell usually means the wine is corked and the cork has gone bad, ruining the wine. It's extremely rare to find these faults in wines poured in the tasting rooms, however, since staffers usually taste each bottle before pouring from it.

JUST A SIP

Once you've checked its appearance and aroma, take a sip—not a swig or a gulp—of the wine. **As you sip wine, gently swish it around in your mouth**—this releases more aromas for your nose to explore. Do the aroma and the flavor complement each other, improve each other? While moving the wine around in your mouth, also think about the way it feels: silky or crisp? Does it coat your tongue or is it thinner? Does it seem to fill your mouth with flavor or is it weak? This combination of weight and intensity is

referred to as body: a good wine may be light-, medium-, or full-bodied.

Do you like it? If not, don't drink it. Even if there is nothing actually wrong with a wine, what's the point of drinking it if you don't like it? A wine can be technically perfect but nevertheless taste strange, unpleasant, or just boring to you. It's possible to learn to appreciate wine that doesn't appeal to your tastes, but unless you like a wine right off the bat, it probably won't become a favorite. In the tasting room, dump what you don't like and move on to the next sample.

The more complex a wine is, the more flavors you will detect in the course of tasting. You might taste different things when you first take a sip ("up front"), when you swish ("in the middle" or "at mid-palate"), and just before you swallow ("at the end" or "on the back-palate"). A good table wine should be neither too sweet nor too tart, and never bitter. Fruitiness, a subtle near-sweetness, should be balanced by acidity, but not to the point that the wine tastes sour or makes your mouth pucker. An astringent or drying quality is the mark of tannins, a somewhat mysterious wine element that comes from grape skins and oak barrels. In young reds this can taste almost bitter—but not quite. All these qualities, together with the wine's aroma, blend to evoke the flavors—not only of fruit but also of unlikely things such as leather, tobacco, or almonds.

SPIT OR SWALLOW?

You may choose to spit out the wine (into the dump bucket or a plastic cup) or swallow it. The pros typically spit, since they want to preserve their palates (and sobriety!) for the wines to come, but you'll find that swallowers far outnumber spitters in the winery tasting rooms. Either way, **pay attention to what happens after the wine leaves your mouth**—this is the finish, and it can be spectacular. What flavors stay behind or appear? Does the flavor fade away quickly or linger pleasantly? A long finish is a sign of quality; wine with no perceptible finish is inferior.

CLOSE UP

Vino Vocabulary

If you've ever read a wine review in *Wine Spectator*, you've probably seen a confounding array of adjectives used to describe wines' aroma and flavor, from "citrus rind," "passion fruit," and "toast" to nose-wrinkling words such as "horsey" and "sweaty." Wine tasters use hundreds of common terms, and even more of their own devising, to try to capture a wine's elusive qualities. You don't need to memorize a laundry list of terms, but becoming familiar with a few of the most common words used by wine tasters will help you to talk wine with the best of them. The following are some of the major categories of aromas you might detect.

■ Chemical: You might be surprised to discover that a subtle odor of diesel or tar is not necessarily considered a bad thing, depending on the varietal and the wine's overall balance of flavors. The smell of skunk, rotten eggs, or fingernail polish remover, though, is a sign that something has gone wrong in the wine-making process.

■ Earthy: Pinot noir is likely to be described as smelling like wet earth or mushrooms. White wines with a high acidity might be called "stoney" or "flinty" or said to have a mineral quality (think of what it might taste like to lick a clean pebble).

■ Floral: White wines might give off a whiff of roses, violets, orange blossoms, or other flowers.

■ Fruity: The number of fruits used to describe wines is almost endless, but those you'll hear most often are citrus (usually lemons or grapefruit), stone fruits (peaches and apricots), tropical fruits (pineapple or lychee), and berries of all sorts.

■ Spicy: The flavor of pepper is commonly detected in gewürztraminer and syrah. Cloves and anise are other spicy flavors often tasted in red wines.

■ Vegetal or herbaceous: White wines, especially sauvignon blanc, are often described as "grassy" if they have a whiff of a new-mown lawn, whereas reds are more likely to be described as reminiscent of tea or pipe tobacco. Good cabernet sauvignons often have an aroma of eucalyptus. But wines that have more than a hint of vegetal characteristics, especially of green pepper or asparagus, are usually frowned upon.

■ Woody: Since many wines are aged in charred wooden barrels, it's not surprising that some have hints of oak, cedar, smoke, or vanilla.

2

TASTING ROOMS AND WINERY TOURS

Some wineries in Napa, Sonoma, and the Central Coast have opulent faux châteaus with vast gift shops; others welcome guests with rough converted barns where you might have to step over the vintner's dog in the doorway. But it doesn't matter if you're visiting an elaborate tasting room complete with art gallery and upscale restaurant, or you're squeezed into the corner of a cinder-block warehouse amid stacked boxes and idle equipment: either way, tasting rooms are designed to introduce newcomers to the pleasures of wine and to inform visitors about the wines made at that winery. So don't worry if you're new to tasting. Relax, grab a glass, and join in for a good time.

Unfortunately, at most California wineries these days you'll have to pay for the privilege of tasting. Though free tastings were the norm 20 years ago, now it's more common to have to pay $5 to $20, and fees of even $25 to $40 aren't unheard-of.

In general, you'll find the highest fees in Napa and slightly lower fees in Sonoma, though there are plenty of exceptions to this rule. And no matter which region you're in, you'll still find the occasional freebie—though it's likely to be at a spot that's off the major tourist thoroughfares and on some little-traveled back road. For some tips on keeping a day of wine tasting from breaking the bank, see the box on money-saving tips on the next page.

TIP TO SIP? **In tasting rooms, tipping is very much the exception rather than the rule. Most frequent visitors to the Wine Country never tip those pouring the wines in the tasting rooms, though if a server has gone out of his or her way to be helpful—by pouring special wines not on the list, for example—leaving $5 or so would be a nice gesture.**

Many wineries are regularly open to the public, usually daily from around 10 AM to 5 PM, though many close as early as 4 or 4:30, especially in winter, so it's best to get a reasonably early start if you want to fit in more than a few spots. ■TIP→ Also keep in mind that most wineries stop serving new visitors 15 to 30 minutes before their posted closing time, so don't expect to skate in at the last moment for a tast-

Barrel sampling at DeLoach Winery in Sonoma's Russian River Valley

ing. Many wineries require reservations to visit, and still others are closed to the public entirely. When in doubt, call in advance.

Though you might have the tasting room all to yourself if you visit midweek in winter, in summer, during crush (harvest season), and on weekends it's likely you'll be bumping elbows with other tasters and vying for the attention of the server behind the bar. If you prefer smaller crowds, look for wineries off the main drags of Highway 29 in Napa and Highway 12 in Sonoma. Also look for wineries that are open by appointment only; they tend to schedule visitors carefully to avoid a big crowd at any one time. Wineries tend to have the least traffic earliest in the morning and get the most crowded between 3 PM and closing, so consider getting an early start.

Finally, remember that those little sips add up, so pace yourself. If you plan to visit several wineries, try just a few wines at each so you don't hit sensory overload, when your mouth can no longer distinguish subtleties. (This is called palate fatigue.) ⚠ **Choose a designated driver for the day: Wine Country roads are often narrow and curvy, and you may be sharing the road with bicyclists and wildlife as well as other wine tourists.** Although wineries rarely advertise it, many will provide a free nonalcoholic drink for the designated driver; it never hurts to ask.

Money-Saving Tips

Those $20 tasting fees can add up awfully quickly if you're not careful, so consider the following tips for whittling down your wine-tasting budget.

■ Many hotels and B&Bs distribute coupons for free or discounted tastings to their guests—don't forget to ask.

■ If you and your travel partner don't mind sharing a glass, servers are happy to let you split a tasting. (This is also a good way to pace yourself and make sure you're not tipsy before lunchtime.)

■ Get off the beaten track. Wineries along heavily traveled routes in Napa and Sonoma typically charge the most. Smaller spots along the back roads often charge less—or sometimes nothing at all.

■ Some wineries will refund all or part of the tasting fee if you buy a bottle. Of course, this can easily lead to spending *more* than you had originally budgeted, but if you're planning on buying some bottles anyway, you can at least get some free tastings out of it.

IN THE TASTING ROOM

In most tasting rooms you'll find on the bar a list of the wines available that day, or you'll receive one from the server. The wines will be listed in a suggested tasting order, starting with the lightest-bodied whites and progressing to the most intense reds. Dessert wines will come at the end.

Most often you'll find an assortment of different wines from the winery's most recently released vintages. There might also be a list of reserve vintages (special wines aged somewhat longer) that you can taste for a separate fee. To create a more cohesive tasting experience, tasting rooms sometimes offer "flights" consisting of three or four particular wines selected to complement or contrast with each other. These might be vertical (several vintages of one wine), horizontal (several different varietals from one vintage, or harvest season), or more intuitively assembled.

Decide which of the wines you'd like to taste. Don't feel the need to tackle them all. In fact, many wineries will indicate at the bottom of the list that you are limited to four or five tastes. (In reality, however, servers will rarely hold you to this limit if the tasting room isn't too crowded and you're showing a sincere interest in learning about the wines.) If you can't decide which wines to choose, tell the server what types of wines you usually like and ask for a recommendation.

The server will pour you an ounce or so of each wine you select. As you taste it, feel free to take notes or ask questions. ■ TIP→ **If you use your list of the wines available for your note taking, you'll have a handy record of your impressions at the end of your vacation, which might help next time you go shopping for wine.** There might be a plate of crackers on the bar; nibble them when you want to clear your palate of one wine's flavor before tasting the next.

Don't be shy—the staff are there to educate you about their wine. If they're not sharing the sort of information you'd like to hear, pipe up. (A few servers have the unfortunate tendency to spout statistics about how their wines have been ranked by "experts," or give you a laundry list of awards their wines have won, neither of which really help you develop your own sense of what sort of wines you like best.) If you don't like a wine, or you've simply tasted enough, feel free to pour the rest into one of the dump buckets usually kept on the bar (if you don't see one, just ask).

TAKING A TOUR

Even if you're not a devoted wine drinker, seeing how grapes turn into wine can be fascinating. Tours tend to be the most exciting (and the most crowded) in September and October, when the harvest and crushing are under way. In harvest season you'll likely see workers picking in the vineyards and hauling fruit bins and barrels around with forklifts. At other times of the year, winery work consists of monitoring the wine, "racking" it (eliminating sediment by transferring it from one tank or barrel to another), and bottling the finished wine.

Depending on the size of the winery, a tour might consist of a few visitors or a large group, following the staff guide from vineyard to processing area and from barrel room to tasting room. The guide explains what happens at each stage of the wine-making process, usually emphasizing the winery's particular approach to growing and wine making. You'll find out the uses for all that complex machinery, stainless-steel equipment, and red-wine-stained oak barrels; feel free to ask questions at any point in the tour. If it's harvest or bottling time, you might see and hear the facility at work. Otherwise, the scene is likely to be quiet, with just a few workers tending the tanks and barrels.

Buying and Shipping Wine

Don't feel obliged to buy a bottle of wine just because the winery has given you a taste, especially if you paid a tasting fee. You should never feel pressured to make a purchase. Still, many visitors like to buy a bottle or two from small wineries as a courtesy, especially when they have taken more than a few minutes of the staff's time.

If you discover a bottle you particularly like, ask about where it's available. Although some wines, especially those made by the bigger operations, are widely distributed, many are available only at the wineries themselves, and perhaps served at a handful of restaurants or sold at wine shops in the San Francisco area. You might want to stock up if you won't be able to get it at home.

If you like several of a winery's bottles, and would like the convenience of having their wines delivered to you, consider joining their wine club, which will periodically send wine to you (except in some states), offer members-only releases, and give you a discount on all of your purchases.

If you're buying wine, ask about the winery's direct-shipment program. Most wineries are happy to ship the wine you buy, as long as you live in a state that lets consumers receive California wine directly from the winery. The rules apply whether you make your purchase in the tasting room, join the wine club, or order online.

Sending wine home is getting easier, especially since the U.S. Supreme Court set a new precedent in 2005. The court found unconstitutional the discriminatory bans on interstate, direct-to-consumer wine shipments in New York and Michigan. More states are opening their borders to such shipments from California, but laws vary greatly from state to state. The penalties for noncompliance with state regulations can be severe, so if you're going to ship wine home, it is wise to do so either through the winery or a professional shipper. (Wineries will also sell you Styrofoam chests you can use to check bottles of wine on your flight home.) ■TIP→ For up-to-date information, check ⊕ www.wineinstitute.org/programs/shipwine.

THE LOUD AND THE RESTLESS. Tasting rooms are for just that—tasting wines, rather than overindulging—and most visitors are on pretty good behavior. If you go to enough wineries, however, you'll eventually run into a loud, rowdy, or tipsy group. Wineries try to avoid these disruptions, often by prohibiting limousines

DID YOU KNOW?

Tasting rooms sometimes offer "flights" consisting of three or four particular wines selected to complement or contrast with each other.

or requiring reservations for groups of more than eight. But once in a while, partyers get in anyway. All that's left to do is wait them out or return to the winery for a quieter visit after they're gone. This is a rare issue, even on Saturday, but you can almost guarantee you won't have a run-in if you visit wineries on a weekday.

Some winery tours, which typically last 30 minutes to an hour, are free, in which case you're usually required to pay a separate fee if you want to taste the wine. If you've paid a fee for the tour—often $10 up to $30—your wine tasting is usually included in that price. ■TIP→ If you plan to take any tours, wear comfortable shoes, since you might be walking on wet floors or stepping over hoses or other equipment. Also, dress appropriately for the weather, preferably in layers, since many tours take place partly outdoors or in wine-making facilities where the temperature may be hot or cold.

At many wineries the basic, introductory tours, typically offered several times daily, are complemented by less frequent specialized tours and seminars focusing on subjects such as viticultural techniques, sensory evaluation, wine blending, and food-and-wine pairing. Prices for these events typically range from $20 to $50, sometimes a bit more if lunch is included. If you're spending a few days in the Wine Country, it's worth reserving at least one of these more in-depth experiences, which may be scheduled only on weekends. Check the wineries' Web sites for more information.

HOW WINE IS MADE

THE CRUSH

The process of turning grapes into wine generally starts at the **crush pad,** where the grapes are brought in from the vineyards. Good winemakers carefully monitor their vineyards throughout the year. Their presence is especially critical at harvest, when regular checks of the grapes' ripeness determines the proper day for picking. Once that day arrives, the crush begins.

Wineries pick their grapes by machine or by hand, depending on the terrain and on the type of grape. Some varietals are harvested at night with the help of powerful floodlights. Why at night? In addition to it being easier on the work-

ers (it often reaches 90°F [32°C] or more during the day in September), the fruit-acid content in the pulp and juice of the grapes peaks in the cool night air. The acids—an essential component during fermentation and aging, and an important part of wine's flavor—plummet in the heat of the day.

Grapes must be handled with care so none of the juice is lost. They arrive at the crush pad in large containers called gondolas and are dropped gently onto a conveyor belt that deposits the grapes into a **stemmer-crusher.** A drum equipped with steel fingers knocks the grapes off their stems and pierces their skins, so the juice can flow off freely. The grapes and juice fall through a grate and are carried via stainless steel pipes to a press or vat. The stems and leaves drop out of the stemmer-crusher and are recycled to the vineyards as natural fertilizer. After this general first step, the production process goes one of four ways to make a white, red, rosé, or sparkling wine.

MAKING WHITE WINES

The juice of white wine grapes goes first to **settling tanks,** where the skins and grape solids sink to the bottom, separating from the clear free-run juice on top. The material in the settling tanks still contains a lot of juice, so after the free-run juice is pumped off, the remains go into a **press.** A modern press consists of a perforated drum containing a Teflon-coated bag. As this bag is inflated like a balloon, it slowly pushes the grapes against the outside wall and the liquids are squeezed from the solids and flow off. Like the free-run juice, the press juice is pumped into a **fermenter,** which is either a stainless-steel tank (which may be insulated to keep the fermenting juice cool) or an oak barrel.

Press juice and free-run juice are fermented separately, but a little of the press juice may be added to the free-run juice for complexity. Because press juice tends to be strongly flavored and may contain undesirable flavor components, winemakers are careful not to add too much of it. White press juice is always fermented in stainless-steel tanks; free-run juice may be handled differently. Most white wines are fermented at 59°F to 68°F (15°C to 20°C). Cooler temperatures, which develop delicacy and fruit aromas, are especially important in fermentation of sauvignon blanc and riesling.

During fermentation, yeast feeds on the sugar in grape juice and converts it to alcohol and carbon dioxide. Wine yeast dies and fermentation naturally stops in two to four weeks, when the alcohol level reaches 15 percent. If there's not enough sugar in the grapes to reach the desired alcohol level, the winemaker can add extra sugar before or during fermentation, in a process called **chaptalization.**

To prevent oxidation, which damages wine's color and flavor, and to kill wild yeast and bacteria, which can produce off flavors, winemakers almost always add sulfur dioxide, in the form of sulfites, before fermenting. A winemaker may also choose to encourage **malolactic fermentation** ("malo") to soften a wine's acidity or deepen its flavor and complexity. This is done either by inoculating the wine with lactic bacteria soon after alcoholic fermentation begins or right after it ends, or by transferring the new wine to wooden vats that harbor the bacteria. Malo, which can also happen by accident, is undesirable in lighter-bodied wines meant to be drunk young.

For richer results, free-run juice from chardonnay, and some from sauvignon blanc, might be fermented in oak barrels, in individual batches, with each vineyard and lot kept separate. **Barrel fermentation** creates more depth and complexity, as the wine picks up vanilla flavors and other harmonious traits from the wood. The barrels used by California winemakers may be imported from France or Eastern Europe, or made domestically of American oak. They are very expensive and can be used for only a few years.

When the wine has finished fermenting, whether in a tank or barrel, it is generally **racked**—moved into a clean tank or barrel to separate it from the lees, the spent yeast and any grape solids that have dropped out of suspension. Sometimes chardonnay and special batches of sauvignon blanc are left on the lees for extended periods of time before being racked to pick up extra complexity. Wine may be racked several times as sediment continues to settle out.

After the first racking, the wine may be **filtered** to take out solid particles that can cloud the wine and any stray yeast or bacteria that can spoil it. This is especially common for whites. Wine may be filtered several times before bottling to help control its development during maturation. This is a common practice among commercial producers, but many fine-wine makers resist filtering, as they believe it leads to less complex wines that don't age as well.

A wine-maker checking on a vintage being aged in barrels

White wine may also be **fined** to clarify it and stabilize its color. In fining, agents such as a fine clay called bentonite or albumen from egg whites are mixed into the wine. As they settle out, they absorb undesirable substances that can cloud the wine. As with filtering, the process is more common with ordinary table wines than with fine wines.

Typically, winemakers blend several batches of new wine together to balance flavor. Careful **blending** gives the winemaker an extra chance to create a perfect single-varietal wine, or to combine several varietals that complement each other in a blend. Premium vintners also make unblended vineyard-designated wines that highlight the attributes of grapes from a single vineyard.

New wine is stored in stainless steel or oak casks or barrels to rest and develop before bottling. This stage, called **maturation or aging,** may last anywhere from a few months to more than a year for white wine. Barrel rooms are kept dark to protect the wine both from light and from heat, either of which can be damaging. Some wineries keep their wines in air-conditioned rooms or warehouses; others use long, tunnel-like **caves** bored into hillsides, where the wine remains at a constant temperature.

If wine is matured or aged for any length of time before bottling, it will be racked and perhaps filtered several times.

CLOSE UP

Its All on the Label

If you look beyond the photograph of a weathered château or the quirky drawing of a cartoon creature on a bottle of wine, it will tell you a lot about what's inside. If you want to decode the details of what's inside, look for the following information:

■ **Alcohol content:** In most cases, U.S. law requires bottles to list the alcohol content, which typically hovers around 13 or 14 percent, but big red wines from California, especially zinfandel, can soar to 16 percent or more.

■ **Appellation:** At least 85 percent of the grapes must have come from the AVA (American Viticultural Area) listed on the bottle. A bottle that says MT. VEEDER, for example, contains mostly grapes that are grown in the compact Mt. Veeder appellation, but if the label simply says CALIFORNIA, the grapes could have come from anywhere in the state.

■ **Estate or Estate Grown:** Wines with this label must be made entirely of grapes grown on land owned or operated by the winery.

■ **Reserve:** An inexact term meaning "special" (and therefore usually costing more) this can refer to how or where the grapes were grown or how the wine was made or even how long it was aged.

■ **Varietal:** If a grape variety is listed on the label, it means that at least 75 percent of the grapes in this wine are of that varietal. If there's no varietal listed, it's almost certainly a blend of various types of grapes.

■ **Vineyard name:** If the label lists a vineyard, then at least 95 percent of the grapes used must have been harvested there. A vineyard name is more commonly, though not exclusively, found on higher-end bottles of wine.

■ **Vintage:** If a year appears on the label, it means that at least 95 percent of the grapes in the wine were harvested in that year (85 percent if the wine is not designated with an AVA). If no vintage is listed, the grapes may come from more than one year's harvest.

■ **Wine name:** Many wineries will give their wines a catchy name, to help consumers pick it out in a crowd.

Once it is bottled, the wine is stored for **bottle aging.** This is done in a cool, dark space to prevent the corks from drying out; a shrunken cork allows oxygen to enter the bottle and spoil the wine. In a few months, most white wines will be ready for release.

MAKING RED WINES

Red wine production differs slightly from that of white wine. Red wine grapes are crushed the same way white wine grapes are, but the juice is not separated from the grape skins and pulp before fermentation. This is what gives red wine its color. After crushing, the red wine **must**—the thick slurry of juice, pulp, and skins—is fermented in vats. The juice is "left on the skins" for varying periods of time, from a few days to two weeks, depending on the grape variety and on how much color the winemaker wants to extract.

Fermentation also extracts flavors and chemical compounds such as **tannins** from the skins and seeds, making red wines more robust than whites. In a red designed for drinking soon after bottling, tannin levels are kept down; they should have a greater presence in wine meant for aging. In a young red not ready for drinking, tannins feel dry or coarse in your mouth, but they soften with age. Over time, a wine with well-balanced tannin will maintain its fruitiness and backbone as its flavor develops. Without adequate tannin, a wine will not age well.

Creating the **oak barrels** that age the wine is a craft in its own right. At Demptos Napa Cooperage, a French-owned company that employs French barrel-making techniques, the process involves several elaborate production phases. The staves of oak are formed into the shape of a barrel using metal bands, and then the rough edges of the bound planks are smoothed. Finally, the barrels are literally toasted to give the oak its characteristic flavor, which will in turn be imparted to the wine.

Red wine fermentation occurs at a higher temperature than that for whites—reds ferment at about 70°F to 90°F (21°C to 32°C). As the grape sugars are converted into alcohol, great amounts of carbon dioxide are generated. Carbon dioxide is lighter than wine but heavier than air, and it forms an **"aerobic cover"** that protects the wine from oxidation. As the wine ferments, grape skins rise to the top and are periodically mixed back in so the wine can extract the maximum amount of color and flavor. This is done either in the traditional fashion by punching them down with a large handheld tool, or by pumping the wine from the bottom of the vat and pouring it back in at the top.

At the end of fermentation, the free-run wine is drained off. The grape skins and pulp are sent to a press, where the remaining wine is extracted. As with the whites, the winemaker may choose to add a little of the press wine to the free-run wine—if he feels it will add complexity to the finished wine. Otherwise the press juice goes into bulk wine—the lower-quality, less expensive stuff. The better wine is racked and then may be fined; some reds are left unfined for extra depth.

Next up is **oak-barrel aging**, which takes a year or longer. Unlike many of the barrels used for aging and fermenting chardonnay, the barrels used for aging red wine are not always new. They may already have been used to age chardonnay, which will have extracted most of the wood's flavors. Oak, like grapes, contains natural tannins, and the wine extracts these tannins from the barrels. Oak also has countless tiny pores through which water in the wine slowly evaporates, making the wine more concentrated. To make sure the aging wine does not oxidize, the barrels have to be regularly **topped off** with wine from the same vintage.

The only way even the best winemaker can tell if a wine is finished is by tasting it. A winemaker constantly tastes wines during fermentation, while they are aging in barrels, and regularly, though less often, while they age in bottles. The wine is released for sale when the winemaker's palate and nose say it's ready.

MAKING SPARKLING WINES

Sparkling wines are, despite the mystique surrounding them, nothing more or less than wines in which carbon dioxide is suspended, making them bubbly. Good sparkling wine will always be fairly expensive, because a great deal of work goes into making it.

White sparkling wines can be made from either white or black grapes. In France, Champagne is traditionally made from pinot noir or chardonnay grapes, whereas in California, pinot blanc, riesling, or sometimes other white grapes might also be used as well. If black grapes are used, they must be picked very carefully to avoid crushing them. The goal is to minimize contact between the inner fruit (which is usually white) and the skins, where the purplish-red color pigments reside. The grapes are rushed to the winery and crushed very gently, and the juice is strained off the skins right away, again, to prevent the juice from coming in contact with pigments and turning red. Even so, some sparklers have more of a pink tinge to them than the wine-maker intends.

The freshly pressed juice and pulp, or must, is **fermented with special yeasts** that preserve the wine's fruit, the character-istic fruit flavor of the grape variety used. Before bottling, this finished "still" wine (wine without bubbles) is mixed with a *liqueur de tirage,* a blend of wine, sugar, and yeast. This mixture causes the wine to ferment again—in the bottle, where it stays for 6 to 12 weeks. **Carbon dioxide,** a by-product of fermentation, is produced and trapped in the bottle, where it dissolves in the wine (instead of escaping into the air, as happens during fermentation in barrel, vat, or tank). This captive carbon dioxide transforms the still wine into a sparkling wine.

Bottles of new sparkling wine are stored on their sides in deep cellars. The wine now ages *sur lie,* or **"on the lees"** (the dead yeast cells and other deposits trapped in the bottle). This aging process enriches the wine's texture and increases the complexity of its bouquet. The amount of time a spar-kling wine ages *sur lie* bears a direct relation to its quality: the longer the aging, the more complex the wine.

The lees must be removed from the bottle before a sparkling wine can be enjoyed. This is achieved in a process whose first step is called **riddling.** In the past, each bottle, head tilted slightly downward, was placed in a riddling rack, an A-frame with many holes of bottleneck size. Riddlers gave each bottle a slight shake and a downward turn, every day if possible. This continued for six weeks, until each bottle rested upside down in the hole and the sediment had col-lected in the neck, next to the cork. Simple as this sounds, it is actually very difficult to do. Hand-riddling is a fine art perfected after much training. Today most sparkling wines are riddled in ingeniously designed machines called gyro palettes, which riddle up to 500 or more bottles at one time, though at a few wineries, such as Schramsberg, the work is still done by hand.

After riddling, the bottles are **disgorged.** The upside-down bottles are placed in a very cold solution, which freezes the sediments in a block that attaches itself to the crown cap that seals the bottle. The cap and frozen plug are removed, and the bottle is topped off with a wine-and-sugar mixture called **dosage** and recorked with the traditional Cham-pagne cork. The dosage determines the final sweetness of a sparkling wine.

Sparkling wines with 1.5 percent sugar or less are labeled **"brut"**; those with 1.2 to 2 percent sugar are called **"extra dry"**; those with 1.7 to 3.5 percent are called **"sec"** (French for "dry"); and those with 3.5 to 5 percent, **"demi-sec"** (half dry). **"Doux"** (sweet) sparkling wine has more than 5 percent sugar. Most sparkling-wine drinkers refuse to admit that they like their bubbly on the sweet side, and this labeling convention allows them to drink sweet while pretending to drink dry. It's a marketing ploy invented in Champagne at least a century ago. A sparkling wine to which no dosage has been added will be bone dry (and taste sour to some) and may be called **"extra-brut"** or "natural."

Most sparkling wines are not vintage dated but are "assembled" (the term sparkling-wine makers use instead of "blended") to create a **cuvée,** a mix of different wines and sometimes different vintages consistent with the house style. However, sparkling wines may be vintage dated in particularly great years.

Sparkling wine may also be made by time- and cost-saving bulk methods. In the bulk **Charmat process,** invented by Eugene Charmat early in the 20th century, the secondary fermentation takes place in large tanks rather than individual bottles. Each tank is basically treated as one huge bottle. After the bubbles have developed, the sediments are filtered from the wine and the wine is bottled. But at a price: although the sparkling wine may be ready in as little as a month, it has neither the complexity nor the bubble quality of the more slowly made sparklers. In the United States, sparkling wine made in this way must be labeled BULK PROCESS or CHARMAT PROCESS. Sparkling wines made in the traditional, time-consuming fashion may be labeled MÉTHODE CHAMPENOISE or WINE FERMENTED IN THIS BOTTLE.

THE FRENCH CONNECTION. Sparkling wines were perfected in Champagne, France's northernmost wine district, where wines tend to be a bit acidic because grapes do not always fully ripen. That's why sparkling wines have traditionally been naturally tart, even austere. Because of their progenitor's birthplace, many sparkling wines are often called Champagne. However, this term designates a region of origin, so it really shouldn't be used for American sparkling wines. That's not to say that Napa and Sonoma County sparkling wines are in any way inferior to French ones. The French Champagne houses are fully aware of

The Russian River Valley, where pinot noir and chardonnay are widely grown

the excellence of the California product and have been quick to cash in on the laurels gathered by such pioneers as Hanns Kornell, Schramsberg, and Iron Horse by establishing sparkling-wine cellars in Sonoma and Napa with American partners.

MAKING ROSÉ WINES

Rosé or blush wines are also made from red wine grapes, but the juicy pulp is left on the skins for a matter of hours—12 to 36—not days. When the winemaker decides that the juice has reached the desired color, it is drained off and filtered. Yeast is added, and the juice is left to ferment. Because the must stays on the skins for a shorter time than the must of red wines, fewer tannins are leached from the skins, and the resulting wine is not as full-flavored as a red. You might say that rosé is a lighter, fruitier version of red wine, not a pink version of white.

A ROSÉ BY ANY OTHER NAME. Rosé has gotten a bad rap in recent years, perhaps because it's sometimes confused with inexpensive, sickly-sweet white zinfandels that are a similar hue, but the French have been making excellent dry rosés for decades. From around 2005 on, many California vintners have jumped on the rosé bandwagon, and it seems like almost every tasting room features at least one of these refreshing wines.

THE SWEET SCIENCE OF VITICULTURE

Most kinds of wine grapes are touchy. If the weather is too hot, they can produce too much sugar and not enough acid, resulting in overly alcoholic wines. Too cool and grapes won't ripen properly, and some will develop an unpleasant vegetal taste. And rain at the wrong time of year can wreak havoc on vineyards, causing grapes to rot on the vine. What's more, the wrong type of soil can leave vines with "wet feet," which can seriously hamper their growth. These and many other conditions must be just right to coax the best out of persnickety wine grapes, and the Central Coast, Napa, and Sonoma have that magical combination of sun, rain, fog, slope, and soil that allow many varieties of wine grape to thrive.

LOCATION, LOCATION, LOCATION

Many California growers and winemakers generally agree that no matter what high-tech wine-making techniques might be used at the winery, in fact the wine is really made in the vineyard. This emphasis on *terroir* (a French term that encompasses the soil, the microclimate, and overall growing conditions of a region) reflects a belief that the quality of a wine is determined by what happens before the grapes are crushed. Even a small winery can produce spectacular wines from small vineyards if it has the right location and grows the grapes best suited to its soil and microclimate. (For a rundown on California's main grape varieties, see the "Winespeak" chapter at the end of this book.)

When a region's terroir is unique in the United States, the Alcohol and Tobacco Tax and Trade Bureau can designate it an AVA, more commonly called an **appellation.** What makes things a little confusing is that appellations often overlap, allowing for increased levels of specificity. California is an appellation, for example, but so is the Napa Valley. Napa and Sonoma counties are each county appellations, but they, too, are divided into even smaller regions, usually called subappellations. Different appellations—there are more than 100 AVAs in California, with 16 in the county of Napa alone—are renowned for different wines.

An appellation always refers to the source of a wine's grapes, not to the place where the wine was made. Wineries can indicate the appellation on a bottle's label only if 85 percent of the grapes used in the wine were grown in that appellation. Many wineries buy grapes from outside their AVA (some don't even have vineyards of their own), so it is quite possible that they will label different wines with the names of different regions.

When it is to their advantage, winemakers make sure to mention prestigious appellations, and even specific vineyards, on their labels. If the grapes have come from multiple AVAs within a given region—say, the North Coast—the wine can be labeled with the name of the whole region. Wines simply labeled CALIFORNIA, then, are usually made of grapes from more than one region.

GEOLOGY 101

Wherever grapes are grown, geology matters. Grapevines are among the few plants that give their best fruit when grown in poor, rocky soil. On the other hand, grapes just don't like wet feet. The ideal vineyard soil is easily permeable by water; this characteristic is even more crucial than its mineral content. Until the 1990s, California growers paid far more attention to climate than geology when deciding where to plant vineyards and how to manage them. As demand for premium wine has exploded, though, winemakers are paying much more attention to the soil part of the terroir equation. Geologists now do a brisk business advising growers on vineyard soil.

Different grape varieties thrive in different types of soil. For instance, cabernet sauvignon does best on well-drained, gravelly soils; soil that's too wet or contains too much heavy clay or organic matter will give the wine an obnoxious vegetative quality that even the best wine-making techniques cannot remove. Merlot grapes, however, can grow in soil with more clay and still be made into a delicious, rich wine. Sauvignon blanc grapes do quite well in heavy clay soils, but the winegrower has to limit irrigation and use some viticultural muscle to keep the grapes from developing unacceptable flavors. Chardonnay likes well-drained vineyards but will also take heavy soil.

The soils below Napa Valley's crags and in the wine-growing valleys of Sonoma County are dizzyingly diverse, which helps account for the unusually wide variety of grapes grown in such a small area. Some of the soils are composed of dense, heavy sedimentary clays washed from the mountains; others are very rocky clays, loams, or silts of alluvial fans. These fertile, well-drained soils cover much of the valleys' floors. Other areas have soil based on serpentine,

Vintage Variables

Oenophiles make much of a wine's vintage—the year in which the grapes were harvested—because the climate in the vineyard has a big impact on a wine's character. From one year to the next, depending on the weather, a single vine can yield very different wines.

It's impossible to generalize about which vintages are best and worst, because growing conditions vary so much from region to region, and sorting out the many elements that influence a wine can be as confusing as untangling a string of last year's Christmas lights. Vines that grow just around the bend from each other can have vastly different weather years.

In very general terms, grapes grown in cool, wet regions tend to do better in warmer years, whereas hotter regions tend to get better results in cooler years. A cool growing season can suppress crop yield, and lower crop yield boosts quality. Grapes ripen more slowly in cool years, gaining more intense flavors and higher acid; the potential of wines meant for aging improves. Cold spring weather, however, can prevent fruit from forming in the first place. Rain can have the same effect. Too much rain any time during the growing season, or any rain at all in late summer, worries growers because it can bring mildew, bunch rot, and off flavors.

All of this comes with caveats. Weather affects different varietals differently: for example, cabernet sauvignon does well in most conditions, but zinfandel and chenin blanc are especially susceptible to bunch rot from late-season rain. The notoriously finicky pinot noir grape suffers in hot weather and can get sunburned, but it is also sensitive to a too-cool growing season. From region to region, a given varietal might respond to similar conditions differently. Frequent fog, for instance, to some extent hardens Central Coast grapes against mildew, and a drizzly day at the wrong time of year can spell doom for a Sonoma crop.

Federal law requires that either 85 or 95 percent of the wine in a bottle labeled with a vintage year be grown that year (the exact percentage depends on whether it's also labeled with an AVA). If you see no vintage on the bottle, what's inside is likely a blend of wines from different years. If you do know the vintage, however, you can glean some information about the wine by knowing the conditions that occurred when and where it was grown. Staff at wine stores and wineries are often a good source for finding out more. Knowing the age of the wine can also help you decide when to open it.

a rock that rarely appears aboveground. In all, there are about 60 soil types in the Napa and Sonoma valleys.

The geology of the Central Coast is less complex: calcareous (calcium-rich) shale predominates at higher elevations, and loamy alluvial soils with fewer nutrients make up flatter land. Good rainfall, soaked up by rocky clay, makes the higher-elevation areas prime spots for dry farming (without irrigation). The sandier, drier flatlands require more irrigation but are much easier to cultivate because of their topography.

In Wine Country you'll hear a lot about limestone, a nutrient-rich rock in which grapevines thrive. Some California winemakers claim to be growing in limestone when in fact they are not. In fact, only small patches of California's Wine Country have significant amounts of limestone. The term is often used to describe the streak of light-colored, almost white soil that runs across the Napa Valley from the Palisades to St. Helena and through Sonoma County from the western flanks of the Mayacamas Mountains to Windsor. The band is actually made of volcanic material that has no limestone content. The error is easily made on the Central Coast, where seashells from a prehistoric ocean floor turned into calcareous shale. Limestone forms in much the same way.

DOWN ON THE FARM

Much like a fruit or nut orchard, a vineyard can produce excellent grapes for decades—even a century—if it's given the proper attention. The growing cycle starts in winter, when the vines are bare and dormant. While the plants rest, the grower works to enrich the soil and repair the trellising system (if there is one) that holds up the vines. This is when **pruning** takes place to regulate the vine's growth and upcoming season's crop size.

In spring, the soil is aerated by plowing, and new vines go in. The grower trains established vines so they grow, with or without trellising, in the shape most beneficial for the grapes. **Bud break** occurs when the first new bits of green emerge from the vines, and a pale green veil appears over the winter's gray-black vineyards. A late frost can be devastating at this time of year. Summer brings the flowering of the vines, when clusters of tiny green blossoms appear, and **fruit set,** when the grapes form from the blossoms. As the vineyards turn luxuriant and leafy, more pruning, along with leaf pulling, keeps foliage in check so the vine directs nutrients to the grapes, and so the sun can reach the fruit. As summer advances, the grower will **thin the fruit,** cutting off (or "dropping") some bunches so the remaining grapes intensify in flavor. A look at the vineyards reveals heavy clusters of green or purple grapes, some pea-size, others marble-size, depending on the variety.

Fall is the busiest season in the vineyard. Growers and wine-makers carefully monitor the ripeness of the grapes, some-times with equipment that tests sugar and acid levels and sometimes simply by tasting them. As soon as the grapes are ripe, **harvest** begins amid the lush foliage. In Califor-nia this generally happens in September and October, but sometimes a bit earlier or later, depending on the type of grape and the climatic conditions. Picking must be done as quickly as possible, within just a day or two, to keep the grapes from passing their peak. Most California grapes are harvested mechanically, but some are picked by hand (⇨ *The Crush, above*). After harvest, the vines start to regenerate for next year.

Sometimes by preference and sometimes by necessity, wine-makers don't grow all the grapes they need. Small wineries with only a few acres of grapes are limited in the varietals and quantities they can grow. (The smallest producers don't even have their own wineries, so they pay to use the equip-ment and storage space at a custom crush facility.) Midsize wineries may aim to get bigger. If it doesn't buy more acre-age, a winery that wants to diversify or expand production has to buy grapes from an independent grower.

Many winemakers purchase at least some of their grapes. Some wineries have negotiated long-term contracts with top growers, buying grapes from the same supplier year after year. This way, the winemaker can control the consistency and quality of the fruit just as if it came from the winery's own vineyard. Other wineries buy from several growers, and many growers sell to more than one winery.

Winemakers who buy from growers face a paradoxical problem: it's possible to make a wine that's too good and too popular. As the demand for a wine—and its price—rises, so will the price of the grapes used to make it. Other wineries sometimes bid up the price of the grapes, with the result that a winemaker can no longer afford the grapes that made a wine famous. This competitiveness among winemakers for specific batches of grapes underscores the faith put in terroir and the importance of growers.

Napa Valley

WORD OF MOUTH

"If you have been to Chianti in Italy, you will have a reasonable idea of what the Napa Valley looks like. . . . In my limited experience, the farther north you go, the better it gets."

—Ackislander

WHEN IT COMES TO WINE PRODUCTION IN THE UNITED STATES, NAPA VALLEY RULES the roost, with more than 275 wineries and many of the biggest brands in the business. Vastly diverse soils and microclimates give Napa winemakers the chance to make a tremendous variety of wines. But what's the area like beyond the glossy advertising and boldface names?

For every blockbuster winery whose name you'll recognize from wine stores and the pages of *Wine Spectator*—Robert Mondavi, Charles Krug, Beringer, and Stag's Leap Wine Cellars, to name a very few—you'll also find a low-frills winery that will warmly welcome you into its modest tasting room. At the other end of the spectrum are Napa's "cult" cabernet producers—Screaming Eagle, Harlan Estate, Dalla Valle, and Dominus Estate among them—whose doors are closed tight to visitors.

The handful of small towns strung along Highway 29 are where wine industry workers live, and they're also where most of the area lodging is. The up-and-coming town of Napa—the valley's largest town—lures with its few cultural attractions and accommodations that are (relatively) reasonably priced. A few miles farther north, compact Yountville is a culinary boomtown, densely packed with top-notch restaurants and hotels, including a few luxury properties. Continuing north, St. Helena teems with elegant boutiques and restaurants; mellow Calistoga, known for spas and hot springs, feels a bit like an Old West frontier town, and has a more casual attitude than many Wine Country towns.

Because the Napa Valley attracts everyone from hard-core wine collectors to bachelorette partyers, it's not necessarily the best place to get away from it all. But there's a reason why it's the number-one California Wine Country destination. The local viticulture has inspired a robust passion for food, and several outstanding chefs have taken root here, sealing Napa's reputation as one of the best restaurant destinations in the country. And here visitors will get a glimpse of California's history, from the wine cellars dating back to the late 1800s to the flurry of Steamboat Gothic architecture dressing up Calistoga. Binding all these temptations together is the sheer scenic beauty of the place. Much of Napa Valley's landscape unspools in orderly, densely planted rows of vines. Even the climate cooperates, as the warm summer days and refreshingly cool evenings that

are so favorable for grape growing make perfect weather for traveling, too.

GETTING AROUND NAPA

Highway 29, the Napa Valley Highway, heads north from Vallejo first as a busy four-lane highway, then narrows to a two-lane road at Yountville. Beyond Yountville, expect Highway 29 to be congested, especially on summer weekends. Traveling through St. Helena can be particularly slow during morning and afternoon rush hours. You'll probably find slightly less traffic on the Silverado Trail, which roughly parallels Highway 29 all the way from the town of Napa to Calistoga. Cross streets connect the two like rungs on a ladder every few miles, making it easy to cross over from one to the other.

NAPA VALLEY APPELLATIONS

Although almost all of Napa County, which stretches from the Mayacamas Mountains in the west to Lake Berryessa in the east, comprises the Napa Valley American Viticultural Area (AVA), this large viticultural region is divided into many smaller AVAs, or subappellations, each with its own unique characteristics.

Four of these—Oak Knoll, Oakville, Rutherford, and St. Helena—stretch clear across the valley floor. Chilled by coastal fog, the **Oak Knoll AVA,** formally recognized in 2004, is one of the coolest appellations in Napa. The **Oakville AVA,** just north of Yountville, is studded by both big-name wineries (such as Robert Mondavi and Opus One) and awe-inspiring boutique labels (such as the super-exclusive Screaming Eagle). Oakville's gravelly, well-drained soil is especially good for cabernet sauvignon.

A sunny climate and well-drained soil make **Rutherford AVA** one of the best locations for cabernet sauvignon in California, if not the world. North of Rutherford, the **St. Helena AVA** is one of Napa's toastiest, as the slopes surrounding the narrow valley reflect the sun's heat. Bordeaux varietals are the most popular grapes grown here—particularly cabernet sauvignon but also merlot. Just north, at the foot of Mt. St. Helena is the newest of the bunch, the **Calistoga AVA,** instituted at the beginning of 2010.

Stags Leap District AVA, a small district on the east side of the valley, is marked by dramatic volcanic palisades. Cab-

The design of the Opus One winery combines space-age and Mayan elements.

ernet sauvignon and merlot are by far the favored grapes. Cool evening breezes encourage a long growing season and intense fruit flavors. Some describe the resulting wines as "rock soft" or an "iron fist in a velvet glove."

Mount Veeder and **Spring Mountain AVAs** each encompass parts of the mountains from which they take their names. And both demonstrate how stressing out grape vines can yield outstanding results; the big winner is cabernet. Growing grapes on these slopes takes a certain recklessness—or foolhardiness, depending on your point of view, especially since many of the vineyards are so steep that they have to be tilled and harvested by hand.

There are plenty of other notable appellations, like up-and-comer Howell Mountain. The climate zones are nearly as much of a crazy quilt as the appellations. The great variability in the climate, as well as the soils, explains why valley vintners can make so many different wines, and make them so well.

NAPA

46 mi northeast of San Francisco via I–80 east and north, Rte. 37 west, and Rte. 29 north.

The town of Napa is the valley's largest, and visitors who get a glimpse of the strip malls and big-box stores from

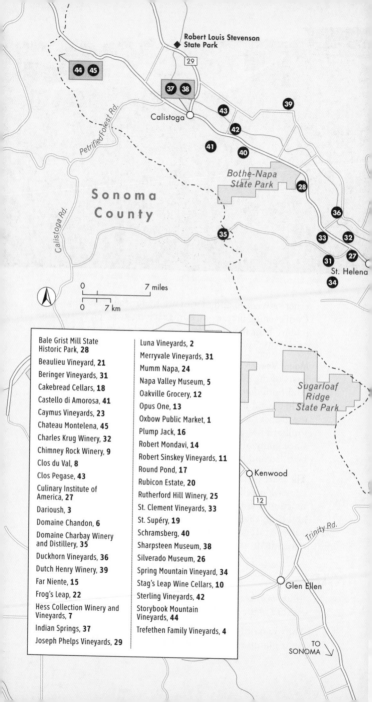

Robert Louis Stevenson State Park

29

44 45

37 38

Petrified Forest Rd.

Calistoga

43

42

39

41

40

Sonoma County

Bothe-Napa State Park

28

Calistoga Rd.

35

36

33 32

31

27

St. Helena

34

0 7 miles
0 7 km

Sugarloaf Ridge State Park

Kenwood

12

Trinity Rd.

Glen Ellen

TO SONOMA

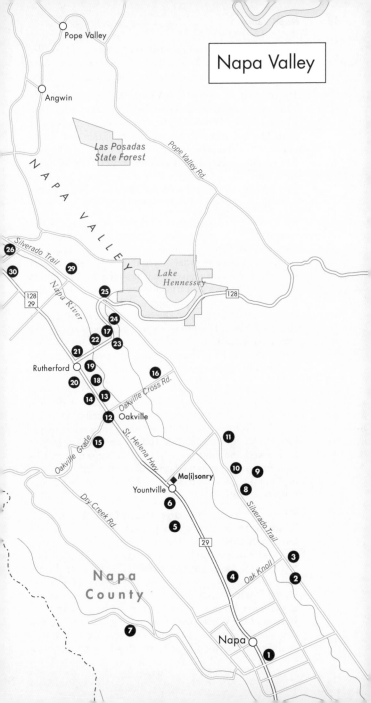

Napa Valley

Highway 29 often speed right past on the way to the smaller and more seductive Yountville or St. Helena. But Napa doesn't entirely deserve its dowdy reputation.

The oldest town in the Napa Valley, Napa was founded in 1848 in a strategic location on the Napa River, where the Sonoma-Benicia Road (Highways 12 and 29) crossed at a ford. The first wood-frame building built that year was a saloon, and the downtown area still preserves an old river-town atmosphere. Many Victorian houses have survived, and in the original business district a few older buildings have been preserved, including the turn-of-the-20th-century courthouse and several riverfront warehouses.

After many years as a blue-collar town that more or less turned its back on the Wine Country scene, Napa has spent the last few years attempting to increase its appeal to visitors, with somewhat mixed results. A walkway that follows the river through town, completed in 2008, makes the city more pedestrian-friendly, and new restaurants and hotels are continually popping up (there are even plans to open a Ritz-Carlton on the river's banks in 2011). But you'll still find a handful of empty storefronts among the wine bars, bookstores, and restaurants, and Napa's biggest tourist attraction, a food- and wine-themed museum and educational center, closed in late 2008.

Although Napa is definitely a work in progress, the town attracts more and more visitors every year, many of them looking for a slightly more reasonably priced place to lay their head after a day of wine tasting than what they'll find farther up the valley. If you set up your home base here, you'll undoubtedly want to spend some time getting out of town and into the beautiful countryside, but don't neglect taking a stroll to see what Napa's least pretentious town has to offer.

Though it's not terribly large, **Oxbow Public Market,** a collection of about 20 small shops, wine bars, and artisanal food producers, is a fun place to begin your introduction to the wealth of food and wine available in the Napa Valley. Swoon over the decadent charcuterie at the Fatted Calf, slurp down some oysters on the half shell at Hog Island Oyster Company, sample a large variety of local olive oils at the Olive Press, or get a whiff of the hard-to-find seasonings at the Whole Spice Company before sitting down to a glass of wine at one of the two wine bars. A branch of the retro fast-food joint Gott's Roadside tempts those who prefer hamburgers to duck-liver mousse. ⊠ *610 and 644 1st St.* ☎ *No phone* ⊕ *www.oxbowpublicmarket.com* ⊡ *Free* ⊙ *Generally weekdays 9–7, weekends 10–6, though hrs of some merchants vary.*

VINEYARDS AROUND NAPA

Luna Vineyards was established in 1995 by veterans of the Napa wine industry intent on making less conventional wines, particularly Italian varieties such as sangiovese and pinot grigio. Though these days you're just as likely to taste a merlot or a cabernet blend, it's still well worth visiting its Tuscan-style tasting room with a coffered ceiling, especially for a nip of late-harvest dessert wine of pinot grigio called Mille Baci ("a thousand kisses" in Italian). ⊠ *2921 Silverado Trail* ☎ *707/255–5862* ⊕ *www.lunavineyards.com* ⊡ *Tasting $15–$25* ⊙ *Sun.–Thurs. 10–5, Fri. and Sat. 10–6.*

Darioush is not quite like any other winery in the valley: you'll know that as soon as you turn into the driveway and see the 16 freestanding, sand-colored columns looming in front of a travertine building that looks like a cross between the Parthenon and a sultan's palace. That grand visitor center—where the opulent gift shop sells luxe housewares, jewelry, and gifty items such as Fabergé wine stoppers—was designed to evoke Persepolis, the capital of ancient Persia. The Persian heritage of owner Darioush Khaledi surfaces in more subtle ways, too, from the Middle Eastern–inflected music playing in the tasting room to the pistachios served with the wines. Although walk-in visitors can taste at the bar, call in advance or book online to sit at a table. In either case, the wines (often a chardonnay, viognier, merlot, cabernet sauvignon, and Duel, a cabernet-shiraz blend) are the same. For a more extensive look at the opulent property and wine-making operations, sign up for the $50 tour and wine and artisan cheese tasting, which is given at 2 PM daily. ⊠ *4240 Silverado Trail* ☎ *707/257–2345* ⊕ *www.darioush. com* ⊡ *$25* ⊙ *Daily 10:30–5, tour by appointment.*

The big terra-cotta-colored building at **Trefethen Family Vineyards** is a remnant of the old Eshcol Winery, built in 1886. It's the only three-story gravity-flow winery built from wood remaining in Napa (other remaining gravity-flow wineries are made from stone, which has weathered the last century much better). Trefethen makes superb chardonnay, cabernet sauvignon, and pinot noir, as well as an excellent dry riesling. If you'd like to find out for yourself how well

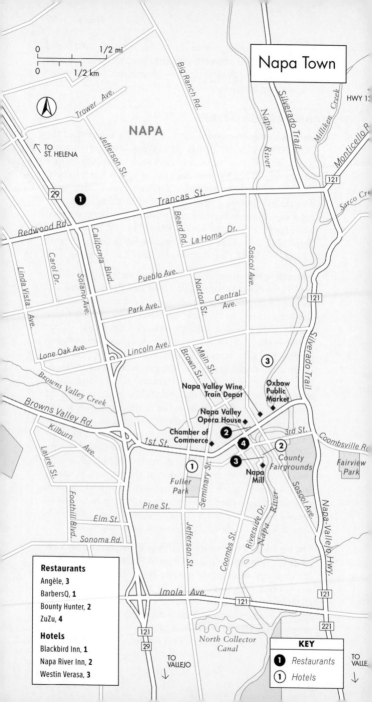

Napa Town

NAPA

TO ST. HELENA

HWY 1

Silverado Trail

Milliken Creek

Monticello R

121

Sarco Cr

Trower Ave.

Big Ranch Rd.

Jefferson St.

Trancas St.

Napa River

29

Redwood Rd.

Beard Rd.

La Homa Dr.

Soscol Ave.

California Blvd.

Carol Dr.

Solano Ave.

Linda Vista Ave.

Pueblo Ave.

Norton St.

Central Ave.

Park Ave.

121

Lone Oak Ave.

Lincoln Ave.

Browns Valley Creek

Silverado Trail

Browns Valley Rd.

Brown St.

Main St.

3

Napa Valley Wine Train Depot

Oxbow Public Market

Kilburn Ave.

Napa Valley Opera House

Chamber of Commerce

2

4

3rd St.

Coombsville Rd

Fairview Park

Laurel St.

Foothill Blvd.

1st St.

Seminary St.

①

3

Napa Mill

2

County Fairgrounds

Soscol Ave.

Napa-Vallejo Hwy.

Fuller Park

Napa River

Pine St.

Elm St.

Sonoma Rd.

Jefferson St.

Coombs St.

Riverside Dr.

Imola Ave.

121

North Collector Canal

121

29

TO VALLEJO

121

221

TO VALLE

their wines age, pay for the reserve tasting, which gets you pours of both limited-release wines and one or two of the older vintages (known as library wines). There's a cork tree planted in the garden outside the tasting room—so *that's* what the stuff looks like before it ends up on the sharp end of your corkscrew. ⊠ *1160 Oak Knoll Ave.* ☎ *707/255–7700* ⊕ *www.trefethen.com* ⊠ *Tasting $10–$25, tour $25* ☉ *Daily 10–4:30, tour daily by appointment at 10:30.*

WHERE TO EAT

$$$ × **Angèle.** An 1890s boathouse with a vaulted wood-beam ceiling sets the scene for romance at this cozy French bistro. Though the style is casual—tables are close together, and the warm, crusty bread is plunked right down on the paper-topped tables—the food is always well executed. Look for classic French dishes such as beef bourguignon, a rib-eye steak with red wine sauce and french fries, or a starter of ris de veau (veal sweetbreads). In fair weather, ask for one of the charming outdoor tables. ⊠ *540 Main St.* ☎ *707/252–8115* ⊕ *www.angelerestaurant.com* ▭ *AE, D, DC, MC, V.*

$ × **BarBersQ.** Hardly a down-home ramshackle barbecue shack, this temple to meat in the middle of a shopping center has a clean, modern aesthetic, with black-and-white photos on the wall and brushed aluminum chairs. (Your average 'cue joint doesn't have a wine list with almost 100 choices on it, either—many of the bottles are from big-name producers just down the road.) The menu of barbecue favorites includes a half or full rack of smoked baby back ribs and a Memphis-style pulled pork sandwich, all served with your choice of three different sauces. The supremely juicy fried chicken, made with free-range chicken and served with mashed potatoes and vinegary collard greens, is also popular. If you can save any room, the root-beer float or sweet potato–pecan pie is a fitting end to a homey meal. Outside seating (on a patio facing the parking lot) is available on fair days. ⊠ *3900D Bel Aire Plaza* ☎ *707/224–6600* ⊕ *www.barbersqu.com* ▭ *AE, MC, V.*

$$$ × **Bistro Don Giovanni.** Co-owner and host Giovanni Scala
★ might be around himself to give you a warm welcome to this lively bistro, where you can peek past the copper pots hanging in the open kitchen to see the 750-degree wood-burning oven. The Cal-Italian food is simultaneously inventive and comforting: an excellent fritto misto of onions, fennel, calamari, and plump rock shrimp; risotto with scal-

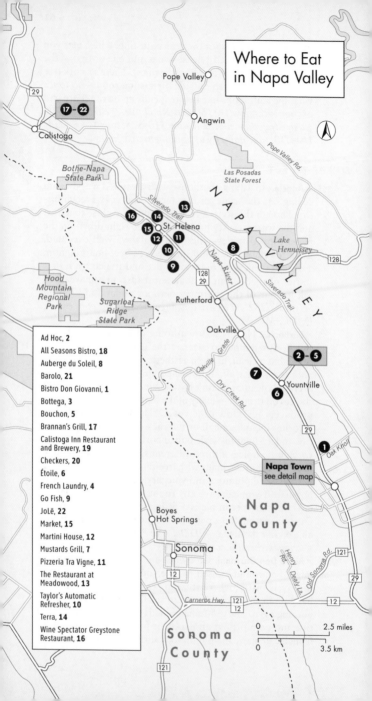

Where to Eat in Napa Valley

Ad Hoc, **2**

All Seasons Bistro, **18**

Auberge du Soleil, **8**

Barolo, **21**

Bistro Don Giovanni, **1**

Bottega, **3**

Bouchon, **5**

Brannan's Grill, **17**

Calistoga Inn Restaurant and Brewery, **19**

Checkers, **20**

Étoile, **6**

French Laundry, **4**

Go Fish, **9**

Jolē, **22**

Market, **15**

Martini House, **12**

Mustards Grill, **7**

Pizzeria Tra Vigne, **11**

The Restaurant at Meadowood, **13**

Taylor's Automatic Refresher, **10**

Terra, **14**

Wine Spectator Greystone Restaurant, **16**

Napa Town
see detail map

0   2.5 miles

0   3.5 km

lops and wild mushrooms; pizza with caramelized onions and Gorgonzola; and tender braised lamb on a bed on fried polenta. Dishes roasted in the wood-burning oven are a specialty. Children are unusually welcome here, catered to with crayons and paper-topped tables and a menu with items such as pizza topped with cheese, french fries, and "no green stuff." Fodors.com Forum users suggest snagging a table on the covered patio for a "more intimate and quiet" experience. ⊠ *4110 Howard La./Rte. 29* ☏ *707/224–3300* ⊕ *www.bistrodongiovanni.com* ⊟ *AE, D, DC, MC, V.*

$$ \times $ **Bounty Hunter.** A triple threat, Bounty Hunter is a wine
★ store, wine bar, and restaurant in one. You can stop by for just a glass of wine from their impressive selection—a frequently changing list with 40 available by the glass in both 2- and 5-ounce pours, and 400 by the bottle—but it's best to come with an appetite. A minuscule kitchen means the menu is also small, but every dish is a standout, including the pulled pork and beef brisket sandwiches served with three types of barbecue sauce, the signature beer-can chicken, and meltingly tender St. Louis–style ribs. The space is whimsically rustic, with stuffed game trophies mounted on the wall and leather saddles standing in for seats at a couple of tables; the pressed-tin ceilings and granite-top café tables also give it a casually chic vibe. ■TIP→ **It's open until midnight on Friday and Saturday, making it a popular spot among locals for a late-night bite.** At this writing, plans to expand into the space next door were in the works. ⊠ *975 1st St.* ☏ *707/226–3976* ⊕ *www.bountyhunterwinebar.com* ⚄ *Reservations not accepted* ⊟ *AE, MC, V.*

$$$ ✕ **ZuZu.** Ocher-color walls, a weathered wood bar, a faded tile floor, and hammered-tin ceiling panels set the scene for a menu composed almost entirely of tapas. These little dishes, so perfect for sharing, and Latin jazz on the stereo help make this place a popular spot for festive get-togethers. Diners down *cava* (Spanish sparkling wine) or sangria with dishes such as white anchovies with endive, ratatouille, and salt cod with garlic croutons. Reservations aren't accepted, so expect a wait on weekends, when local young adults flood the zone. The bocadillos (Spanish-style sandwiches) and empanadas available at lunch make it an inexpensive stop for a midday snack. ⊠ *829 Main St.* ☏ *707/224–8555* ⚄ *Reservations not accepted* ⊕ *www.zuzunapa.com* ⊟ *AE, MC, V* ☉ *No lunch weekends.*

Napa Valley's Wine Train

Turn the driving over to someone else—a train conductor. The **Napa Valley Wine Train** (✉ 1275 McKinstry St., Napa ☎ 707/253–2111 or 800/427–4124 ⊕ www.winetrain.com) runs a scenic route between Napa and St. Helena with several restored 1915–17 Pullman railroad cars. The ride often includes a meal, such as brunch or dinner; it can also include a winery tour or some other kind of special event such as a murder mystery dinner or a visit with a local vintner. Although it's no bargain (starting at around $90 for lunch, $100 for dinner) and can feel a bit hokey, the train gives you a chance to enjoy the vineyard views without any driving worries.

WHERE TO STAY

$-$$ ☒ **Blackbird Inn.** Arts and Crafts style infuses this 1905 building, from the lobby's enormous fieldstone fireplace to the lamps that cast a warm glow over the impressive wooden staircase. The style is continued in the attractive guest rooms, with sturdy turn-of-the-20th-century oak beds and matching night tables, which nonetheless are updated with spacious, modern bathrooms, most with spa bathtubs. The inn is within walking distance of Napa's historic, restaurant-rich downtown area. It tends to book up quickly, so reserve well in advance. **Pros:** gorgeous architecture and period furnishings; convenient to downtown Napa; free DVD library. **Cons:** must be booked well in advance; some rooms are on the small side. ✉ 1755 1st St. ☎ 707/226–2450 or 888/567–9811 ⊕ www.blackbirdinnnapa.com ➪ 8 rooms ☖ In-room: a/c, DVD, Wi-Fi. In-hotel: some pets allowed (fee) ▤ AE, D, DC, MC, V ⫼ CP.

$$$$ ☒ **Milliken Creek Inn.** Wine and cheese at sunset set a romantic mood in the intimate lobby, with its terrace overlooking the Napa River and a lush lawn. The chic rooms take a page from the stylebook of British-colonial Asia, with a khaki-and-cream color scheme and gauzy canopies over the beds in some rooms, alongside hydrotherapy spa tubs and some of the fluffiest beds in the Wine Country. All but one have a gas-burning fireplace. A tiny deck overlooking the river is the spot for massages and private yoga classes. In the serene spa, all the treatment rooms, including one used for popular couple's treatments, have river views.

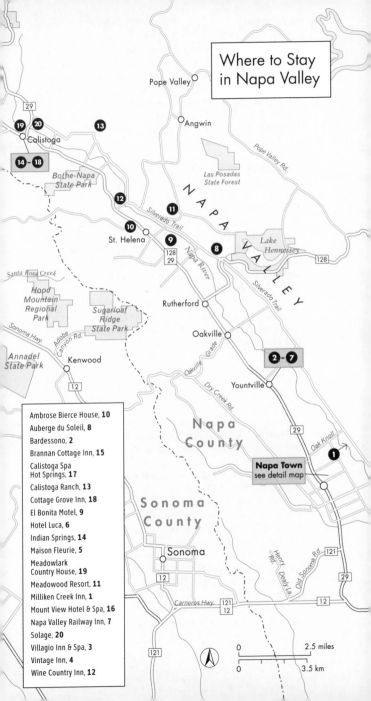

Where to Stay in Napa Valley

Ambrose Bierce House, **10**

Auberge du Soleil, **8**

Bardessono, **2**

Brannan Cottage Inn, **15**

Calistoga Spa
Hot Springs, **17**

Calistoga Ranch, **13**

Cottage Grove Inn, **18**

El Bonita Motel, **9**

Hotel Luca, **6**

Indian Springs, **14**

Maison Fleurie, **5**

Meadowlark
Country House, **19**

Meadowood Resort, **11**

Milliken Creek Inn, **1**

Mount View Hotel & Spa, **16**

Napa Valley Railway Inn, **7**

Solage, **20**

Villagio Inn & Spa, **3**

Vintage Inn, **4**

Wine Country Inn, **12**

Pros: soft-as-clouds beds; serene hotel-guests-only spa; breakfast delivered to your room (or wherever you'd like to eat on the grounds); gratuities not accepted (except at the spa). **Cons:** expensive; road noise can be heard from the admittedly beautiful outdoor areas. ✉ *1815 Silverado Trail* ☎ *707/255–1197 or 800/835–6112* ⊕ *www.milliken-creekinn.com* 🛏 *12 rooms* ⚲ *In-room: a/c, safe, refrigerator, DVD, Wi-Fi. In-hotel: spa, no kids under 18* ⊟ *AE, D, DC, MC, V* ⊺○⊺ *CP.*

\$\$–\$\$\$ 🖫 **Napa River Inn.** Almost everything's close here: this waterfront inn is part of a complex of restaurants, shops, a gallery, and a spa, all within easy walking distance of downtown Napa. Guest rooms spread through three neighboring buildings. Those in the 1884 Hatt Building, in Victorian style, are arguably the most romantic, with deep-red walls, original architectural details such as maple hardwood floors, and old-fashioned slipper tubs. Brighter colors dominate in the rooms of the Plaza and Embarcadero buildings; many of the rooms have river views. Baked goods from the neighboring bakery are delivered to your door for breakfast. **Pros:** a pedestrian walkway connects the hotel to downtown Napa; unusual pet-friendly policy; wide range of room sizes and prices. **Cons:** river views could be more scenic; some rooms get noise from nearby restaurants. ✉ *500 Main St.* ☎ *707/251–8500 or 877/251–8500* ⊕ *www.napariverinn. com* 🛏 *65 rooms, 1 suite* ⚲ *In-room: a/c, safe, refrigerator, DVD (some), Wi-Fi. In-hotel: 4 restaurants, bar, gym, spa, bicycles, laundry service, Internet terminal, some pets allowed (fee)* ⊟ *AE, D, DC, MC, V* ⊺○⊺ *CP.*

\$\$\$–\$\$\$\$ 🖫 **Westin Verasa.** Across the street from the Wine Train depot and just behind the Oxbow Public Market is this spacious hotel-condo complex, which considerably expanded the city's once-limited options for full-service hotels when it opened in 2008. Although its style is hardly cutting-edge, its look is sophisticated and soothing, all pristine white bedding and furniture in warm earth tones. Gadgets such as Xbox 360s, iPod docking stations, and 32-inch flat-screen televisions are a convenient perk for the technologically inclined, whereas the heated saltwater pool and hot tub and boccie court are there for those who want to unplug. The attached restaurant, Ken Frank's acclaimed La Toque, is one of the best in town. It's open for dinner only, but a more casual café and wine bar is also open for breakfast and lunch. **Pros:** centrally located in downtown Napa;

well-equipped kitchenettes; spacious double-headed showers. **Cons:** annoying "amenities fee" charged in addition to room rate. ⊠ *1314 Mckinstry St.* ☎ *707/257–1800* ⊕ *www. westin.com/napa* ⇆ *130 rooms, 50 suites* ⚿ *In-room: a/c, safe, kitchen (some), refrigerator (some), DVD, Internet, Wi-Fi. In-hotel: 2 restaurants, room service, bar, pool, gym, laundry service, some pets allowed* ⊟ *AE, D, DC, MC, V* ⊙❘ *EP.*

NIGHTLIFE AND THE ARTS

Napa nightlife tends toward the sleepy side, but locals sip wine and listen to live music (mostly jazz, but also rock, blues, and more) from Wednesday through Saturday at **Silo's,** next to the Napa River Inn in the Historic Napa Mill. The cover varies, but it's generally $10–$25. ⊠ *530 Main St.* ☎ *707/251–5833* ⊕ *www.silosjazzclub.com.*

The interior of the 1879 Italianate Victorian **Napa Valley Opera House** isn't quite as majestic as the façade, but the intimate 500-seat venue is still an excellent place to see all sorts of performances, from Pat Metheny and Mandy Patinkin to various dance and theater companies and, yes, even the occasional opera. ⊠ *1030 Main St.* ☎ *707/226–7372* ⊕ *www. napavalleyoperahouse.org.*

SHOPPING

Napa doesn't have a slew of cute boutiques like St. Helena, but if you wander around the downtown area you're sure to find an interesting bookstore, clothing boutique, or wine shop. Just around the corner from the opera house, **Bounty Hunter Rare Wine and Provisions** (⊠ *975 First St.* ☎ *707/255– 0622*) stocks Napa cult cabernets and other hard-to-find wines. The store shares space with a charming wine bar with exposed-brick walls and a stamped-tin ceiling. **Shackford's Kitchen Store** (⊠ *1350 Main St.* ☎ *707/226–2132*) looks something like a hardware store (the floors are concrete), but there's no better place in town for all your cooking needs, whether it's ceramic serving pieces or a chef's jacket. Even visitors who are zipping right past Napa for destinations farther up the valley are sometimes tempted to turn off the highway at **Napa Premium Outlets** (⊠ *629 Factory Stores Dr.* ☎ *707/226–9876* ⊕ *www.premiumoutlets.com*)where national chains such as Kenneth Cole, Coach, J. Crew, and Levi's sell their wares at 25%–65% off.

Wine Country Balloon Rides

Thought those vineyards were beautiful from the highway? Try viewing them from an altitude of about a thousand feet, serenely drifting along with the wind, the only sound the occasional roar of the burners overhead.

Many companies organize hot-air ballooning trips over Napa and Sonoma, offering rides that usually cost between $200 and $250 per person for a one-hour flight, which typically includes brunch or lunch afterward. If you were hoping for the ultimate in romance—a flight with no one else but your sweetie (and an FAA-approved pilot) on board—be prepared to shell out two to four times as much.

Flights typically take off at the crack of dawn, when winds are the lightest, so be prepared to make an early start and dress in layers. Flights are dependent on weather, and if there's rain or too much fog, expect to be grounded.

The following are a few of the many outfits offering rides. Many hotels can also hook you up with companies in their vicinity, some of whom can pick you up from your lodgings.

■ **Balloons Above the Valley** (☎ 707/253–2222 or 800/464–6824 ⊕ www.balloonrides.com). **Napa Valley Balloons** (☎ 707/944–0228 or 800/253–2224 ⊕ www.napavalleyballoons.com). **Napa Valley Drifters** (☎ 707/252–7210 or 877/463–7438 ⊕ www.napavalleydrifters.com).

SPORTS AND THE OUTDOORS

GOLF

The 27 holes at the **Chardonnay Golf Club** (✉ 2555 Jameson Canyon Rd. ☎ 707/257–1900), which meander through vineyards, can by golfed in three different 18-hole combinations. The greens fee varies but is generally $50 to $84, depending on the season and time of day, and discounts are available for booking well in advance. The prices include a cart.

YOUNTVILLE

13 mi north of the town of Napa on Rte. 29.

These days Yountville is something like Disneyland for food lovers. It all started with Thomas Keller's French Laundry, one of the best restaurants in the United States, and the only spot in all of Northern California to wrest a coveted three-star ranking from Michelin when it published its first guide to the San Francisco area in 2006. Now Keller is also behind two more casual restaurants a few blocks from his mother ship—and that's only the tip of the iceberg. You could stay here for a week and not exhaust all the options in this tiny town with a big culinary reputation.

Yountville is full of small inns and luxurious hotels that cater to those who prefer to be able to stagger a short distance home after a decadent dinner. But it's also well located for excursions to many big-name Napa wineries. Near Yountville, along the Silverado Trail, the Stags Leap District helped put Napa on the wine-making map with its big, bold cabernet sauvignons. Volcanic soil predominates on the eastern slopes of Stags Leap, apparent from the towering volcanic palisades and crags hovering over the vineyards here.

On the other side of Highway 29 from Yountville rises the Mayacamas Range. Unlike on the valley floor, where wineries stand cheek by jowl along Highway 29 and the Silverado Trail, here wineries are fewer and farther between, hidden among the stands of oak, madrone, and redwood trees. Even though the Mount Veeder AVA gets more rain than the Napa Valley (as witnessed by those redwoods), soils are poor and rocky and the water runs off quickly, forcing grape vines planted here to grow deep roots. Vines thus stressed produce grapes that are smaller, with a higher ratio of grape surface to liquid volume, resulting in intensely flavored wines. This comes at a price: the vines on the steep slopes of the 2,677-foot volcanic peak of Mt. Veeder must be laboriously picked by hand. Merlot and syrah thrive in these conditions, but the big winner is cabernet.

Though many visitors use Yountville as a home base, touring wineries by day and returning to town for dinner, you could easily while away a few hours in town, picking up picnic fixings at a bakery.

At one end of town is the **Pioneer Cemetery and Indian Burial Ground** (✉ *Lincoln and Jackson Sts.*), which was established in 1848. George Yount is buried here, and the cemetery is still used by the remaining members of the local Wappo tribe.

A combination art gallery and tasting room, **Ma(i)sonry** (✉ *6711 Washington St.* ☎ *707/944–0889* ⊕ *www.maisonry. com*) occupies an atmospheric stone manor house constructed in 1904. In fair weather, tasting flights ($15–$35) from about 10 different limited-production wineries can be sampled in the beautiful garden, in a private nook, or at the long communal redwood table, or indoors among the various artwork and objets. Many of the pieces, which range from 17th-century furnishings to industrial lamps to slabs of petrified wood, were collected by the owner on his travels to Europe, but contemporary painters, sculptors, and other artists are shown on a rotating basis as well.

In between bouts of eating and drinking, you might stop by **V Marketplace** (⊠ 6525 Washington St. ☎ 707/944–2451). The vine-covered brick complex, which once housed a winery, livery stable, and distillery, contains a smattering of clothing boutiques, art galleries, and gift stores. NapaStyle, a large store, deli, and wine bar, sells cookbooks, luxury food items, and kitchenware, as well as an assortment of prepared foods perfect for picnics. The complex's signature restaurant, Bottega, features the food of celebrity chef Michael Chiarello.

It's not worth a long detour, but if you need a break from wine tasting, you can visit the **Napa Valley Museum** (⊠ 55 Presidents Circle ☎ 707/944–0500 ⊕ www.napavalleymuseum.org ⊠ $4.50 ⊙ Wed.–Mon. 10–5) next to Domaine Chandon on the grounds of the town's Veterans Home. Downstairs you'll find exhibits on local history, from the Wappo Indians through the pioneer period to modern wine making, and upstairs are rotating art exhibits.

VINEYARDS NEAR YOUNTVILLE

NEAR DOWNTOWN YOUNTVILLE

French-owned **Domaine Chandon** claims one of Yountville's prime pieces of real estate, on a knoll west of downtown where whimsical sculptures sprout out of the lawn and ancient oaks shade the winery. Basic tours of the sleek, modern facilities are available for $12 (not including a tasting), but other tours ($30 each), which focus on various topics (food-and-wine pairing or pinot production, for example), end with a seated tasting. The top-quality sparklers are made using the laborious *méthode champenoise*. To complete the experience, you can order hors d'oeuvres to accompany the wines in the tasting room, which can be ordered either by tasting flights or by the glass. Although Chandon is best known for its bubblies, still wines such as their chardonnay, pinot noir, and rosé are also worth a try. ⊠ 1 California Dr., west of Rte. 29 ☎ 707/944–2280 ⊕ www.

CLOSE UP

The Wine Country by Bicycle

Thanks to the scenic country roads that wind through the region, bicycling is a practically perfect way to get around the Wine Country (lack of designated bike lanes notwithstanding). And whether you're interested in an easy spin to a few wineries or a strenuous haul up a mountainside, there's a way to make it happen.

Bike shops in most towns will rent you a bike and helmet by the day. In addition to doling out maps and advice on the least-trafficked roads, bike-shop staffers can typically recommend a route based on your interests and fitness level.

If you're at all concerned about the logistics of your trip, consider springing for a one-day or multiday bike tour, which usually includes lunch, a guide, and a "sag wagon" in case you poop out before you reach your destination.

Some of your best bets for bike rentals:

Calistoga Bikeshop (✉ *1318 Lincoln Ave., Calistoga* ☎ *707/942–9687*) offers a self-guided Calistoga Cool Wine Tour package ($79), which includes free tastings at a number of small wineries. Best of all, they'll pick up any wine you purchase along the way if you've bought more than will fit in the handy bottle carrier on your bike.

Napa Valley Bike Tours (✉ *6488 Washington St., Yountville* ☎ *707/944–2953*) will deliver the bikes, which go for $30 to $70 a day, to many hotels in the Napa Valley if you're renting at least two bikes for a full day. One-day guided winery tours are $149.

St. Helena Cyclery (✉ *1156 Main St., St. Helena* ☎ *707/963–7736*) rents bikes by the hour, as well as by the day (hybrids $35, road bikes $60).

Wine Country Bikes (✉ *61 Front St., Healdsburg* ☎ *707/473–0610*), in downtown Healdsburg, is perfectly located for treks out into the Dry Creek and Russian River valleys, two of the better destinations for those on two wheels. Bikes, including tandems, go for $33 to $95 a day. One-day tours start at $129.

3

Domaine Chandon

chandon.com 🖩 *Tasting $5.50–$25 by the glass, $16–$22 by the flight* ⊙ *Daily 10–6; tours daily at 11, 1, and 3.*

MT. VEEDER

★ **Fodor's**Choice The **Hess Collection Winery and Vineyards** is a delightful discovery on Mt. Veeder 9 mi northwest of the city of Napa. (Don't give up; the road leading to the winery is long and winding.) The simple limestone structure, rustic from the outside but modern and airy within, contains Swiss owner Donald Hess's personal art collection, including mostly large-scale works by such contemporary European and American artists as Robert Motherwell, Andy Goldsworthy, and Frank Stella. Cabernet sauvignon is the real strength here, though Hess also produces some fine chardonnays. Self-guided tours of the art collection and guided tours of the winery's production facilities are both free. ⊠ *4411 Redwood Rd., west of Rte. 29, Napa* ☎ *707/255–1144* ⊕ *www.hesscollection.com* 🖩 *Tasting $10–$30* ⊙ *Daily 10–5:30; guided tours daily, hourly 10:30–3:30.*

STAGS LEAP

Austere **Clos du Val** doesn't seduce you with dramatic architecture or lush grounds, but it doesn't have to: the wines, crafted by winemaker John Clews, have a wide following, especially among those who are patient enough to cellar the wines for a number of years. Though Clews's team makes great pinot noir and chardonnay (grown in the nearby Car-

The Hess Collection Winery

neros region), the real claim to fame is the intense reserve cabernet, made with fruit from the Stags Leap District. The few picnic tables fill up early on summer weekends, and anyone is welcome to try a hand at the boccie-style French game of pétanque. ⊠ *5330 Silverado Trail, Napa* ☎ *707/259–2200* ⊕ *www.closduval.com* ✇ *Tasting $10–$20* ⊙ *Daily 10–5, tour by appointment.*

Chimney Rock Winery is usually easily spotted from the road—unless the poplar trees surrounding it are in full leaf, hiding it from view. In the somewhat ornate Cape (as in Cape of Good Hope) Dutch style of the 17th century, it seems out of place amid the austere Stags Leap landscape. But you have to love a winery that gradually took over a golf course, putting the land to a much nobler use. Most of its grapes go into a cabernet sauvignon, which tends to be softer and more supple than other cabernets hereabouts, but there's also a very fine sauvignon blanc and sauvignon gris blend and a dry rosé of cabernet franc (the latter, produced in small quantities, is available only at the winery). The comfortable tasting room's decor mirrors the exterior, with high, wood-beamed ceilings and a fireplace that warms it in winter. ⊠ *5350 Silverado Trail, Napa* ☎ *707/257–2641* ⊕ *www.chimneyrock.com* ✇ *Tasting $20–$30, tour $35* ⊙ *Daily 10–5, tour by appointment.*

It was the 1973 cabernet sauvignon produced by **Stag's Leap Wine Cellars** that put the winery—and the California wine industry—on the map by placing first in the famous Paris tasting of 1976. A visit to the winery is a no-frills affair; visitors in the tasting room are clearly serious about tasting wine and aren't interested in distractions like a gift shop. It costs $30 to taste the top-of-the-line wines, including their limited-production estate-grown cabernets, a few of which sell for well over $100. If you're interested in more modestly priced wines, try the $15 tasting, which usually includes a sauvignon blanc, chardonnay, merlot, and cabernet. ⊠ *5766 Silverado Trail, Napa* ☎ *707/265–2441* ⊕ *www.cask23.com* ⊠ *Tasting $15–$30, tour $40* ☉ *Daily 10–4:30, tour by appointment.*

Robert Sinskey Vineyards makes well-regarded cabernet blends from their all-organic, certified biodynamic vineyards, as well as a dry, refreshing pinot gris, gewürztraminer, riesling, and pinot blanc blend. However, it's best known for its intense, brambly pinot noirs, grown in the cooler Carneros District, where the grape thrives. The influence of Robert's wife, Maria Helm Sinskey—a chef and cookbook author—is evident during the tastings, which come with a few bites of food paired with each wine (her books and other culinary items are also available in the gift shop, next to the open kitchen). But for the best sense of how Sinskey wines pair with food, reserve a spot on the culinary tour, which ends with local cheeses and charcuterie served with the wines. ⊠ *6320 Silverado Trail Napa* ☎ *707/944–9090* ⊕ *www.robertsinskey.com* ⊠ *Tasting $25, tours $30–$50* ☉ *Daily 10–4:30, tour by appointment.*

WHERE TO EAT

★ Fodor's Choice ✕ **Ad Hoc.** When superstar chef Thomas Keller
$$–$$$ opened this relatively casual spot in 2006, he meant to run it for only six months until he opened a burger joint in the same space—but locals were so charmed by the homey food that they clamored for the stopgap to stay. Now a single, seasonal fixed-price menu ($49) is served nightly, with a slightly less expensive menu but equally hearty meal served for Sunday brunch. The selection might include a juicy pork loin and buttery polenta, served family-style, or a delicate panna cotta with a citrus glaze. The dining room is warmly low-key, with zinc-top tables, wine served in tumblers, and rock and jazz on the stereo. If you just can't wait to know what's going be served before you visit, you can call a day in advance for the menu. ⊠ *6476 Washington St.*

Ad Hoc, Thomas Keller's casual restaurant in Yountville

☎ 707/944–2487 ⊕ *www.adhocrestaurant.com* ▤ *AE, MC, V* ⊗ *No lunch Mon.–Sat.; no dinner Tues. and Wed.*

★ **Fodor'sChoice** ✕**Bottega.** In 2008 celebrity chef Michael
$$$ Chiarello made a much-heralded return to the restaurant business with this lively trattoria. The menu is simultaneously soulful and inventive, transforming local ingredients into regional Italian dishes with a twist. The antipasti in particular shine: you can order olives grown on Chiarello's own property in St. Helena, house-made charcuterie, or a creamy burrata, mozzarella cheese wrapped around a creamy center, which is served with meaty mushrooms and topped with beads of "caviar" made from balsamic vinegar. Potato gnocchi might be served with duck and a chestnut ragu, and hearty main courses such as braised short ribs may come on a bed of spinach prepared with preserved lemons. The vibe is more festival than formal, with exposed brick walls, an open kitchen, and paper-topped tables, but service is spot on, and the reasonably priced wine list offers lots of interesting choices from both Italy and California. ⊠ *6525 Washington St.* ☎ *707/945–1050* ⊕ *www.bottegana-pavalley.com* ▤ *AE, MC, V* ⊗ *No lunch Mon.*

$$$ ✕**Bouchon.** The team that brought French Laundry to its current pinnacle is also behind this place, where everything—the lively and crowded zinc bar, the elbow-to-elbow seating, the traditional French onion soup—could have come straight from a Parisian bistro. Roast chicken with mustard greens and fingerling potatoes and steamed mus-

DID YOU KNOW?

These tomatoes are headed for the kitchen of The French Laundry, one of Napa Valley's most famous restaurants, where dinner will set you back $250 if you can get a reservation.

sels served with crispy, addictive frites (french fries) are among the hearty dishes served in the high-ceilinged room. ■TIP→ **Late-night meals from a limited menu are served until 12:30 AM—a rarity in the Wine Country, where it's often difficult to find a place to eat after 10.** ⊠ *6534 Washington St.* ☎ *707/944–8037* ⊕ *www.bouchonbistro.com* ⊟ *AE, MC, V.*

$$$ × **Étoile.** Housed at Domaine Chandon, this quietly elegant stunner seems built for romance, with delicate orchids on each table and views of the beautiful wooded winery grounds from the large windows. After a few years of being off the radar of many local critics, the restaurant has gotten more attention lately under the young chef Perry Hoffman, who turns out sophisticated California cuisine. Starters such as poached lobster with radishes, Asian pear, and pearl barley play with a variety of textures, and luxe ingredients such as shavings of black truffle dress up a perfectly cooked beef tenderloin. Four- and six-course tasting menus can be ordered with or without wine pairings. The wine list naturally features plenty of Domaine Chandon sparklers, but it's strong in wines from throughout California as well. ⊠ *1 California Dr.* ☎ *888/242–6366* ⊕ *www.chandon.com/etoile-restaurant* ⊟ *AE, D, MC, V* ☉ *Closed Tues., Wed., and Jan.*

★ Fodor'sChoice × **French Laundry.** An old stone building laced **$$$$** with ivy houses the most acclaimed restaurant in Napa Valley—and, indeed, one of the most highly regarded in the country. The restaurant's two prix-fixe menus (both $250), one of which is vegetarian, vary, but "oysters and pearls," a silky dish of pearl tapioca with oysters and white sturgeon caviar, is a signature starter. Some courses rely on luxe ingredients such as foie gras, whereas others take humble foods like fava beans and elevate them to art. Reservations at French Laundry are hard-won and not accepted more than two months in advance. ■TIP→ **Call two months ahead to the day at 10 AM on the dot. Didn't get a reservation? Call on the day you'd like to dine here to be considered if there's a cancellation.** ⊠ *6640 Washington St.* ☎ *707/944–2380* ⚑ *Reservations essential* 🎩 *Jacket required* ⊕ *www.frenchlaundry.com* ⊟ *AE, MC, V* ☉ *Closed 1st 2 or 3 wks in Jan. No lunch Mon.–Thurs.*

$$ × **Mustards Grill.** There's not an ounce of pretension at Cindy Pawlcyn's longtime Napa favorite, despite the fact that it's booked solid every day and night with fans of her hearty cuisine. The menu mixes updated renditions of traditional American dishes, such as baby back pork ribs and a lemon-lime tart piled high with browned meringue, with innovative choices such as sweet corn tamales with tomatillo-avocado salsa and pumpkin seeds. A black-and-white marble tile floor and upbeat artwork set a scene that one Fodors.com reader describes as "pure fun, if not fancy." ⊠ *7399 St. Helena Hwy./Rte. 29, 1 mi north of town* ☎ *707/944–2424* ⊕ *www.mustardsgrill.com* ⌂ *Reservations essential* ▭ *AE, D, DC, MC, V.*

WHERE TO STAY

$$$$ ☲ **Bardessono.** It bills itself as the "greenest luxury hotel in America" (it's run partially on solar and geothermal energy, and 70% of the construction materials were recycled or reclaimed, to name just a few of the eco-conscious moves). Still, the large, spare rooms, arranged around four landscaped courtyards, are anything but spartan, with luxurious organic white bedding, gas fireplaces, and huge bathrooms with walnut floors (large enough for a massage table, should you opt for an in-room massage). It's got all the high-tech touches you'd expect for a property that opened in 2009—speakers for your iPhone, a flat-panel TV, and fancy spa tubs—and a few you wouldn't, such as motion sensors that detect when you're gone and adjust the blinds for energy efficiency. Service is smooth, from the valet who takes your car to the folks who staff the 75-foot-long rooftop lap pool area April through October, serving food and drinks to guests lounging on the cabanas. At the hotel's restaurant, chef Sean O'Toole uses largely local ingredients (some grown by the hotel itself) to concoct a seasonal menu of California fare with an adventurous twist. **Pros:** large rooftop lap pool; exciting restaurant on-site; polished service. **Cons:** expensive. ⊠ *6526 Yount St.* ☎ *707/204–6000* ⊕ *www.bardessono.com* ⌖ *50 rooms, 12 suites* ⌂ *In-room: a/c, safe, Internet, Wi-Fi. In-hotel: restaurant, room service, bar, pool, spa, bicycles, laundry service, some pets allowed (fee)* ▭ *AE, D, DC, MC, V* ⏻ *CP.*

$$$–$$$$ ☲ **Hotel Luca.** Although this 20-room newcomer to Yountville just opened in December 2009, the property embodies a rustic Tuscan style through and through, with dark-wood furniture and soothing decor in brown and sage. Rooms are clustered around a courtyard, which is warmed by a fireplace when the weather demands it. Uncommonly spacious bathrooms with large tubs and separate showers, warmed by radiant floor heating, invite lingering in the fluffy robes and slippers. A wide variety of spa services are available in the small spa or in your room. The hotel's excellent restaurant, Cantinetta Piero, serves soul-warming Tuscan fare, such as pastas, house-made preserved meats, and thin-crust pizzas from a wood-burning oven. **Pros:** extremely comfortable beds; attentive service; breakfast, included in rates, is served in the restaurant or delivered to your room. **Cons:** rooms are soundproofed, but outdoor areas get some traffic noise. ⊠ *6774 Washington St.,* ☎ *707/944–8080* ⊕ *www.hotellucanapa.com* ⤴ *20 rooms* ⟁ *In-room: a/c, refrigerator, safe, Wi-Fi. In-hotel: restaurant, room service, bar, pool, spa, gym, laundry service* ⊟ *AE, D, MC, V* ⫲*BP.*

¢–$ ☗ **Maison Fleurie.** If you'd like to be within easy walking distance of most of Yountville's best restaurants, and possibly score a great bargain, look into this casual, comfortable inn. Rooms share a French country style (picture toile bedspreads, wooden armoires, and trompe-l'oeil paintings on the walls) but vary dramatically in size and amenities. The largest have a private entrance, deck, fireplace, and jetted bathtub big enough for two. ■TIP→ **For a much lower rate, however, you can get one of the tiny but well-kept rooms with a small shower but no bathtub—and save for a French Laundry meal instead.** **Pros:** smallest rooms are some of the most affordable in town; free bike rental; refrigerator stocked with free soda. **Cons:** breakfast room can be crowded at peak times; bedding could be nicer. ⊠ *6529 Yount St.* ☎ *800/788–0369* ⊕ *www.maisonfleurienapa.com* ⤴ *13 rooms* ⟁ *In-room: a/c, refrigerator (some), DVD (some), no TV (some), Wi-Fi. In-hotel: pool, bicycles* ⊟ *AE, D, MC, V* ⫲*CP.*

¢   ☗ **Napa Valley Railway Inn.** Budget-minded travelers and guests with kids appreciate these basic accommodations just steps way from most of Yountville's best restaurants. Actual railcars, more than 100 years old, house nine long, narrow rooms that have a bit more charm than your average motel. Most have armoires or other turn-of-the-century furniture, as well as small flat-panel TVs and sparkling-clean bathrooms. A coffee shop in an adjacent railcar sells beverages and pastries. **Pros:** central Yountville location; you have access to adjacent gym. **Cons:** minimal service, since the office is often unstaffed; rooms on the parking-lot side get some noise. ⊠ *6523 Washington St.* ☎ *707/944–2000* ⊕ *www.napavalleyrailwayinn.com* ⤴ *9 rooms* ⟁ *In-room: no phone, a/c, refrigerator, Wi-Fi.* ⊟ *AE, MC, V* ⫲*EP.*

$$$–$$$$ ☗ **Villagio Inn & Spa.** The luxury here is quiet and refined, not flashy. Stroll past the fountains and clusters of low buildings to reach the pool, where automated misters cool the sunbathers. Streamlined furnishings, subdued color

schemes, and high ceilings enhance a sense of spaciousness in the guest rooms. Each room also has a fireplace and, beyond louvered doors, a balcony or patio. The spa has huge "suites" big enough for small groups, as well as individual treatment rooms, spread out over 13,000 square feet. Rates include afternoon tea, a bottle of wine, and a generous buffet breakfast—and because the hotel's near the town center, you'll be right next to all those outstanding restaurants. **Pros:** amazing buffet breakfast; no extra charge for hotel guests to use the spa facilities; steps away from Yountville's best restaurants. **Cons:** can be bustling with large groups; you can hear the highway from many of the room's balconies or patios. ⊠ *6481 Washington St.* ☎ *707/944–8877 or 800/351–1133* ⊕ *www.villagio. com* ⊅ *86 rooms, 26 suites* ◊ *In-room: a/c, refrigerator, DVD, Internet, Wi-Fi. In-hotel: room service, bar, tennis courts, pool, spa, bicycles, laundry service* ⊟ *AE, D, DC, MC, V* ⫯⊙⫯ *CP.*

$$$–$$$$ ⊡ **Vintage Inn.** Rooms in this lavish inn are housed in two-story villas scattered around a lush, landscaped 3½-acre property. French fabrics and plump upholstered chairs outfit the spacious, airy guest rooms. Those on the second floor have vaulted beam ceilings, and all have a private patio or balcony, a fireplace, and a whirlpool tub in the bathroom. Some private patios have vineyard views. Rates include a bottle of wine, a buffet breakfast, and afternoon tea and scones. **Pros:** spacious bathrooms with spa tubs; lavish breakfast buffet; luscious bedding. **Cons:** some exterior rooms get highway noise; pool area is smaller than the one at its sister property, the Villagio Inn & Spa. ⊠ *6541 Washington St.* ☎ *707/944–1112 or 800/351–1133* ⊕ *www.vintageinn.com* ⊅ *68 rooms, 12 suites* ◊ *In-room: a/c, refrigerator, DVD, Internet, Wi-Fi. In-hotel: room service, bar, tennis courts, pool, bicycles, laundry service, some pets allowed (fee)* ⊟ *AE, D, DC, MC, V* ⫯⊙⫯ *CP.*

OAKVILLE

2 mi northwest of Yountville on Rte. 29.

Barely a blip on the landscape as you drive north on Route 29, Oakville is marked only by its grocery store. Oakville's small size belies the big mark it makes in the wine-making world. Slightly warmer than Yountville and Carneros to the south, but a few degrees cooler than Rutherford and St. Helena to the north, the Oakville area benefits from gravelly, well-drained soil in most locations. This allows roots to go deep—sometimes more than 100 feet deep—so that the vines produce intensely flavored grapes.

The winemakers who have staked their claim here are an intriguing blend of the old and the new. Big-name wineries such as Far Niente, Robert Mondavi, and Opus One have been producing well-regarded wines—mostly notably cabernet sauvignon—for decades. But upstarts such as PlumpJack are getting just as much press these days.

The **Oakville Grocery** (⊠ *7856 St. Helena Hwy./Rte. 29* ☎ *707/944–8802*), built in 1881 as a general store, now carries a surprisingly wide range of unusual and chichi groceries and prepared foods. Unbearable crowds pack the narrow aisles on weekends, but it's still a fine place to sit on a bench out front and sip an espresso between winery visits.

Along the mountain range that divides Napa and Sonoma, the **Oakville Grade** (⊠ *West of Rte. 29*) is a twisting half-hour route with breathtaking views of both valleys. Although the surface of the road is good, it can be difficult to negotiate at night, and the continual curves mean that it's not ideal for those who suffer from motion sickness.

OAKVILLE VINEYARDS

The combined venture of the late California winemaker Robert Mondavi and the late French baron Philippe de Rothschild, **Opus One** produces only one wine: a big, inky Bordeaux blend that was the first of Napa's ultra-premium wines, fetching unheard-of prices before it was overtaken by cult wines like Screaming Eagle. The winery's futuristic limestone-clad structure, built into the hillside, seems to be pushing itself out of the earth. Although the tour, which focuses on why it costs so much to produce this exceptional wine, can come off as "stuffy" (in the words of one Fodors. com reader), the facilities are undoubtedly impressive, with gilded mirrors, exotic orchids, and a large semicircular cellar modeled on the Château Mouton Rothschild winery in France. You can also taste the current vintage without the tour ($30), as long as you've called ahead for a reservation. ■TIP→ **Take your glass up to the rooftop terrace if you want to appreciate the views out over the vineyards.** ⊠ *7900 St. Helena Hwy./Rte. 29* ☎ *707/944–9442* ⊕ *www. opusonewinery.com* ⊡ *Tour $35* ☉ *Daily 10–4, tasting and tour by appointment.*

Opus One

The arch at the center of the sprawling Mission-style build-ing at **Robert Mondavi** perfectly frames the lawn and the vineyard behind, inviting a stroll under the lovely arcades. If you've never been on a winery tour before, the compre-hensive 70- to 90-minute tour ($25), followed by a seated tasting, is a good way to learn about oenology, as well as the late Robert Mondavi's role in California wine mak-ing (shorter tours are also available). You can also head straight for one of the two tasting rooms. Serious wine lov-ers should definitely consider springing for the $30 reserve-room tasting, where you can enjoy four tastes of Mondavi's top-of-the-line wines, including both the current vintage and several previous vintages of the reserve cabernet that cemented the winery's reputation. Concerts, mostly jazz and R&B, take place in summer on the lawn; call ahead for tickets. ⊠ *7801 St. Helena Hwy./Rte. 29* ☎ *888/766–6328* ⊕ *www.robertmondaviwinery.com* ⌛ *Tasting $15–$30, tours $15–$50* ☉ *Daily 10–5, tour times vary.*

★ **Fodor's Choice** Though the fee for the combined tour and tast-ing is at the high end, **Far Niente** is especially worth visiting if you're tired of elbowing your way through crowded tast-ing rooms and are looking for a more personal experience. Here you're welcomed by name and treated to a glimpse of one of the most beautiful Napa properties. Small groups are shepherded through the historic 1885 stone winery, including some of the 40,000 square feet of caves, for a les-

Far Niente

son on the labor-intensive method for making Far Niente's two wines, a cabernet blend and a chardonnay. (The latter is made without undergoing malolactic fermentation, so it doesn't have that buttery taste that's characteristic of many California chards.) The next stop is the Carriage House, where you can see the founder's gleaming collection of classic cars. The tour ends with a seated tasting of wines and cheeses, capped by a sip of the spectacular Dolce, a late-harvest dessert wine made by Far Niente's sister winery. ✉ *1350 Acacia Dr.* ☎ *707/944–2861* ⊕ *www.farniente.com* 💰 *$50* ⊙ *Tasting and tour by appointment.*

If Opus One is the Rolls-Royce of the Oakville District— expensive, refined, and a little snooty—then **PlumpJack** is the Mini Cooper: fun, casual, and sporty. With its metal chandelier and wall hangings, the tasting room looks like it could be the stage set for a modern Shakespeare production. (The name "PlumpJack" is a nod to Shakespeare's Falstaff.) Dave Matthews, rather than Mozart, plays on the sound system. The reserve chardonnay has a good balance of baked fruit and fresh citrus flavors, and a merlot is blended with a bit of cabernet sauvignon, giving the wine enough tannins to ensure it can be aged for another five years or more. If the tasting room is crowded, take a breather under the shady arbor on the back patio, where you can enjoy a close-up view of the vines. ✉ *620 Oakville Cross Rd.* ☎ *707/945–1220* ⊕ *www. plumpjack.com* 💰 *Tasting $10* ⊙ *Daily 10–4.*

RUTHERFORD

2 mi northwest of Oakville on Rte. 29.

You could drive through the tiny community of Rutherford, at the intersection of Highway 29 and Rutherford Cross Road, in the blink of an eye, but this may well be one of the most important wine-related intersections in the United States. With its singular microclimate and soil, Rutherford is an important viticultural center, with more big-name wineries than you can shake a corkscrew at, including Beaulieu, Caymus Vineyards, and Rubicon Estate.

Cabernet sauvignon is king here. The well-drained, loamy soil is ideal for those vines, and since this part of the valley gets plenty of sun, the grapes develop exceptionally intense flavors. Legendary winemaker André Tchelistcheff's famous claim that "it takes Rutherford dust to grow great cabernet" is now quoted by just about every winery in the area that produces the stuff. That "Rutherford dust" varies from one part of the region to another, but the soils here are primarily gravel, sand, and loam, a well-drained home for cabernet grapes that don't like to get their feet wet.

WORD OF MOUTH. "For wineries to visit, Napa is Cab Country. Mondavi, BV, Inglenook (now Rubicon), and Heitz helped put the Napa Valley on the world's wine map. Others now include Silver Oak, Clos du Val, Stag's Leap, Opus One, Groth, and Caymus. . . . You should take a tour somewhere. Both Mondavi and Groth give good tours about cabernet production." —Otis_B_Driftwood

It's not all grapevines here—you can switch your fruit focus to olives at **Round Pond.** This small farm grows five varieties of Italian olives and three types of Spanish olives. Within an hour of being handpicked, the olives are crushed in the mill on the property to produce pungent, peppery oils that are later blended and sold. Call at least a day or two in advance to arrange a tour of the mill followed by an informative tasting, during which you can sample several types of oil, both alone and with Round Pond's own red wine vinegars and other tasty foods. ■TIP→ If you can arrange to visit between mid-November and the end of December, you might be lucky enough to see the mill in action. ✉ *877 Rutherford Rd.* ☎ *888/302–2575* ⊕ *www.roundpond.com* ✇ *Tour $25* ⊗ *Tour by appointment.*

Round Pond

RUTHERFORD VINEYARDS

Jack and Dolores Cakebread snapped up the property at **Cakebread Cellars** in 1973, after Jack fell in love with the area while visiting on a photography assignment. Since then, they've been making luscious chardonnays, as well as merlot, a great sauvignon blanc, and a beautifully complex cabernet sauvignon. You must make an appointment for a tasting, which might take place during a stroll through the winery's barrel room and crush pad and past Dolores's kitchen garden, or it could be a seated event in the winery's modern wing, where an elevator is crafted out of a stainless-steel fermentation tank and the ceiling is lined with thousands of corks. You can also book in advance for a variety of more in-depth tours and tastings, which might focus on pairing food with wine or Cakebread's library wines. ✉ *8300 St. Helena Hwy.* ☎ *707/963–5221* ⊕ *www.cakebread.com* 🍷 *Tasting $10–$30, tour $25* ☉ *Daily 10–4:30, tasting and tour by appointment.*

Your instinct may be to enter the beautifully restored 1882 Queen Anne Victorian at **St. Supéry** looking for the tasting room; actually the wines are being poured in the building behind it, a bland, unappealing, officelike structure. But you'll likely forgive the atmosphceric lapse once you taste their fine sauvignon blancs, merlots, and chardonnays, as well as a couple of unusual wines that are made primarily

Frog's Leap vineyard's red barn

of either cabernet franc or petit verdot, both of which are usually used for blending with cabernet sauvignon. An excellent, free self-guided tour also allows you a peek at the barrel and fermentation rooms, as well as a gallery of rotating art exhibits. At the "Smell-a-Vision" station you can test your ability to identify different smells that might be present in wine. If you have some extra time, ask to borrow the pétanque balls and play a round of the game outside. ⊠ *8440 St. Helena Hwy. S/Rte. 29* ☎ *707/963–4507* ⊕ *www. stsupery.com* ☛ *Tasting $15–$25* ☉ *Daily 10–5.*

It's the house *The Godfather* built. Filmmaker Francis Ford Coppola began his wine-making career in 1975, when he bought part of the historic, renowned Inglenook estate. He eventually reunited the original Inglenook land and snagged the ivy-covered 19th-century château to boot. In 2006 he renamed the property **Rubicon Estate**, intending to focus on his premium wines, including the namesake cabernet sauvignon–based blend. (The less expensive wines are showcased at the Francis Ford Coppola Winery in Sonoma County's Geyserville.) The many tours cover topics that include the history of the estate, the Rutherford climate and geology, and food and wine pairings, but many just come to taste in the opulent, high-ceilinged tasting room. ⊠ *1991 St. Helena Hwy./Rte. 29* ☎ *707/963–9099* ⊕ *www.rubiconestate.com* ☛ *$15–$50* ☉ *Daily 10–5; call for tour times.*

The cabernet sauvignon produced at the ivy-covered **Beau-lieu Vineyard** is a benchmark of the Napa Valley. The legendary André Tchelistcheff, who helped define the California style of wine making, worked his magic here from 1938 until his death in 1973. This helps explain why Beaulieu's flagship, the Georges de Latour Private Reserve Cabernet Sauvignon, still garners high marks from major wine publications. The zinfandels, merlots, and chardonnays being poured in the main tasting room are notably good. Still, it's worth paying the extra money to taste that special cabernet in the more luxe, less crowded reserve tasting room. ⊠ *1960 St. Helena Hwy./Rte. 29* ☎ *707/967–5200* ⊕ *www. bvwines.com* ☜ *Tasting $10–$30* ⊙ *Daily 10–5.*

★ **Fodor's Choice Frog's Leap** is the perfect place for wine novices
ℭ to begin their education. The owner, John Williams, maintains a goofy sense of humor about wine that translates into an entertaining yet informative experience. You'll also find some fine zinfandel, cabernet sauvignon, merlot, chardonnay, sauvignon blanc, rosé, and the dessert wine Frögenbeerenauslese, their whimsically named take on the German wine Trockenbeerenauslese. The organization prides itself on the sustainability of their operation, and the tour guides can tell you about their dry farming and solar power techniques. The winery includes a red barn built in 1884, 5 acres of organic gardens, an eco-friendly visitor center, and, naturally, a frog pond topped with lily pads. Tastings accompanied by the highly recommended tour are free, but if you just want a seated tasting of their wines (on a porch overlooking the garden, weather permitting), you pay $15. ⊠ *8815 Conn Creek Rd.* ☎ *707/963–4704* ⊕ *www. frogsleap.com* ☜ *Tasting and tour free; tasting alone, $15* ⊙ *Mon.–Sat. 10–4, tour by appointment.*

Caymus Vineyards is run by wine master Chuck Wagner, who started making wine on the property in 1972. His family, however, had been farming in the valley since 1906. Though they make a fine zinfandel and sauvignon blanc, cabernet is the winery's claim to fame, a ripe, powerful wine that's known for its consistently high quality. ■TIP→ **There's no tour and you have to reserve to taste, but it's still worth planning ahead to visit, because the low-key seated tasting (limited to 10 guests) is a great opportunity to learn about the valley's cabernet artistry.** ⊠ *8700 Conn Creek Rd.* ☎ *707/967–3010* ⊕ *www.caymus.com* ☜ *Tasting $25* ⊙ *Sales daily 10–4, tasting by appointment.*

Mumm Napa is one of California's best-known sparkling-wine producers. But enjoying the bubbly from the light-filled tasting room—available in either single flutes ($8–$15) or by the flight ($16–$20)—isn't the only reason to visit. There's also an excellent photography gallery with 30 Ansel Adams prints and rotating exhibits. You can even take that glass of wonderfully crisp Brut Rosé with you as wander. For a leisurely tasting of a flight of their library wines while seated on the outdoor terrace ($30), reserve in advance. ⊠ 8445 Silverado Trail ☎ 707/967–7700 ⊕ www.mumm-napa.com ⚏ Tasting $8–$30, tour free–$20 ⊗ Daily 10–5; tour daily at 10 (free, tasting not included), 11, 1, and 3 ($20, tasting included).

Rutherford Hill Winery is a merlot lover's paradise in a cabernet sauvignon world. When the winery's founders were deciding what grapes to plant, they discovered that the climate and soil conditions of their vineyards resembled those of Pomerol, a region of Bordeaux where merlot is king. The wine caves here are some of the most extensive of any California winery—nearly a mile of tunnels and passageways. You can get a glimpse of the tunnels and the 8,000 barrels inside on the tours, then cap your visit with a picnic in their oak, olive, or madrone groves. With views over the valley from a perch high on a hill, the picnic grounds are more charming than many others in Napa, which tend to be rather close to one of the busy thoroughfares. ⊠ 200 Rutherford Hill Rd., east of Silverado Trail ☎ 707/963–1871 ⊕ www.rutherfordhill.com ⚏ Tasting $15–$30, tour $20 ⊗ Daily 10–5; tour weekdays at 11:30, 1:30, and 3:30, weekends at 11:30, 12:30, 1:30, 2:30, and 3:30.

WHERE TO STAY AND EAT

★ Fodor's Choice ⊠ **Auberge du Soleil.** Taking a cue from the olive tree–studded landscape, this renowned hotel cultivates a Mediterranean look. It's luxury as simplicity: earth-tone tile floors, heavy wood furniture, and terra-cotta colors. This spare style is backed with lavish amenities, though, such as private terraces and truly grand bathrooms, many with jetted soaking tubs and extra-large showers with multiple showerheads (they also have their own flat-panel TVs). The Auberge du Soleil restaurant has an impressive wine list and serves a Mediterranean-inflected menu that relies largely on local produce. Be sure to ask for a table on the terrace in fair weather. The bar serves less expensive fare until

$$$$

10 or 11 PM nightly. **Pros:** stunning views over the valley; spectacular pool and spa areas; the most expensive suites are fit for a superstar. **Cons:** stratospheric prices; the two least expensive rooms (in the main house) get some noise from the bar and restaurant. ✉ *180 Rutherford Hill Rd., off Silverado Trail north of Rte. 128,* ☎ *707/963–1211 or 800/348–5406* ⊕ *www.aubergedusoleil.com* ↘ *31 rooms, 21 suites* ♿ *In-room: a/c, safe, refrigerator, DVD, Internet, Wi-Fi. In-hotel: 2 restaurants, room service, bar, tennis court, pool, gym, spa, laundry service* ▭ *AE, D, DC, MC, V* ⑩ *BP.*

ST. HELENA

5 mi northwest of Oakville on Rte. 29.

Downtown St. Helena is a symbol of how well life can be lived in the Wine Country. Sycamore trees arch over Main Street (Route 29), where chic-looking visitors flit between boutiques, cafés, and storefront tasting rooms housed in sun-faded redbrick buildings. Genteel St. Helena pulls in rafts of Wine Country tourists during the day, though like most Wine Country towns it more or less rolls up the sidewalks after dark.

Many visitors never get away from the Main Street magnets—dozens of great restaurants and boutiques selling women's clothing, food and wine, and upscale housewares—but you should explore a bit farther and stroll through quiet residential neighborhoods. A few blocks west of Main Street you'll be surrounded by vineyards, merging into the ragged wilderness edge of the Mayacamas Mountains. Several blocks east of Main Street, off Pope Street, is the Napa River, which separates St. Helena from the Silverado Trail and Howell Mountain.

Around St. Helena the valley floor narrows between the Mayacamas and Vaca mountains. These slopes reflect heat onto the 9,000 or so acres below, and since there's less fog and wind, things get pretty toasty. In fact, this is one of the hottest AVAs in Napa Valley, with midsummer temperatures often reaching the mid-90s. Bordeaux varietals are the most popular grapes grown here—especially cabernet sauvignon but also merlot. You'll also find chardonnay, petite sirah, and pinot noir in the vineyards.

Unlike many other parts of the Napa Valley, where milling grain was the primary industry until the late 1800s,

St. Helena took to vines almost instantly. The town got its start in 1854, when Henry Still built a store. Still wanted company, and donated land lots on his town site to anyone who wanted to erect a business here. Soon his store was joined by a wagon shop, a shoe shop, hotels, and churches. Dr. George Crane planted a vineyard in 1858, and was the first to produce wine in commercially viable quantities. A German winemaker named Charles Krug followed suit a couple of years later, and other wineries soon followed.

In the late 1800s, phylloxera had begun to destroy France's vineyards, and Napa Valley wines caught the world's attention. The increased demand for Napa wines spawned a building frenzy in St. Helena. Many of the mansions still gracing the town's residential neighborhoods were built around this time. During the same period, some entrepreneurs attempted to turn St. Helena into an industrial center to supply specialized machinery to local viticulturists. Several stone warehouses were built near the railroad tracks downtown. Other weathered stone buildings on Main Street, mostly between Adams and Spring streets and along Railroad Avenue, date from the same era. Modern façades sometimes camouflage these old-timers, but you can study the old structures by strolling the back alleys.

If you have a soft spot for author Robert Louis Stevenson, you could also hit the modest **Silverado Museum,** which displays one of the best collections of Stevenson memorabilia in the world. Early editions of his books in glass-fronted bookcases and paintings and photographs covering the walls make the room resemble a private library. Display cases exhibit manuscripts as well as a lock of his hair. Stevenson's book *Silverado Squatters* was inspired by his months spent in an abandoned mining town on the slopes of nearby Mt. St. Helena. ✉ *1490 Library La.* ☎ *707/963– 3757* ⊕ *www.silveradomuseum.org* 🖃 *Donations accepted* ☉ *Tues.–Sun. noon–4.*

The West Coast headquarters of the **Culinary Institute of America,** the country's leading school for chefs, are in the **Greystone Winery,** an imposing building that was the largest stone winery in the world when it was built in 1889. The upper floors are reserved for students and teachers, but on the ground floor you can check out the quirky corkscrew display and shop at a well-stocked culinary store that tempts aspiring chefs with gleaming gadgets and an impressive selection of cookbooks. One-hour cooking demonstrations take place regularly, usually twice a day on weekends and occasionally more often; call or visit the Web site for times and reservations. (You can also have dinner at the Mediterranean-inspired Wine Spectator Greystone Restaurant. See details under Where to Eat, below.) ⊠ *2555 Main St.* ☎ *707/967–1100* ⊕ *www.ciachef.edu* ⊠ *Free, demonstrations $15* ⊙ *Restaurant Sun.–Thurs. 11:30–9, Fri. and Sat. 11:30–10; store and museum daily 10–6.*

If it's the weekend and you're looking for a break from swirling, sniffing, and spitting, drive 3 mi north of town, off Highway 29, to visit the **Bale Grist Mill State Historic Park,** whose water-powered mill was built in 1846 and partially restored in 1925. A short trail from the parking lot leads to the mill and granary, where exhibits explain the milling process and docents occasionally offer milling demonstrations. A trail leads from the park to Bothe–Napa Valley State Park, where you can pick up a number of hiking trails or linger for a picnic. ⊠ *Hwy. 29, 3 mi north of St. Helena* ☎ *707/942–4575* ⊠ *Park free, mill buildings $3* ⊙ *Weekends 10–5.*

VINEYARDS AROUND ST. HELENA

★ **Fodor's**Choice Although an appointment is required to taste at **Joseph Phelps Vineyards,** it's worth the trouble. In fair weather the casual, self-paced wine tastings are held on the terrace of a huge, modern barnlike building with stunning views down the slopes over oak trees and orderly vines. Though the sauvignon blanc and viognier are good, the blockbuster wines are reds. The 2002 vintage of their superb Bordeaux-style blend called Insignia was selected as *Wine Spectator*'s wine of the year, immediately pushing up prices and demand. Luckily, you'll get a taste of the current vintage of Insignia (it's fairly rare that tasting rooms will pour such highly coveted wines, in this case one that goes for around $200 a bottle). A variety of 90-minute seminars, available by appointment, are $30. One of the most popular is the blending seminar, during which you get to try your hand at mixing the varietals that go into Insignia. ⊠ *200 Taplin Rd.* ☎ *707/963–2745* ⊕ *www.jpvwines.com* ⊠ *Tasting $20* ⊙ *Weekdays 9–5, weekends 9–4; tasting by appointment.*

Right next door to the fieldstone buildings of the Tra Vigne restaurant complex sits the ivy-covered **Merryvale Vineyards.** It's a good place to save for the end of a day, since the win-

Joseph Phelps Vineyards

ery stays open until around 6 or 6:30 PM, considerably later than most others. Chardonnay and cabernet are its claims to fame, though you'll also find a bit of pinot noir and merlot here as well. The red Meritage blend called Profile is their top-of-the-line wine; though it's not typically poured in the tasting room, it's worth asking if there's an open bottle around so you can taste it. For the full Merryvale experience, reserve a spot in the weekend Wine Component Tasting seminar ($25). A walk through the winery winds up in the enchanting Cask Room, where the guides focus on wine's essential components—sugar, alcohol, acid, and tannins—and discuss how these elements are balanced by the vintner. (The fourth weekend of the month features a food-and-wine-pairing seminar instead.) ✉ *1000 Main St.* ☎ *707/963–2225* ⊕ *www.merryvale.com* ✉ *$5–$15* ☉ *Daily 10–6 or 6:30, weekend seminars at 10:30.*

Arguably the most beautiful winery in Napa Valley, the 1876 **Beringer Vineyards** is also the oldest continuously operating property. In 1884 Frederick and Jacob Beringer built the Rhine House Mansion to serve as Frederick's family home. Today it serves as the reserve tasting room, where you can sample four wines amid the Belgian art-nouveau hand-carved oak and walnut furniture and stained-glass windows, choosing from among wines such as a limited release chardonnay, a few big but very drinkable cabernets, and a luscious white dessert wine named Nightingale. Another, less expensive tasting takes place in the less atmospheric but also historic original stone winery. Because of its big reputation and lovely grounds, the winery gets crowded in high season. ■TIP→ **If you're looking for an undiscovered gem, pass this one by, but first-time visitors to the valley will learn a lot about the history of wine making in the region on the introductory tour.** Longer tours, which might pass through a demonstration vineyard or end with a seated tasting in the wine-aging tunnels, are also offered a few times a day. ✉ *2000 Main St./Rte. 29* ☎ *707/963–4812* ⊕ *www.beringer.com* 🍷 *Tasting $15–$25, tour $15–$40* ☾ *May 30–Oct. 23, daily 10–6; Oct. 24–May 29, daily 10–5; call for tour times.*

The first winery founded in the Napa Valley, **Charles Krug Winery,** opened in 1861 when Count Haraszthy lent Krug a small cider press. Today the Peter Mondavi family runs it. At this writing, tours have been suspended indefinitely because a major earthquake retrofit project is in the works, but you can still come for tastings. Though the tasting room is fairly modest, the knowledgeable and friendly servers ensure a relaxed visit. They are best known for their lush red Bordeaux blends, but their zinfandel is also good—or you can go for something unusual with their New Zealand–style sauvignon blanc. Its zingy flavor of citrus and tropical fruit is rare in wines from this area. ✉ *2800 N. Main St.* ☎ *707/963–5057* ⊕ *www.charleskrug.com* 🍷 *Tasting $10–$20* ☾ *Daily 10:30–5.*

At **St. Clement Vineyards,** the beautifully restored Rosenbaum House, built in 1878, houses a tiny tasting room. The mansion is notable for its splendid views from the swing and café tables on the front porch. Tours of the property reveal details about the mansion's history, as well as the workings of the winery in back. Only about 10 percent of the fruit for their wines is grown on the estate; instead, they purchase grapes from about a dozen different vineyards to produce their sauvignon blanc, chardonnay, merlot, and cabernet sauvignon. Their most impressive offering is a full-bodied Bordeaux-style blend called Oroppas, a holdover from the days when the winery was owned by Sapporo (read it backward). ✉ *2867 St. Helena Hwy.* ☎ *707/963–7221* ⊕ *www.stclement.com* 🍷 *Tasting $10–$25, tour $20* ☾ *Daily 10–5, tour daily at 10:30 and 2:30 by appointment.*

Hidden off a winding road behind a security gate, **Spring Mountain Vineyard** has the feeling of a private estate in the countryside, even though it's only a few miles from downtown St. Helena. Though some sauvignon blanc, pinot noir, and syrah is produced, the calling card here is cabernet—big, chewy wines that demand some time in the bottle but promise great things. Tours meander through the beautiful property, from the cellars, a portion of which were dug by Chinese immigrants in the 1880s, to a 120-year-old-barn, to the beautifully preserved 1885 mansion. If you're interested in finding out what their wines taste like after years in the bottle, set aside at least an hour and a half for your visit and spring for the $50 reserve tasting, when they'll pour wines of various vintages while you're seated in the mansion's dining room. ⊠ *2805 Spring Mountain Rd.* ☎ *707/967–4188* ⊕ *www.springmtn.com* ☜ *Tour and tasting $25–$50* ☉ *Tour and tasting by appointment.*

Most people who have heard of **Domaine Charbay Winery and Distillery** know of their flavored vodkas, infused with ingredients such as blood oranges, Meyer lemons, and green tea, but there's much more going on at this rustic property 5 mi uphill from St. Helena. During the casual one-hour distilling presentation tour you'll learn about their other passions, such as crafting small batches of rum, whiskey, tequila, and pastis. You're likely to meet one or more members of the Karakasevic family, the owners, who have been in the distilling business for 13 generations. Though most of the distilling is actually done in Mendocino County, the tour here lets you see an alembic copper pot still and learn the basics of distillation. They make a small quantity of wine and port, as well as excellent, not-too-sweet aperitifs. By law they're not allowed to offer tastings of their distilled spirits, but the presentation concludes with a wine tasting. ⊠ *4001 Spring Mountain Rd.* ☎ *707/963–9327* ⊕ *www.charbay.com* ☜ *Tour and tasting $20* ☉ *Daily 10–4, by appointment.*

Although the reputation of merlot still hasn't completely recovered after the mockery it took in the 2004 movie *Sideways,* **Duckhorn Vineyards** is a favorite of those who don't mind paying around $50 to $100 a bottle for some of the finest merlots made anywhere. In fact, Duckhorn fans tend to be so dedicated to their merlots that they sometimes forget there is some fine sauvignon blanc (their only white wine) and cabernet sauvignon produced here as well. The airy, high-ceilinged tasting room looks like a sleek restaurant, and you'll be seated at a table and served by staffers who make the rounds to pour. In fair weather, you'll be seated on the lovely wraparound porch overlooking a vineyard. Reservations are required for tours and tastings, although walk-ins are often accommodated on weekdays. ✉ *1000 Lodi La.* ☎ *707/963–7108* ⊕ *www. duckhorn.com* 🍷 *Tasting $15–$25, tour $35* ⊙ *Daily 10–4, tour daily at 11 and 2.*

WHERE TO EAT

★ Fodor's Choice ✕ **Go Fish.** Prolific restaurateur Cindy Pawlcyn
$$ is the big name behind one of the few restaurants in the Wine Country to specialize in seafood. You can either sit at the long marble bar and watch the chefs whip up inventive sushi rolls and raw-bar bites, or head into the dining room to study the mouthwatering menu, with such choices as a French-inflected sole amandine and Asian-inspired dishes such as miso-marinated black cod. Hearty sandwiches like the bigeye tuna Reuben are popular at lunch. The large, lively space works a modern-chic look, with stainless-steel lamps and comfortable banquettes. ✉ *641 Main St.* ☎ *707/963–0700* ⊕ *www.gofishrestaurant.net* ▭ *AE, D, DC, MC, V.*

$$ ✕ **Market.** The fieldstone walls and friendly service would set a homey mood here even if the menu didn't present comfort food's greatest hits, including fried chicken with mashed potatoes and the signature macaroni and cheese, made even richer with the addition of bacon. Locals know that it's a casual spot to socialize over oysters on the half shell at the full bar, or a leisurely dinner of slow-braised lamb shanks. The reasonable prices are even better when you take into account the fact that they don't charge a corkage fee for bringing in your own wine. ✉ *1347 Main St.* ☎ *707/963– 3799* ⊕ *www.marketsthelena.com* ▭ *AE, MC, V.*

$$$$ ✕ **Martini House.** Beautiful and boisterous, St. Helena's most stylish restaurant fills a converted 1923 Craftsman-style home, where earthy colors are made even warmer by the glow of three fireplaces. Woodsy ingredients such as chanterelles or juniper berries might accompany braised veal sweetbreads or a hearty grilled loin of venison. Inventive salads and delicate desserts such as the blood-orange sorbet demonstrate chef–owner Todd Humphries's range. In warm weather, angle for a table on the patio, where lights sparkle in the trees. If you don't have a reservation, ask for a seat at the bar downstairs, where you can order from either the small (but much less expensive) bar menu or the full menu. ✉ *1245 Spring St.* ☎ *707/963–2233* ⊕ *www.martinihouse. com* ▭ *AE, DC, MC, V* ⊙ *No lunch Mon.–Thurs.*

Napa's Back Roads

It's not hard to escape the summer crowds on Highway 29, despite Napa Valley's being the most visited Wine Country destination. East of Calistoga and St. Helena, over a ridge from the Napa Valley floor, the Chiles Valley and Howell Mountain AVAs seem a universe away from the rest of Napa County. Instead of being stuck in traffic behind a BMW convertible, you're more likely to have to slow down for lumbering farm machinery or a deer darting across the road. (Also watch out for cyclists, who are drawn by the lack of traffic in the area.)

The rugged heights of the Howell Mountain AVA are spread out over 14,000 acres, but a mere 600 or so are planted with vines. However, this will surely change in the next several years, as vintners vie for coveted permits to clear the dense forests of the high, rolling plateau and plant vines. Though visitors are still few and far between here—in part because many of the wineries are not open to the public—Howell Mountain seems poised to become the next big thing.

Grapes were first planted in Chiles Valley and neighboring Pope Valley in 1854. Today the forest has reclaimed formerly cultivated land, but you can still tell the course of the old road by the moss-covered

stone walls along its margins. Here and there in the woods you'll discover the ruins of an abandoned winery, and you may stumble over an ancient vine persisting among the oaks, laurels, and pines.

■TIP→ **If you want to schedule a day in this blissfully rural area, the Web site ⊕ www.napavalleybackroads. com is extremely helpful. It provides some background on the Pope and Chiles valleys, a handy list of wineries, and an interactive map that will help you plan your itinerary.**

The region's one quirky tourist attraction is **Litto's Hubcap Ranch** (Pope Valley Road, near Pope Valley Winery), a private home where every fence, tree, and building is plastered with hubcaps. The creator of this odd folk-art project, Emanuele "Litto" Dimonte, died in 1985, but his family has kept the thousands of hubcaps he spent years collecting. Though the property is strictly off-limits to visitors, you can appreciate Litto's handiwork glinting in the sun as you drive by.

The following are some of the wineries in the area that are open to the public:

Langtry Estate & Vineyards. Just north of the Howell Mountain AVA, in the Guenoc AVA, is a long driveway leading to this hilltop winery. The main building was built to resemble the old Langtry barn that still stands about 2 mi south of the winery, but with a difference—the newer facility is the size of a football field. Langtry owns a whopping 21,000 acres and produces about 250,000 cases a year. Still, it feels like a much smaller operation, and the fact that so few visitors make it here makes for a leisurely experience in the tasting room. A tasting of their mostly moderately priced wines is $5, and they are open daily 11 to 5. ⊠ *21000 Butts Canyon Rd., Middletown* ☎ *707/987–9127* ⊕ *www.langtryestate.com.*

Pope Valley Winery. You may have to peek into the barrel room to find someone to pour wines for you in this simple tasting room with a corrugated tin roof—and don't be surprised if the person serving you is the winemaker himself. This rustic little winery producing about 4,000 cases a year doesn't get that many visitors. If you visit from Thursday to Sunday from 11 to 5, though, you'll be warmly welcomed with free tasting of their wines. Tours are not regularly scheduled, but you can ask whether anyone has time to show you around the small, rough-hewn cave dug into the hillside next to the tasting room. To fully appreciate the slow Pope Valley lifestyle, plan to bring a picnic and ask to play a game of boccie. ⊠ *6613 Pope Valley Rd., Pope Valley* ☎ *707/965–1246* ⊕ *www.popevalleywinery.com.*

RustRidge Winery. Though it's only a 20-minute drive from the Napa that most visitors know, secluded RustRidge seems more like Colorado or Montana than the California Wine Country. Signs on Lower Chiles Valley Road point you toward their property, where you'll wind your way past barns, horse paddocks, and farm equipment before finding the tasting room. The property was purchased by the Meyer family in 1972 as a thoroughbred-horse ranch, and one of the owners continues to breed and train horses here. The family also runs a five-room ranch-style bed-and-breakfast on-site. Tastings are $15, $25 if you choose to share. Though it's open daily from 10 to 4, you might have to stop by the office or poke around the winery to find someone to pour wines for you. ⊠ *2910 Lower Chiles Valley Rd., St. Helena* ☎ *707/965–9353* ⊕ *www.rustridge.com.*

3

A carefully composed plate at the Restaurant at Meadowood

$ ✕ **Pizzeria Tra Vigne.** Early in the evening, families with kids flock to the outdoor tables at this casual pizzeria. Later on, young couples gather around the pool table or watch the game on the TV. At any time of day you'll find fabulous, crisp, thin-crust pizzas, such as the unusual Positano, with sautéed shrimp and crescenza cheese. Salads and pasta round out the menu. Service is friendly, if not particularly speedy, and the lack of a corkage fee makes it a good place for an inexpensive meal with that bottle of sangiovese you picked up at one of the wineries. ✉ *1016 Main St.* ☎ *707/967–9999* ⊕ *www.travignerestaurant.com* ▭ *D, MC, V.*

★ **Fodor's**Choice ✕ **The Restaurant at Meadowood.** Chef Christo-
$$$$ pher Kostow has garnered rave reviews for transforming seasonal local products (some grown right on the property) into elaborate, elegant fare. The "composition of carrots," constructed of the tiniest carrots imaginable accompanied by delicate shavings of chocolate, foie gras, and candied tangerine (it sounds odd, but it works), is just one example of Kostow's inventiveness and playfulness. The slow-cooked black cod with chorizo and lamb demonstrates an earthier approach. The chef's menu ($155, $260 with wine pairings), composed of eight or so courses, is the best way to appreciate the experience, but the gracious and well-trained servers provide some of the best service in the valley even if you're ordering a less extravagant three-, four-, or five-course menu. ✉ *900 Meadowood La.* ☎ *707/967–1205*

⊕ *www.meadowood.com* ☐ *AE, D, DC, MC, V* ☻ *Closed Sun. No lunch.*

¢–$ ✕**Gott's Roadside.** A slick 1950s-style outdoor hamburger stand goes upscale at this hugely popular spot (previously called Taylor's Automatic Refresher), where locals are willing to brave long lines to order juicy burgers, root-beer floats, and garlic fries. There are also plenty of choices you wouldn't have found 50 years ago, such as the ahi tuna burger and chicken club with pesto mayo. Try to get here early or late for lunch, or all the shaded picnic tables on the lawn might be filled with happy throngs. Lines are usually shorter at the Gott's in downtown Napa's Oxbow Public Market. ☒ *933 Main St.* ☎ *707/963–3486* ⊕ *gottsroadside. com* ☐ *AE, MC, V.*

$$$$ ✕**Terra.** St. Helena may have newer, flashier, and more dramatic restaurants, but for old-school romance and service, many diners return year after year to this quiet favorite in an 1884 fieldstone building. Since 1988, chef Hiro Sone has been giving unexpected twists to Italian and southern-French cuisine in dishes such as the mussel soup with caramelized onions and garlic croutons, heavily perfumed with the scent of saffron. A few, such as the signature sake-marinated black cod in a shiso broth, draw on Sone's Japanese background. Inventive desserts, courtesy of Sone's wife, Lissa Doumani, might include a maple bread pudding served in a baked apple. The gracious staff unobtrusively attends to every dropped fork or half-full water glass. ☒ *1345 Railroad Ave.* ☎ *707/963–8931* ⊕ *www.terrarestaurant.com* ☖ *Reservations essential* ☐ *AE, DC, MC, V* ☻ *Closed Tues. and 1st 2 wks in Jan. No lunch.*

$$$ ✕**Wine Spectator Greystone Restaurant.** The Culinary Institute of America runs this place in the handsome old Christian Brothers Winery. Century-old stone walls house a spacious restaurant that bustles at both lunch and dinner, with several cooking stations in full view. On busy nights you might find the hard-at-work chefs (who, incidentally, are generally full-fledged chefs rather than mere students) more entertaining than your dinner partner. On fair days the tables on the terrace, shaded by red umbrellas, are away from the action but equally appealing. The menu has a Mediterranean spirit and emphasizes locally grown produce. Typical main courses include pan-roasted scallops with spinach and shiitake mushrooms and house-made pasta with a sherry-thyme cream sauce. ☒ *2555 Main St.* ☎ *707/967–1010* ⊕ *www. ciachef.edu* ☐ *AE, D, DC, MC, V.*

WHERE TO STAY

$-$$ ⬚ **Ambrose Bierce House.** Writer and professional curmudgeon Ambrose Bierce lived here until 1910, when he became bored with the peaceful wine valley and vanished into Pancho Villa's Mexico, never to be seen or heard from again. The vibe at his namesake inn is full-blown Victorian—floral bedspreads and white lace curtains, with pretty turn-of-the-century antique oak furnishings throughout—but the amenities in the four rooms are strictly up-to-date, from small satellite TVs to gleaming bathrooms, most with jetted bathtubs. If you're interested in Bierce's writings, you can browse the inn's bookshelves for a few of his books. **Pros:** hot tub; free port and chocolates in each room; within walking distance of downtown St. Helena and its many restaurants. **Cons:** breakfast served only at 9 AM; fire-station siren across the street occasionally goes off. ⊠ *1515 Main St.* ☎ *707/963–3003* ⊕ *www.ambrosebiercehouse.com* ⇨ *3 rooms, 1 suite* ⌂ *In-room: a/c, Wi-Fi.* ⊟ *D, MC, V* ⑩ *BP.*

¢–$ ⬚ **El Bonita Motel.** Only in St. Helena would a basic room in a roadside motel cost around $200 a night in high season. Still, for budget-minded travelers the tidy rooms here are pleasant enough, and the landscaped grounds and picnic tables elevate the property over similar places. There's even a small sauna next to the hot tub and swimming pool, which is heated year-round. ■TIP→ **Family-friendly pluses include roll-away beds and cribs for a modest charge. Its location right on Route 29 makes it convenient, but light sleepers should ask for rooms farthest from the road.** **Pros:** cheerful rooms; hot tub; microwaves and mini-refrigerators. **Cons:** road noise is a problem in some rooms. ⊠ *195 Main St./Rte. 29* ☎ *707/963–3216 or 800/541–3284* ⊕ *www.elbonita.com* ⇨ *38 rooms, 4 suites* ⌂ *In-room: a/c, refrigerator, Wi-Fi. In-hotel: pool, Internet terminal, some pets allowed (fee)* ⊟ *AE, D, DC, MC, V* ⑩ *CP.*

★ Fodor'sChoice ⬚ **Meadowood Resort.** Everything at Meadowood
$$$$ seems to run seamlessly, starting with the gatehouse staff who alert the front desk to arrivals so that a receptionist is ready for each guest. A rambling lodge and several gray-clapboard bungalows are scattered across the sprawling property, giving it the air of an exclusive New England retreat. Guest rooms have views over these wooded grounds from expansive windows. The supremely comfortable beds defy you to get up and pursue the golf, tennis, hiking, croquet, or other activities on offer. In recent years the elegant but unstuffy dining room has won rave reviews,

Meadowood Resort

becoming a destination restaurant (see ⇨ The Restaurant at Meadowood *in* Where to Eat, above). **Pros:** site of one of Napa's best restaurants; lovely hiking trail on the property; the most gracious service in all of Napa. **Cons:** very expensive; most bathrooms are not as extravagant as those at other similarly priced resorts. ⊠ *900 Meadowood La.* ☎ *707/963–3646 or 800/458–8080* ⊕ *www.meadowood. com* ⌖ *40 rooms, 45 suites* ⚘ *In-room: a/c, refrigerator, DVD, Internet, Wi-Fi. In-hotel: 2 restaurants, room service, bar, golf course, tennis courts, pools, gym, children's programs (ages 6–12, summer only)* ☰ *AE, D, DC, MC, V.*

$$$–$$$$ ☖ **Wine Country Inn.** A pastoral landscape of vine-covered hills surrounds this retreat, which was styled after the traditional New England inns its owners liked to visit in the 1970s. Rooms are comfortably done with homey furniture such as four-poster beds topped with quilts, and many have a wood-burning or gas fireplace, a large jetted tub, and a patio or balcony overlooking the vineyards. A hearty breakfast is served buffet-style in the sun-splashed common room, and wine and appetizers are available in the afternoon next to the wood-burning cast-iron stove. Though it's not the most stylish lodging in the area, the thoughtful staff and the vineyard views from several rooms encourage many people to return year after year. **Pros:** free shuttle to some restaurants (reserve early); lovely grounds; swimming pool is heated year-round. **Cons:** some rooms let in noise from neighbors; some areas could use updating.

TOP PICNIC SPOTS

Local parks are often picnic-friendly, but a picnic at a winery is better yet. Many wineries have outdoor tables shaded by trees, and some sell snacks as well. (It's polite to buy a bottle of wine if you're using their picnic facilities, and almost all wineries prohibit drinking wines made elsewhere on their grounds.) Here are three terrific choices.

■ **Napa Valley:** Stock up on gourmet staples such as pâté and imported cheeses at the Dean & Deluca store on the St. Helena highway, 1½ mi south of downtown Napa.

Then drive up to Rutherford Hill Winery to eat under their olive trees with a view of the valley.

■ **Sonoma Valley:** Snap up local breads, cheeses, and other supplies at the stores around Sonoma's plaza, such as the Sonoma Cheese Factory. Take your haul to Gundlach-Bundschu Winery, where the views from the slopes are unbeatable.

■ **Russian River Valley:** Hit the Oakville Grocery on Healdsburg's main plaza, and then have your spread at the tables at Rochioli Vineyards.

✉ *1152 Lodi La., east of Rte. 29* ☎ *707/963–7077* ⊕ *www. winecountryinn.com* ↪ *24 rooms, 5 suites* ⚄ *In-room: a/c, refrigerator (some), no TV, Wi-Fi. In-hotel: pool* ⊟ *MC, V* ⧆ *BP.*

NIGHTLIFE AND THE ARTS

A nightcap at one of St. Helena's great restaurants serves as all the nightlife most visitors need, but if you want to let your hair down, **Ana's Cantina** (✉ *1205 Main St.* ☎ *707/963–4921*) serves cocktails, Thursday-night karaoke, and occasional live music to a raucous crowd of locals. The art-nouveau **Cameo Cinema** (✉ *1340 Main St.* ☎ *707/963–9779* ⊕ *www. cameocinema.com*) screens first-run and art-house movies, as well as occasional live performances. Beautifully restored under the direction of Charlotte Wagner, one of the owners of Caymus Vineyards, the 140-seat theater has several love seats for the romantically inclined.

SHOPPING

Most of St. Helena's stores are clustered along bucolic Main Street, where 19th-century redbrick buildings recall the town's past and make it a particularly pleasant place to while away an afternoon window-shopping.

Contemporary American, European, and Latin American paintings and sculptures are illuminated by a skylight in the **Caldwell Snyder** (✉ *1328 Main St.* ☎ *707/200–5050*) gallery.

Dean & Deluca (✉ *607 St. Helena Hwy. S/Rte. 29* ☎ *707/967–9980*), a branch of the famous Manhattan store, is crammed with everything you need in the kitchen—including terrific produce and deli items—as well as a large wine selection.

Footcandy (✉ *1239 Main St.* ☎ *707/963–2040*) will thrill foot fetishists with its displays of precarious stilettos and high-heeled boots.

The airy **I. Wolk Gallery** (✉ *1354 Main St.* ☎ *707/963–8800*) has works by established and emerging American artists, with abstract and contemporary realist paintings and high-quality works on paper and sculpture.

Fine French table linens, custom-embroidered aprons, and other high-quality housewares fill **Jan de Luz** (✉ *1219 Main St.* ☎ *707/963–1550*).

The **Spice Islands Marketplace** (✉ *Culinary Institute of America, 2555 Main St.* ☎ *888/424–2433*) is the place to shop for cookbooks, kitchenwares, and everything else related to cooking and preparing food.

Elaborate confections handmade on the premises are displayed like miniature works of art at **Woodhouse Chocolate** (✉ *1367 Main St.* ☎ *707/963–8413*), a lovely shop that resembles an 18th-century Parisian salon.

CALISTOGA

3 mi northwest of St. Helena on Rte. 29.

False-fronted shops, 19th-century hotels, and unpretentious cafés lining the main drag of Lincoln Avenue give Calistoga a slightly rough-and-tumble feel that's unique in the Napa Valley. With Mt. St. Helena rising to the north and visible from downtown, it looks a bit like a cattle town tucked into a remote mountain valley. It's easier to find a bargain here than farther down the valley, making Calistoga's quiet, tree-shaded streets and mellow bed-and-breakfasts a relatively affordable home base for exploring the surrounding vineyards and back roads.

Ironically, Calistoga was developed as a ritzy vacation getaway. In 1859 Sam Brannan—Mormon missionary, entrepreneur, and vineyard developer—learned about a place in the upper Napa Valley, called Agua Caliente by the settlers, that was peppered with hot springs and even had an "old faithful" geyser. He snapped up 2,000 acres of prime property and laid out a resort. Planning a place that would rival New York's famous Saratoga Hot Springs, he built an elegant hotel, bathhouses, cottages, stables, an observatory, and a distillery (a questionable choice for a Mormon missionary). Brannan's gamble didn't pay off as he'd hoped, but Californians kept coming to "take the waters," supporting a sprinkling of small hotels and bathhouses built wherever a hot spring bubbled to the surface. Many of them are still going, and you can come for an old-school experience of a mud bath or a dip in a warm spring-fed pool.

Indian Springs has welcomed clients to mud baths, mineral pools, and steam rooms, all supplied with mineral water from its three geysers, since 1871. You can choose from the various spa treatments and volcanic-ash mud baths, or soak in the Olympic-size mineral-water pool (kept at 92°F (33°C) in the summer, and a toasty 102°F (39°C) in the winter). Those who visit the spa also get access to a small Zen-inspired garden out back, where you can relax after your treatment. If you're planning several sessions, you might want to overnight in one of the lodge rooms or bungalows ($–$$$). Reservations are recommended for spa treatments. ⊠ *1712 Lincoln Ave./Rte. 29* ☎ *707/942–4913* ⊕ *www.indianspringscalistoga.com* ☉ *Daily 9–8.*

Founded by Ben Sharpsteen, an animator for Walt Disney who retired to Calistoga, the small **Sharpsteen Museum** has a detailed diorama of the Calistoga Hot Springs Resort in its heyday. Other permanent and rotating exhibits cover the region's past, from the indigenous Wappo people who once lived here to World War II. Next to the museum is the Sam Brannan Cottage, built by the town's founder in the 1860s and one of only three in town to survive from the era. Take a peek at the lavishly furnished period interior. The small gift shop specializes in books focusing on local history. ⊠ *1311 Washington St.* ☎ *707/942–5911* ⊕ *www. sharpsteen-museum.org* ☒ *$3 donation* ☉ *Daily 11–4.*

☾ The **Petrified Forest** contains the remains of the volcanic eruptions of Mt. St. Helena 3.4 million years ago: petrified giant redwoods. Pick up a brochure before starting off on the leisurely 15-minute walk around the property, which takes you by the largest specimen, "The Queen of the Forest," a 65-by-8-foot petrified log. The site isn't worth a long detour unless you're a geology buff. For the best experience, consider taking a meadow hike, which leads through the woodland until you have a view of Mt. St. Helena. The 45-minute excursion, led by a naturalist, is offered on Sunday at 11 am and by appointment, weather permitting. ⊠ *4100 Petrified Forest Rd., 5 mi west of Calistoga* ☎ *707/942–6667* ⊕ *www.petrifiedforest.org* ⊠ *$8* ☉ *Mid-Apr.–mid-Sept., daily 9–7; mid-Sept.–mid-Apr., daily 9–5.*

VINEYARDS AROUND CALISTOGA

The tasting room at **Dutch Henry Winery** isn't much more than a nook in the barrel room between towering American and French oak barrels full of their excellent cabernet sauvignon, merlot, and zinfandel. Their chardonnay and a charming rosé also have their fervent fans. The winery produces about 6,000 cases annually—sold mostly on-site and through their wine club—which explains the simple facilities, but the wines are truly top-notch. Sometimes the tasting-room staffers can be playfully crotchety, but the lack of crowds and casual style make it a welcome change of pace from some of its overly serious neighbors. ⊠ *4310 Silverado Trail* ☎ *707/942–5771* ⊕ *www.dutchhenry.com* ⊠ *Tasting $10* ☉ *Daily 10–5.*

★ **Fodor'sChoice** **Schramsberg**, hidden on the hillside near Route 29, is one of Napa's oldest wineries. Founded in the 1860s, it now produces a variety of bubblies made using the traditional *méthode champenoise* process (which means, among other things, that the wine undergoes a second fermentation in the bottle before being "riddled," or turned every few days over a period of weeks, to nudge the sediment into the neck of the bottle). If you want to taste, you must tour first, but what a tour: in addition to getting a glimpse of the winery's historic architecture, you get to tour the cellars dug in the late 19th century by Chinese laborers, where a mind-boggling 2.5 million bottles are stacked in gravity-defying configurations. The tour fee includes generous pours of several very different sparkling wines. ⊠ *1400 Schramsberg Rd.* ☎ *707/942–4558* ⊕ *www.schramsberg.com* ⊠ *Tasting and tour $40* ☉ *Tasting and tour by appointment.*

Possibly the most astounding sight in Napa Valley is your first glimpse of the **Castello di Amorosa,** which looks for

An underground aging room at Schramsberg Vineyards

all the world like a medieval castle, complete with drawbridge and moat, a chapel, stables, and secret passageways. There's even a chapel where Mass is celebrated in Latin every Sunday morning. Opened in 2007 after 14 years of construction, this brainchild of Dario Sattui, who also owns several properties in Tuscany, shows his passion for Italy and for medieval architecture down to the last obsessive detail. Some of the 107 rooms contain replicas of 13th-century frescoes, and the dungeon has an actual iron maiden from Nuremberg, Germany. You must pay for the tour to see the most of the extensive eight-level property, though paying for a tasting allows you access to a small portion of the astounding complex, as well as tastes of several of their excellent Italian-style wines. ■ TIP→ **Prices for tastings and tours are $5 higher on Fridays and weekends (a rarity in the Wine Country), so schedule this stop for a weekday, if possible.** ✉ *4045 N. St. Helena Hwy.* ☎ *707/967–6272* 🌐 *www.castellodiamorosa.com* *Tasting $10–$27, tour $25–$42* ⏲ *March–Nov., daily 9:30–6; Dec.–Feb., daily 9:30–5; tour by appointment.*

The approach to **Sterling Vineyards**, perched on a hilltop about a mile south of Calistoga, is the most spectacular in the valley. Instead of driving up to their tasting room, you board an aerial tramway to reach the pristine white buildings that recall those in the Greek islands (the winery's founder once lived on Mykonos). The views from

Best Wine Country Spas

Whether you want to experience the mud baths of Calistoga or a grape-centered spa experience, you don't have to look far to find a Wine Country spa that will massage, scrub, or soak you into a blissed-out stupor.

■ **Dr. Wilkinson's.** The oldest spa in Calistoga. Although it's the least chic of the bunch, it's still well loved for its reasonable prices and its friendly, unpretentious vibe. Their mud baths are a mix of volcanic ash and peat moss. ⊠ *1507 Lincoln Ave., Calistoga* ☎ *707/942–4102* ⊕ *www.drwilkinson.com.*

■ **Fairmont Sonoma Mission Inn & Spa.** The largest such destination in the Wine Country. The vast complex covers every amenity you could want in a spa, including several pools and Jacuzzis fed by local thermal mineral springs. ⊠ *100 Boyes Blvd./Rte. 12, Boyes Hot Springs* ☎ *707/938–9000* ⊕ *www.fairmont.com/sonoma.*

■ **Health Spa Napa Valley.** Focuses on health and wellness, with personal trainers and an outdoor pool in addition to the usual spa fare. The grape-seed mud wrap, during which you're slathered with mud mixed with crushed Napa Valley grape seeds, is a more indulgent alternative to a mud bath. ⊠ *1030 Main St., St. Helena* ☎ *707/967–8800* ⊕ *www. napavalleyspa.com.*

■ **Kenwood Inn & Spa.** The prettiest spa setting in the Wine Country, thanks to the vineyards across the road and the Mediterranean style of the inn. The "wine wrap" body wrap is followed by a slathering of lotion made from various grape-seed oils and red wine extract. ⊠ *10400 Sonoma Hwy./ Rte. 12, Kenwood* ☎ *707/833–1293* ⊕ *www.kenwoodinn.com.*

■ **The Spa Hotel Healdsburg.** Larger hotel spas have more bells and whistles, but this intimate spot provides plush Frette robes, an outdoor Jacuzzi, and soothing minimalist decor, making it a tranquil choice for massages, body wraps, facials, and hand and foot treatments. ⊠ *327 Healdsburg Ave., Healdsburg* ☎ *707/433–4747* ⊕ *www. hotelhealdsburg.com.*

■ **Spa at Villagio.** This 13,000-square-foot spa with fieldstone walls and a Mediterranean theme has all the latest gadgets, including men's and women's outdoor hot tubs and showers with an extravagant number of showerheads. Huge spa suites—complete with flat-panel TV screens and wet bars—are perfect for couples and groups. ⊠ *6481 Washington St., Yountville* ☎ *707/948–5050* ⊕ *www.villagio.com.*

3

the winery are superb, although the quality of the wines doesn't necessarily match the vista. Still, the short tram ride is the rare kid-friendly attraction in this area (and those under 21 pay only $10 admission). ✉ *1111 Dunaweal La.* ☎ *707/942–3300* ⊕ *www.sterlingvineyards.com* ⛱ *$20–$25, including tramway, self-guided tour, and tasting* ☉ *Daily 10–4:30.*

Designed by postmodern architect Michael Graves, the **Clos Pegase** winery is a one-of-a-kind "temple to wine and art" packed with unusual art objects from the collection of owner and publishing entrepreneur Jan Shrem. After tasting the wines, which include a bright sauvignon blanc, fruity chardonnays, and mellow pinot noir, merlot, and cabernet (they're made in a soft, approachable style and meant to be drunk somewhat young), be sure to check out the surrealist paintings near the main tasting room, which include a Jean Dubuffet painting you may have seen on one of their labels. Better yet, bring a picnic and have lunch in the courtyard, where a curvaceous Henry Moore sculpture is one of about two-dozen works of art. ✉ *1060 Dunaweal La.* ☎ *707/942–4981* ⊕ *www.clospegase.com* ⛱ *Tasting $15, tour free* ☉ *Daily 10:30–5, tour daily at 11:30 and 2.*

Tucked into a rock face in the Mayacamas range, **Storybook Mountain Vineyards** is one of the more beautiful wineries in Napa, with vines rising steeply from the winery in dramatic tiers. Zinfandel is king here, and they even make a Zin Gris, an unusual dry rosé of zinfandel grapes. (In Burgundy, *vin gris*—pale rosé—is made from pinot noir grapes.) The owners have discovered that zinfandel grapes, which are usually prone to mildew because the grapes grow in such tight clusters, thrive on the eastern-facing slopes on their property. Tastings are preceded by a low-key tour, during which you take a short walk up the hillside into the picture-perfect vineyard and then visit the atmospheric tunnels, parts of which have the same rough-hewn look as they did when Chinese laborers painstakingly dug them around 1888. ✉ *3835 Highway 128* ☎ *707/942–5310* ⊕ *www.storybookwines.com* ⛱ *Free* ☉ *Tour and tasting by appointment.*

Château Montelena is an architectural mash-up. The 19th-century, vine-covered building suggests France, but the lake below it is surrounded by Chinese-inspired gardens and dotted with islands topped by Chinese pavilions. You'll get the best view of this quirky combination as you walk up the hill from the driveway, up past the duck-filled pond. From here the château, with its little turrets and ornamental crenellations, looks like it's straight out of a fairy tale. (And if you've seen the movie *Bottle Shock*, you might recognize it as well. The movie, although largely fictional, was based on events that took place here around 1976.) In the tasting room, make a beeline for the bright chardonnay and the estate-grown cabernet sauvignon. If you want to participate in a tasting of library wines ($40), reserve in advance. Reservations are also required for the Bottle Shock tour, offered three mornings a week, on which you'll see some of the locations used in the movie and learn which events in the film actually took place. ⊠ *1429 Tubbs La.* ☎ *707/942–5105* ⊕ *www.montelena.com* ⊑ *Tasting $20* ☉ *Daily 9:30–4.*

Robert Louis Stevenson State Park encompasses the summit of **Mt. St. Helena.** It was here, in the summer of 1880, in an abandoned bunkhouse of the Silverado Mine, that Stevenson and his bride, Fanny Osbourne, spent their honeymoon. This stay inspired the writer's travel memoir *The Silverado Squatters,* and Spyglass Hill in *Treasure Island* is thought to be a portrait of Mt. St. Helena. The park's approximately 3,600 acres are mostly undeveloped except for a trail leading to the site of the bunkhouse—which is marked with a marble memorial in the form of an open book on top of a pedestal—and a fire trail to the summit beyond. ■TIP→ If you're planning to attempt the hike to the top, a 10-mi roundtrip, bring plenty of water and dress appropriately: the trail is steep and lacks shade in spots, but the summit is often cool and breezy. ⊠ *Rte. 29, 7 mi north of Calistoga* ☎ *707/942–4575* ⊕ *www.parks.ca.gov* ⊑ *Free* ☉ *Daily sunrise–sunset.*

WHERE TO EAT

★ **Fodor's**Choice ✕ **All Seasons Bistro.** Bistro cuisine takes a California spin in this cheerful sun-filled space, where tables topped with flowers stand on an old-fashioned black-and-white checkerboard floor. The seasonal menu might include seared scallops with a cauliflower purée or fettuccine puttanesca. Homey desserts include crème brûlée and rum-raisin bread pudding. You can order reasonably priced wines from their extensive list, or buy a bottle at the attached wine shop and have it poured at your table. Attentive service contributes to the welcoming atmosphere. ⊠ *1400 Lincoln Ave.* ☎ *707/942–9111* ⊕ *www.allseasonsnapavalley.net* ⊟ *AE, D, MC, V* ☉ *Closed Mon.*

$$

$$ ✕ **Barolo.** In 2006 Calistoga got a little more urbane with the addition of this Italian-inflected wine bar in the Mount View Hotel. With red-leather seats, artsy light fixtures, and a marble bar indoors and café seating out, it's a stylish, modern spot for a glass of wine, with many from small producers you probably haven't heard of. Small plates that could have come straight from Tuscany—fried calamari, risotto croquettes, a selection of salumi—are great for sharing. A handful of well-executed large plates, such as the pappardelle (pasta) with shrimp and veal scaloppine, round out the menu. ⊠ *1457 Lincoln Ave.* ☎ *707/942–9900* ⊟ *AE, MC, V* ⊕ *www.barolocalistoga.com* ⊙ *No lunch.*

$$$ ✕ **Brannan's Grill.** Arts and Crafts–style lamps cast a warm glow over the booths and tables at this popular spot. The hearty cooking will satisfy hungry meat eaters, who can tackle substantial dishes such as a red-wine-braised lamb shank served with a porcini-risotto cake, or smoked pork shoulder served with rich polenta. (Vegetarians will do better elsewhere.) An attractive, well-stocked bar is a congenial spot for cocktails, and live jazz on Friday and Saturday nights makes it one of the livelier places in town for a night out. ⊠ *1374 Lincoln Ave.* ☎ *707/942–2233* ⊕ *www. brannansgrill.com* ⊟ *AE, D, MC, V.*

$$$ ✕ **Calistoga Inn Restaurant and Brewery.** On pleasant days this riverside restaurant and its sprawling, tree-shaded patio come into their own. At lunchtime, casual plates such as a grilled turkey-and-Brie sandwich or a Chinese chicken salad are light enough to leave some energy for an afternoon of wine tasting. And at night, when there's often live jazz played on the patio during the warm months, you'll find heartier dishes such as braised lamb shank or grilled Sonoma duck breast with a fennel-and-Parmesan stuffing. Service can be a bit lackadaisical, so order one of the house-made brews and enjoy the atmosphere while you're waiting. ⊠ *1250 Lincoln Ave.* ☎ *707/942–4101* ⊕ *www. calistogainn.com* ⊟ *AE, MC, V.*

$ ✕ **Checkers.** A large spot filled with both locals and visitors with children in tow, this restaurant comes across as casual and cheerful, with light-brown walls and huge French advertising posters. The Cal-Italian menu consists mostly of pasta (rigatoni with broccoli, linguini carbonara) and pizzas. One unusual but very popular pick is the Thai pizza with chicken, cilantro, and peanuts. Some of the best dishes are the hearty salads, such as the sweet and tangy Napa salad, served with apples, candied walnuts,

Gorgonzola, and a poppy-seed dressing. ⊠ *1414 Lincoln Ave.* ☎ *707/942–9300* ⊟ *AE, D, MC, V.*

$$ ✕ **Jolē.** Husband and wife team Matt and Sonjia Spector are the force between this stylish newcomer off the lobby of the Mount View Hotel (it opened in 2008). The small space feels casual, with servers in jeans and white shirts and jazz on the stereo, but the food is a cut above. The owners' "farm to table" philosophy means that you'll find lots of local ingredients used for their California fare with a Mediterranean flair, such as the crispy pork belly served with quince and ginger-infused sauce, and a lamb T-bone with a chickpea-and-chorizo stew. The "small plates" format (dishes are meant to be shared) mean the bill can add up quickly, and the eclectic wine list (divided into "Old World," "New World," and "Our World") tends toward expensive bottles, but for expertly prepared and sometimes adventurous dishes, you can't do better in somewhat staid Calistoga. ⊠ *1457 Lincoln Ave.* ☎ *707/942–5938* ⊕ *www. jolerestaurant.com* ⊟ *AE, D, DC, MC, V* ⊗ *No lunch.*

WHERE TO STAY

¢–$ ☖ **Brannan Cottage Inn.** The pristine Victorian house with lacy white fretwork, large windows, and a shady porch is the only one of Sam Brannan's 1860 resort cottages still standing on its original site. Each room has individual touches, such as a four-poster bed, a claw-foot tub, or a velvet settee. **Pros:** innkeepers go the extra mile; most rooms have fireplaces; a five-minute walk from most of Calistoga's restaurants. **Cons:** owners' dog may be a problem for those with allergies; beds may be too firm for some. ⊠ *109 Wapoo Ave.* ☎ *707/942–4200* ⊕ *www.brannancottageinn.com* ⊅ *6 rooms* ⚭ *In-room: no phone, a/c, no TV (some), Wi-Fi. In-hotel: some pets allowed (fee)* ⊟ *AE, MC, V* ⊠ *BP.*

$$$$ ☖ **Calistoga Ranch.** A sister property of the Auberge du Soleil in Rutherford, this posh resort shares a similar wide-open feel. Spacious cedar-shingle bungalows throughout the wooded property have outdoor living areas, and even the restaurant, spa, and reception area have outdoor seating areas and fireplaces. Though it has a more casual, ranchlike feel than the more European Auberge, the lodges are still supremely luxurious, with large bathrooms, a large, romantic outdoor shower, beds dressed with down bedding, and a minibar stocked with free drinks and snacks. **Pros:** almost half the cottages have private hot tubs on the deck; lovely hiking trails on the property; guests have reciprocal privileges at Auberge du Soleil. **Cons:** very expensive; innovative indoor-outdoor organization works better in fair weather than in rain or cold; staff, though friendly, sometimes seems inexperienced. ⊠ *580 Lommel Rd.* ☎ *707/254–2800 or 800/942–4220* ⊕ *www.calistogaranch.com* ⌁ *46 rooms* ⊗ *In-room: a/c, safe, refrigerator, DVD, Internet, Wi-Fi. In-hotel: restaurant, room service, bar, pool, gym, spa, bicycles, laundry service, some pets allowed (fee)* ═ *AE, D, MC, V* ⊚ *EP.*

¢ ⊺ **Calistoga Spa Hot Springs.** Though the rooms are standard motel issue, their well-equipped kitchenettes and the four outdoor heated mineral pools make this a popular spot for those who want to enjoy Calistoga's famed waters on a budget. An on-site spa offers massages, mud baths that use volcanic ash, and other services at reasonable rates (although without the deluxe facilities you'll find at pricier spas). The location on a quiet side street one block from Calistoga's main drag is another plus. Fodors.com users suggest staking out a prime lounging spot next to the pools before the day-trippers are admitted each morning. **Pros:** a rare family-friendly spot in Napa Valley; some rooms equipped with barbecue grills. **Cons:** dated and drab rooms; children at the mineral pools can spoil tranquility; kitchenettes lack microwaves. ⊠ *1006 Washington St.* ☎ *707/942–6269* ⊕ *www.calistogaspa.com* ⌁ *51 rooms, 1 suite* ⊗ *In-room: a/c, kitchen, Wi-Fi. In-hotel: pools, gym, spa, laundry facilities* ═ *MC, V* ⊚ *EP.*

$$$ ⊺ **Cottage Grove Inn.** A long driveway lined with 16 free-standing cottages, each shaded by elm trees and with rocking chairs on the porch, looks a bit like Main Street USA, but inside the skylit buildings are all the perks you could want for a romantic weekend away. There are overstuffed chairs in front of a wood-burning fireplace, flat-panel TVs, and an extra-deep two-person whirlpool tub. Each cottage also has its own variation on the overall comfy-rustic look, with telltale names such as Fly Fishing Cottage and Provence. Spas and restaurants are within walking distance. Rates include afternoon wine and cheese. **Pros:** bicycles available for loan; freestanding cottages offer lots of privacy; bathtubs so big you could swim in them. **Cons:** no pool; decor may seem a bit frumpy for some. ⊠ *1711 Lincoln Ave.* ☎ *707/942–8400 or 800/799–2284* ⊕ *www. cottagegrove.com* ⌁ *16 rooms* ⊗ *In-room: a/c, safe, refrigerator, DVD, Internet, Wi-Fi. In-hotel: bicycles, Internet terminal* ═ *AE, D, DC, MC, V* ⊚ *CP.*

$–$$ 🖼 **Indian Springs.** Since 1871, this old-time spa has welcomed clients to its mud baths, mineral pool, and steam room, all of them supplied with mineral water from its four geysers. Rooms in the lodge, though quite small, are beautifully done up a simple Zen style, with Asian-inspired furnishings, Frette linens on the bed, and flat-panel televisions. The cottages dotted around the property have anything from a small kitchenette to a fully equipped kitchen, encouraging longer stays (book well in advance for these). A boccie ball court, shuffleboard, and croquet lawn outside your door provide entertainment when you're not indulging in various spa treatments and volcanic-ash mud baths, or soaking in the toasty Olympic-size mineral-water pool. **Pros:** lovely grounds with outdoor seating areas; stylish for the price; enormous mineral pool. **Cons:** lodge rooms are small; oddly uncomfortable pillows. ⊠ *1712 Lincoln Ave.* ☎ *707/942–4913* ⊕ *www.indianspringscalistoga.com* ➵ *24 rooms, 17 suites* ⚍ *In room: no phone, kitchen (some), refrigerator (some), Wi-Fi. In-hotel: tennis court, pool, spa* ⊟ *D, MC, V* ⧉ *EP.*

★ **Fodors**Choice 🖼 **Meadowlark Country House.** Twenty hillside
$–$$ acres just north of downtown Calistoga surround this decidedly laid-back but sophisticated inn. Rooms in the main house and guest wing each have their own charms: one has a deep whirlpool tub looking onto a green hillside, and others have a deck with a view of the mountains. Many rooms have fireplaces, and all but one have a whirlpool tub large enough for two. A spacious two-story guesthouse opens directly onto the clothing-optional pool, hot tub, and sauna area, which is open to all guests and enjoyed by a diverse crowd (the inn is welcoming to all, gay and straight). Fodors.com readers point out that "Kurt and Richard are delightful, helpful hosts." **Pros:** sauna next to the pool and hot tub; welcoming vibe attracts diverse guests; some of the most gracious innkeepers in Napa. **Cons:** clothing-optional pool policy isn't for everyone. ⊠ *601 Petrified Forest Rd.* ☎ *707/942–5651 or 800/942–5651* ⊕ *www. meadowlarkinn.com* ➵ *5 rooms, 5 suites* ⚍ *In-room: a/c, no phone, kitchen (some), refrigerator (some), DVD (some), Wi-Fi. In-hotel: pool, Internet terminal, some pets allowed* ⊟ *AE, MC, V* ⧉ *BP.*

$–$$ 🖼 **Mount View Hotel & Spa.** A National Historic Landmark built in 1917 in the Mission-revival style, the Mount View nevertheless feels up-to-date, after renovations in 2008 resulted in repainted rooms (some are a dramatic red and black), feather duvets, and high-tech touches such as iPod

DID YOU KNOW?

Silverado Trail runs parallel to Highway 29 from the town of Napa to Calistoga and is popular with bicyclists because it has a bit less traffic than the more heavily traveled highway.

alarm clocks. A full-service spa provides state-of-the-art pampering, and three cottages are each equipped with a private redwood deck, whirlpool tub, and wet bar. The hotel's location on Calistoga's main drag, plus the two excellent restaurants off the lobby, mean you won't need to go far if your spa treatment has left you too indolent to drive. **Pros:** convenient location; excellent spa treatments. **Cons:** ground-floor rooms dark; mediocre continental breakfast; some bathrooms could use updating. ⊠ *1457 Lincoln Ave.* ☎ *707/942–6877 or 800/816–6877* ⊕ *www.mountviewhotel.com* ⇩ *18 rooms, 13 suites* ⚼ *In-room: a/c, refrigerator (some), DVD, Wi-Fi. In-hotel: restaurant, bar, pool, spa* ⊟ *AE, D, MC, V* ⦿*CP.*

$$$$ ⊺ **Solage.** A resort for sociable sorts who like to lounge at the bar overlooking the large pool or play a game of boccie after lunch at the excellent indoor-outdoor restaurant, this Calistoga newcomer sprawls over 22 acres. The cottages don't look particularly luxurious from the outside, but inside they flaunt a Napa-Valley-barn-meets-San-Francisco-loft aesthetic, with high ceilings, polished concrete floors, recycled walnut furniture, and all-natural fabrics in soothing muted colors. Sports and fitness are a high priority here: in addition to a large, well-equipped spa and "mud bar" where you can indulge in mud-bath variations, there's a packed schedule of fitness activities that include yoga, Pilates, and biking and hiking excursions. ■TIP→ **If you want to be in the middle of the action, ask for a room facing the pool. For more seclusion, ask for one of the quieter rooms near the oak grove.** **Pros:** great service; bike cruisers parked at every cottage for guests' use; separate pools for kids and adults. **Cons:** new landscaping looks a little bleak; some rooms don't have tubs. ⊠ *755 Silverado Trail* ☎ *866/942–7442* ⊕ *www.solagecalistoga.com* ⇩ *89 rooms* ⚼ *In-room: a/c, safe, refrigerator, DVD, Wi-Fi. In-hotel: restaurant, room service, bar, pools, gym, spa, bicycles, laundry service* ⊟ *AE, D, DC, MC, V* ⦿*EP.*

NIGHTLIFE AND THE ARTS

Brannan's Grill (⊠ *1374 Lincoln Ave.* ☎ *707/942–2233*) has talented mixologists behind the mahogany bar, making it a good stop for an after-dinner cocktail. While you're there, take a look at the vaulted ceiling, redwood beams, and hard-forged iron trestles; the building was constructed in 1903 as a garage. On Friday and Saturday nights a superb jazz vibraphone player provides entertainment.

A Great Napa Drive

Traffic permitting, it would be easy to zip from one end of the valley to the other along Highway 29 in about 45 minutes, passing scores of wineries along the way. Indeed, that's what plenty of visitors do, but a much better strategy is to appreciate the wineries at a more leisurely pace.

From the town of Napa, start around 10 AM and drive north on Highway 29 to the Trancas Street/Redwood Road exit. Take the shady Redwood Road (to the left), and when it narrows from four lanes to two, stay to your left. Just after a sharp curve, look for the Hess Winery sign. When you see it, turn sharply left to stay on Redwood Road; you'll see the entrance to the winery almost immediately. (The trip from Napa to Hess should take about 15 minutes.) Here you'll want to allow at least an hour or so to browse the excellent modern art collection before you pass through the tasting room on your way out.

After your visit, turn right out of the winery back onto Redwood Road. At the next T, turn left onto Mt. Veeder Road. Next, turn right on Oakville Grade, and you'll be twisting and turning your way downhill to Highway 29. (Take your time, and pack the Dramamine if you're prone to car sickness.) Turn left on Highway 29 and you'll see the driveway to Robert Mondavi almost immediately on your left. Their introductory tour is particularly good for wine newbies, but if you've arranged to take an afternoon tour at Schramsberg, you'll have to skip the tour and head straight to one of the two tasting rooms.

After your stop at Mondavi, head north on Highway 29 for about five minutes to Dean & Deluca, where you can find the most decadent picnic items possible: imported cheeses and charcuterie, locally made pastries and chocolates, and more condiments than you might know what to do with. Pop into the funky, modern Flora Springs tasting room next door, taste what's on offer, and pick up a bottle before heading to the picnic tables on the back patio for a leisurely lunch.

If you've made a reservation for one of the excellent afternoon tours at Schramsberg, head north on Highway 29 to Peterson Road, where you'll turn left and then make a quick right onto narrow, winding Schramsberg Road. After touring their extensive caves and tasting their sparklers, return to Highway 29 and turn right (south) to return to St. Helena. You'll have an hour or two to browse the shops along Main Street before they close for the evening.

Live music, a laid-back atmosphere, and the garden patio make the **Calistoga Inn Restaurant and Brewery** (⊠ *1250 Lincoln Ave.* ☎ *707/942–4101*) a popular spot for a house-brewed beer on warm summer nights.

SHOPPING

Shops and restaurants along Lincoln Avenue in downtown Calistoga tend to cater to locals rather than visitors, and you'll find few of the high-priced boutiques that line the main street of St. Helena. The **Calistoga Depot** (⊠ *1458 Lincoln Ave.* ☎ *No phone*) is a small cluster of gift shops, a café, and a wine shop and tasting room housed in an old train depot and its six restored railway cars. The sandwiches and small selection of prepared foods at the café are picnickers' best bet in Calistoga.

Enoteca Wine Shop (⊠ *1348B Lincoln Ave.* ☎ *707/942–1117*), on Calistoga's main drag, displays almost all of their wines with extensive tasting notes. This makes it easier to choose from among this unusually fine collection, which includes both hard-to-find bottles from Napa and Sonoma and many rare French wines.

The **Wine Garage** (⊠ *1020 Hwy. 29* ☎ *707/942–5332*) is the stop for bargain hunters, since all their bottles go for $25 or less. It's a great way to discover the work of smaller wineries producing undervalued wines. The unusually helpful staffers are happy to share information on all the wines they stock.

The Carneros District

WORD OF MOUTH

"Artesa, between Napa and Sonoma, is on top of a hill and on a clear day you can see all the way to the San Franciso Bay."

—boom_boom

THE CARNEROS AVA HAS A BUZZ about it. Also known as Los Carneros, this compact viticultural region stretches across the cool lower reaches of Sonoma and Napa counties. *Carneros* means "sheep" in Spanish, and the slopes now covered with vines were once thought to be good only as pasture. Today, however, the only sheep you're likely to see are the metal sheep sculptures grazing in front of di Rosa, as winemakers have snapped up almost every available acre, sending land values through the roof. Though vintners have clearly wised up to the value of the Carneros region, visitors have been slower to catch on. Most zip right through in their haste to get to big-name spots to the north—but if you check out a few of these places, odds are you'll become a convert.

To understand how different the Carneros is from the other California wine-producing regions, you must approach it from the roads that border the water. From San Francisco, travel north on U.S. 101 to Novato and take the Highway 37 turnoff to the east, which will take you along the northern reaches of San Francisco Bay, at this point called San Pablo Bay. On a gray day, the flat marshes and low hills near the bay look moody, more like Scottish moor than a California shore. During summer and autumn, strong west winds blow in from the ocean each afternoon, tempering the hot days.

The soils here are shallow and not particularly fertile, which means that the vines struggle to produce fruit. Though it seems that this would be a drawback, it's in fact a plus. Vines that grow slowly and yield less fruit tend to produce concentrated, high-acid grapes that are ideal for wine making. Grape growers in the mid-19th century recognized this and planted vast tracts here. Because of the low yields, some of the land was allowed to revert to sheep pasture after phylloxera destroyed the vines in the 1890s. But the reputation of the grapes survived, and shortly after the repeal of Prohibition, vines once again began to spread across the hills.

Pinot noir and chardonnay grapes are considered king here, as they thrive in the moderate temperatures of the exposed, windy slopes. These days, however, winemakers are also trying out merlot and syrah, which are also considered well suited to the cool winds, thin soil, and low rainfall. (Carneros generally gets less rain than elsewhere in Napa and Sonoma.) Even warm-climate grapes such as cabernet sauvignon can ripen well in favored Carneros locations. Though many of these grapes are cultivated by small Carneros wineries that use them to make estate wines, some are instead purchased by wineries elsewhere in Napa and Sonoma. High-profile places such as Robert Sinskey, Domaine Chandon, and Beaulieu Vineyard have all tapped the Carneros grape supply to make wines of great complexity and depth.

GETTING AROUND CARNEROS

The Carneros region is closer to San Francisco than any other part of the Wine Country: on a good day you can be sipping wine here within 45 minutes of crossing the Golden Gate Bridge. The main route through the region is the east–west Carneros Highway, also known as Highway 121 or the Sonoma Highway. This connects Highway 12, the main north–south route through Sonoma Valley, with Highway 29, the main north–south route through Napa Valley.

WESTERN CARNEROS

37 mi from San Francisco via U.S. 101 north to Rte. 37 east.

The western stretches of the Carneros District, from the foot of the Sonoma Mountains to the breezy banks of San Pablo Bay, fall in Sonoma County. The cool air and early-afternoon fog are perfectly suited to cool-climate varieties such as the pinot noir and chardonnay. Here they are often turned into still wines, but about 20% of those grapes are transformed into lively sparkling wines, like the crisp and citrusy ones you'll find at Gloria Ferrer Caves and Vineyards.

The gently rolling hills of western Carneros are still relatively undeveloped, and visitors tend to pass through quickly on their way to destinations farther up Sonoma Valley. And though compact Carneros has very few restaurants and lodgings, the towns of Sonoma and Napa are rarely more than a 15-minute drive away.

If you happen to be driving north along Highway 121 from San Francisco, you might be mystified to see a whimsical sculpture on the right side of the road, a full-size tree covered with 80,000 baby-blue Christmas balls. The "Blue Tree" marks your arrival at **CornerStone Sonoma,** a 9-acre complex of shops, galleries, a café, tasting rooms, a Sonoma

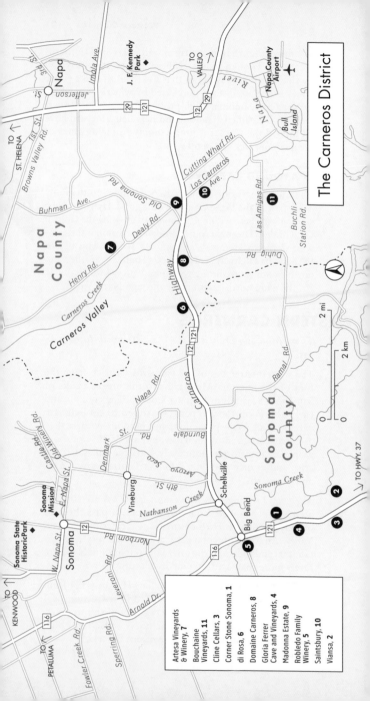

The Carneros District

Artesa Vineyards & Winery, 7
Bouchaine Vineyards, 11
Cline Cellars, 3
Corner Stone Sonoma, 1
di Rosa, 6
Domaine Carneros, 8
Gloria Ferrer Cave and Vineyards, 4
Madonna Estate, 9
Robledo Family Winery, 5
Saintsbury, 10
Viansa, 2

The gardens at CornerStone Sonoma

Valley Visitors Bureau office, and many different "architectural gardens." About 20 landscape artists were each given a small plot of land and carte blanche to create an installation, and it's worth taking the time to explore these sometimes whimsical, sometimes pretentious, always interesting landscapes. The Sonoma Children's Garden offers a large sandbox, climbing structure, and room for the little ones to run around and play. ✉ *23570 Hwy. 121/Arnold Dr., Sonoma* ☎ *707/933–3010* ⊕ *www.cornerstonesonoma. com* ✐ *Free* ☺ *Architectural gardens daily 10–4, hours of other attractions vary.*

VINEYARDS

Although many Carneros wineries specialize in pinot noir and chardonnay, **Cline Cellars** goes its own way by focusing on Rhône varietals, such as syrah, roussanne, and viognier, all grown here in Carneros, as well as mourvèdre and carignane, which are cultivated in Contra Costa County. They're also known for their Ancient Vines Zinfandel, produced from vines that are around 100 years old. (Older vines are often pulled out because their grape yields decrease over time, but many believe that the concentrated flavor of the grapes is well worth the tradeoff.) The 1850s farmhouse that houses the tasting room has a pleasant wraparound porch for enjoying the weeping willows, ponds, fountains, and thousands of rosebushes on the property. Pack a picnic and plan to stay for a while, if you have the time. ✉ 24737 Hwy. 121/Arnold Dr., Sonoma ☎ 707/940–4030 ⊕ www. clinecellars.com ☞ Tasting free–$1 per reserve wine, tour free ☉ Daily 10–6; tour daily at 11, 1, and 3.

The Spanish hacienda–style architecture recalls the native country of the Ferrer family, who make both sparkling and still wines at **Gloria Ferrer Caves and Vineyards.** The Spanish sparkling-wine maker Freixenet was the first winery to start producing Carneros fizz, establishing this site in 1982. Winemaker Bob Iantosca crafts superb sparkling wines from his beloved chardonnay and pinot noir grapes, but still finds the time to make a small quantity of still wines, making him something of a rarity among winemakers. The daily tours here include the cellar, where several feet of earth maintain a constant temperature, and a glimpse of some antique wine-making equipment. You can enjoy the tasting either seated indoors or out on the terrace. ✉ 23555 Carneros Hwy./Rte. 121, Sonoma ☎ 707/996–7256 ⊕ www. gloriaferrer.com ☞ Tasting $2–$10, tour $10 ☉ Daily 10–5; tours daily at 11, 1, and 3.

The **Robledo Family Winery,** founded by Reynaldo Robledo Sr., a former migrant worker from Michoacán, Mexico, is truly a family affair. You're likely to encounter one of the charming Robledo sons in the tasting room, where he'll proudly tell you the story of the immigrant family while pouring tastes of their sauvignon blanc, pinot noir, merlot, cabernet sauvignon, and other wines, including a chardonnay that comes from the vineyard right outside the tasting room's door. All seven Robledo sons and two Robledo daughters, as well as matriarch Maria, are involved in the winery operations. If you don't run into them on your visit to the winery, you'll see their names and pictures on the bottles of wine, such as the Dos Hermanas late-harvest dessert wine, or one of the ports dedicated to Maria Robledo. ✉ 21901 Bonness Rd., Sonoma ☎ 707/939–6903 ⊕ www. robledofamilywinery.com ☞ Tasting $5–$10 ☉ Mon.–Sat. 10–5, Sun. 11–4.

Reminiscent of a Tuscan villa, with ocher-color buildings surrounded by olive trees and colorful flower beds, sprawling **Viansa** focuses on Italian varietals such as sangiovese, nebbiolo, and tocai friulano. Fodor's readers are generally split when summing up the charms of the winery. Some love the market on the premises that sells sandwiches and deli foods to complement the Italian-style wines, as well as a large selection of dinnerware, cookbooks, and condiments. Others find the crowds that tend to congregate here off-putting (it's a popular spot for large parties and weddings). Regardless, the many picnic tables, some of which overlook a wetland preserve below, are a fine place to enjoy a glass of wine while bird-watching (only food and wines sold on the premises are permitted). ⊠ *25200 Arnold Dr., Sonoma* ☏ *707/935–4700* ⊕ *www.viansa.com* ⊟ *Tasting $5–$20, tour $10 (tasting fee additional)* ⊙ *Daily 10–5, tour daily at 11, 2, and 3.*

EASTERN CARNEROS

42 mi northeast of San Francisco via U.S. 101 north to Rte. 37 east to Rte. 29 north and east.

Stretching from the Sonoma County line to the Napa River in the town of Napa, the eastern half of the Carneros region generally shares the same wine-growing climate and soils with the western half. Though you'll find the same rustic, relatively undeveloped atmosphere in eastern Carneros, wineries pop up more frequently along Highway 121 here, and the route is lined with vineyards where bits of shiny reflective tape, tied to the vines to keep the birds away, flicker in the sunlight.

To take a break from wine tasting, grab a picnic lunch and take Cuttings Wharf Road south to the Napa River, stop at the public boat ramp, and dangle your feet in the river. Keep a lookout for white egrets, great blue herons, wood ducks, and other waterfowl. But beware, as these waters are tricky and rise and fall with the tide. If the bleak marshes to the south look familiar, there's a reason: Francis Ford Coppola shot some of the Mekong Delta scenes for *Apocalypse Now* here.

★ Fodor's Choice While you're driving along the Carneros Highway on your way to Napa from San Francisco, it would be easy to zip by one of the region's best-kept secrets: **di Rosa.** Metal sculptures of sheep grazing in the grass mark the entrance to this sprawling, art-stuffed property. Thousands of 20th-century artworks by hundreds of Northern California artists crop up everywhere—in galleries, in the former di Rosa residence, on every lawn, in every courtyard, and even on the lake. Some of the works were commissioned especially for the preserve, such as Paul Kos's meditative *Chartres Bleu*, a video installation in a chapel-like setting

Organic Wines

If, as many grape growers insist, a wine is only as good as the vineyard it comes from, those who have adopted sustainable, biodynamic, or organic viticulture methods may be on to something.

But what do vintners mean by "organic"? Although organic viticulture is governmentally recognized and regulated, it is vaguely defined and its value is hotly debated—just like the rest of organic farming. It boils down to a rejection of chemical fertilizers, pesticides, and fungicides. Biodynamic farming, meanwhile, is a trademarked term for a similar anti-artificial approach with a spiritual slant.

Partly because it is difficult and expensive to qualify for official certification, partly because organic vineyards have smaller yields, and partly because it is hard to grow grapes organically except in warm, dry climates, organic viticulture remains the exception rather than the rule in the industry, although more vineyards are being certified organic every year.

Even rarer than wines produced from organically grown grapes are completely organic wines. To make an organic wine, not only do the grapes have to come from organic vineyards, but processing must use a minimum of chemical additives. Some winemakers argue that

it is impossible to make truly fine wine without using at least some additives, such as sulfur dioxide (sulfites), an antioxidant that protects the wine's color, aroma, bright flavors, and longevity. And, of course, organic wine making is more expensive.

Many wineries that might qualify as partially organic resist the label, wary of its impact on their reputation. Still, the movement is gaining momentum. Many major players, even if they are not certified organic, have taken steps to reduce their use of pesticides or implement other eco-friendly policies. Others, such as Frog's Leap and Hess, grow some or all of their grapes organically. Very few producers—and none of the big names in Napa and Sonoma Valley—make completely organic wine. If you're interested in trying some, you might seek out wines made by Frey Vineyards, in Mendocino County.

If demand for organic products continues to grow, supply will no doubt follow suit. In the meantime, if you want organic wine, read the label carefully. To be labeled organic, a wine must contain 100% certified organic grapes and have no added sulfites. Wines that contain sulfites can indicate that they are made from certified organic grapes.

di Rosa Preserve

that replicates a stained-glass window of the cathedral in Chartres, France. If you stop by without a reservation, you'll gain access only to the Gatehouse Gallery, where there's a small collection of riotously colorful figurative and abstract sculpture and painting. ■TIP→ **To see the rest of the property and artwork, you'll have to sign up for one of the various tours of the grounds (from 1 to 2½ hours).** Reservations for the tours are recommended, but they can sometimes accommodate walk-ins. ⊠ *5200 Sonoma Hwy./Carneros Hwy., Napa* ☎ *707/226–5991* ⊕ *www.dirosaart.org* ✉ *Free, tours $10–$15* ☉ *Wed.–Fri. 9:30–3; Sat. by reservation; call for tour times.*

VINEYARDS

With its modern, minimalist look in the tasting room, which is dug into a Carneros hilltop, and contemporary sculptures and fountains on the property, **Artesa Vineyards & Winery** is a far cry from the many faux French châteaus and rustic Italian-style villas in the region. Although the Spanish owners once made only sparkling wines, now they produce primarily still wines, mostly chardonnay and pinot noir, but also cabernet sauvignon and a smattering of other limited-release wines such as syrah and albariño. Call ahead to reserve a spot on one of the specialty tours, such as a wine and cheese pairing or the walk through the vineyard ($40). ⊠ *1345 Henry Rd., north off Old Sonoma*

Bouchaine Vineyards

Rd. and Dealy La., Napa ☎ *707/224–1668* ⊕ *www.artesawinery.com* ✉ *Tasting $10–$15, tour $20* ☉ *Daily 10–5, tour daily at 11 and 2.*

Just a few miles off the Carneros Highway but seeming much farther off the beaten path, tranquil **Bouchaine Vineyards** lies between Carneros and Huichica creeks and the tidal sloughs of San Pablo Bay. The alternately breezy and foggy weather works well for the Burgundian varietals pinot noir and chardonnay, which account for most of their vines, but look for their syrah and an excellent late-harvest chardonnay called Bouche d'Or as well. The exceptionally friendly staffers charge $15 for a tasting standing at the bar, but consider paying $30 for a seated tasting (accompanied by nibbles of cheeses, olives, and nuts) on the lovely back patio. From there you're likely to see hawks, starlings, or even golden eagles soaring above the vineyards (they have to place netting over the vines to keep the birds away from the fruit). The commitment to sustainable practices is evident everywhere, from the use of organic compost in their vineyards to the construction of the winery's redwood façade, made from their original wine tanks. ■ TIP➔ **Pick up a brochure if you're interested in taking a self-guided ¾-mi walk through the vineyards, behind the tasting room.** ✉ *1075 Buchli Station Rd., Napa* ☎ *707/252–9065* ⊕ *www.bouchaine.com* ✉ *Tasting $15–$30* ☉ *Daily 10:30–4.*

The main château at Domaine Carneros

The majestic château of **Domaine Carneros** looks for all the world like it belongs in France, and in fact it does: it's modeled after the Château de la Marquetterie, an 18th-century mansion owned by the Taittinger family near Epernay, France. Carved into the hillside beneath the winery, Domaine Carneros's cellars produce delicate sparkling wines reminiscent of those made by Taittinger, using only grapes grown locally in the Carneros wine district. The winery sells full glasses, flights, and bottles of their wines, which also include still wines such as a handful of pinot noirs and a merlot, and serves them with cheese plates or caviar to those seated in the Louis XV–inspired salon or on the terrace overlooking the vineyards. Though this makes a visit here a tad more expensive than some stops on a winery tour, it's also one of the most opulent ways to enjoy the Carneros district, especially on fair days, when the views over the vineyards are spectacular. ⊠ *1240 Duhig Rd., Napa* ☎ *707/257–0101* ⊕ *www.domainecarneros.com* ⬚ *Tasting $6.50–$25, tour $25* ☉ *Daily 10–6; tour daily at 11, 1, and 3.*

Winemaker Andrea Bartolucci, whose family has been growing grapes in Napa since 1922, oversees the 160 gently rolling acres of vines at **Madonna Estate.** Here he uses organic and dry farming techniques to grow nearly a dozen kinds of grapes. (Dry farming, which leaves established vines to rely on rainwater, stresses the plants, resulting in a smaller yield but more intensely flavored grapes.) Though the winery's location, right on Highway 121, is less scenic than some and the tasting room is modest, it's worth a visit for a taste of their crisp, lean pinot grigio, with a fresh melony aroma; the smoky, creamy chardonnay aged in French oak; and the earthy pinot noir. The muscat canelli, gewürztraminer, and riesling (the latter two made in a fairly dry style) are particularly good, although they often sell out, since they are produced in small quantities. ✉ *5400 Old Sonoma Rd., Napa* ☎ *707/255–8864* ⊕ *www.madonnaestate.com* ✎ *Tasting $5–$15* ☉ *Daily 10–5, tours by appointment.*

Back in 1981, when **Saintsbury** released its first pinot noir, conventional wisdom was that only the French could produce great pinot. No matter that a few cutting-edge winemakers, such as Beaulieu's André Tchelistcheff, had been making pinot from Carneros grapes since the late 1930s. But what a difference a few decades make: the Carneros region is now thought to produce some of the best pinots in the world. If you're still in doubt, try Saintsbury's earthy, intense Brown Ranch pinot noir. Their other pinot noirs tend to be lighter in style and more fruit-forward. Named for the English author and critic George Saintsbury (he wrote *Notes on a Cellar-Book*), the winery also makes chardonnay, syrah, and a delightful vin gris. You must make an appointment to taste or take a tour, and the tasting room is fairly utilitarian, but the quality of the wines makes it well worth a visit if you're a fan of pinot noir. ✉ *1500 Los Carneros Ave., Napa* ☎ *707/252–0592* ⊕ *www.saintsbury.com* ✎ *Tasting $15–$20, tour free* ☉ *Mon.–Sat. by appointment only.*

WHERE TO STAY AND EAT

★ Fodor's Choice ✕ **Boon Fly Café.** Part of the Carneros Inn complex, west of downtown Napa, this small spot melds rural charm with industrial chic. Outside, swings occupy the porch of a modern red barn; inside, things get sleek with high ceilings and galvanized steel tabletops. The small menu of three squares a day updates American classics, with dishes such as Dungeness crab cakes with a lemon-and-sesame vinaigrette, a New York strip steak served with Blue Lake green beans, and flatbread topped with bacon, Point Reyes blue cheese, and sautéed mushrooms. If there's a wait for a table, never fear: belly up to the bar, where you'll find good selection of wines by the glass in addition to a full bar. ■TIP→ Since it's the rare Wine Country restaurant

$$

that's open all day (from 7 AM to 9 PM), it makes a convenient midday stop when you need a break from wine tasting. ✉ *4048 Sonoma Hwy., Napa* ☎ *707/299–4872* ♿ *Reservations not accepted* ▭ *AE, D, MC, V.*

★ Fodor'sChoice 🍸 **Carneros Inn.** Freestanding board-and-batten
$$$$ cottages with rocking chairs on each porch are simultaneously rustic and chic at this luxurious property. Inside, each cottage is flooded with natural light but still manages to maintain privacy, with windows and French doors leading to a private garden. (The suites are actually two-cottage clusters.) Wood-burning fireplaces, ethereal beds topped with Italian linens and pristine white down comforters, and spacious bathrooms with heated slate floors and large indoor-outdoor showers may make it difficult to summon the will to leave the cottage and enjoy the hilltop infinity swimming pool and hot tub. The Hilltop Dining Room, with views of the neighboring vineyards, is open to guests only for breakfast and lunch, but Boon Fly Café (see above) and FARM, their public restaurants, are popular with visitors throughout the Wine Country. **Pros:** cottages have lots of privacy; beautiful views from the hilltop pool and hot tub; heaters on each private patio encourage lounging outside in the evening. **Cons:** a long drive from destinations up-valley; smallish rooms with limited seating options, annoying $15 per night resort fee. ✉ *4048 Sonoma Hwy.,* ☎ *707/299–4900* ⊕ *www.thecarnerosinn.com* ⟿ *76 cottages, 10 suites* ♿ *In-room: a/c, refrigerator, DVD, Internet. In-hotel: 3 restaurants, room service, bar, pool, gym, spa, laundry service* ▭ *AE, D, DC, MC, V* ⧀ *EP.*

Sonoma Valley

WORD OF MOUTH

"In contrast to its more famous neighbor to the east (Napa), you will find the Sonoma wineries more inviting and less hectic—I actually like them better. . . . [And i]n Sonoma, they seem to go out of their way to invite you to use their facilities."

—StuDudley

ALTHOUGH THE SONOMA VALLEY may not have quite the cachet of the neighboring Napa Valley, wineries here entice with their unpretentious attitude and smaller crowds. The glitzy Napa-style tasting rooms with enormous gift shops and $25 tasting fees are the exception here rather than the rule. Sonoma's landscape seduces, too, its roads gently climbing and descending on their way to wineries hidden from the road by trees.

That's not to suggest that Sonoma is exactly undiscovered territory. On the contrary, along the main corridor through the Sonoma Valley—Highway 12 from Sonoma to Santa Rosa—you'll spot sophisticated inns and spas between the ubiquitous wineries. And in high season the towns of Glen Ellen and Kenwood are filled with well-heeled wine buffs. Still, the pace of life is a bit slower here than in Napa— you'll see as many bicyclists as limos zipping from one winery to the next. And the historic Sonoma Valley towns offer glimpses of the past. The town of Sonoma, with its atmospheric central plaza, is rich with 19th-century build- ings. Glen Ellen, meanwhile, has a special connection with author Jack London.

Bounded by the Mayacamas Mountains on the east and Sonoma Mountain on the west, this scenic valley extends north from San Pablo Bay nearly 20 mi to the eastern outskirts of Santa Rosa. The varied terrain, soils, and cli- mate (cooler in the south because of the bay influence and hotter toward the north) allow grape growers to raise cool-weather varietals such as chardonnay and pinot noir as well as merlot, cabernet sauvignon, and other heat- seeking vines.

GETTING AROUND SONOMA VALLEY

Highway 12, also called the Sonoma Highway, is the main thoroughfare through the Sonoma Valley, running north– south through Sonoma, Glen Ellen, and Kenwood. Traffic tends to move fairly smoothly along this route, except on some summer weekends. To get to Napa from the Sonoma Valley, you can drive south of the town of Sonoma and fol- low Highway 121/Highway 12, also known as the Carneros Highway, east, or you can pick up Trinity Road, which turns into Oakville Grade Road, for a beautiful—but slow and winding—trip over the Mayacamas range.

SONOMA VALLEY APPELLATIONS

Although Sonoma *County* is a large, diverse growing region encompassing several different appellations, the much smaller Sonoma *Valley*, at the southern end of Sonoma County, is comparatively compact and consists mostly of the **Sonoma Valley AVA**, which stretches from southeast of Santa Rosa south toward San Pablo Bay. The weather and soils here are unusually diverse. Pinot and chardonnay are most likely to be found in the southernmost parts of the AVA, which is cooled by fog from San Pablo Bay, whereas zinfandel, cabernet, and sauvignon blanc are popular farther north, near Glen Ellen and Kenwood, which tend to be a few degrees warmer.

The **Sonoma Mountain AVA** rises to the west of Glen Ellen on the western border of the Sonoma Valley AVA. Benefiting from a sunny mountain location and poor rocky soil, the vineyards here produce deep-rooted vines and intensely flavored grapes that are made into unique, complex red wines, especially hearty cabernet sauvignons.

With only 650 acres planted with vines, the idyllic **Bennett Valley AVA** is one of the smallest appellations in California. Surrounded by the mountains on three sides but cooled by coastal breezes that sneak through the Crane Canyon wind gap, it's ideal for cooler-weather grapes such as pinot noir and chardonnay, but also does well with syrah, cabernet sauvignon, and sauvignon blanc.

SONOMA

14 mi west of Napa on Rte. 12; 45 mi northeast of San Francisco via U.S. 101 to Rte. 37 to Rte. 121/12.

The town of Sonoma, the valley's cultural center, is the oldest town in the Wine Country. Founded in the early 1800s, when California was still part of Mexico, it is built around a large, tree-filled plaza. One of the few towns in the valley with many attractions not related to food and wine, Sonoma has plenty to keep you busy for a couple of hours before you head out to tour the wineries. On your way into town from the south, you pass through the Carneros wine district, which straddles the southern sections of Sonoma and Napa counties.

FAIR PLAY. Wonder why the stone city hall, built on Sonoma's plaza in 1906, looks the same from all angles? Its four sides were

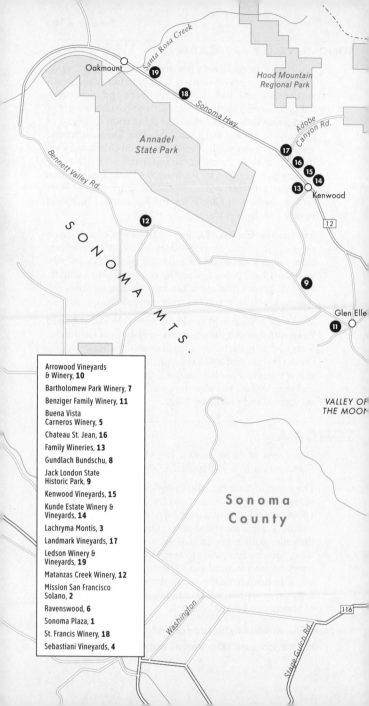

Oakmount

Santa Rosa Creek

19

Hood Mountain
Regional Park

18

Sonoma Hwy.

Adobe
Canyon Rd.

Annadel
State Park

17

16

15

14

13

Kenwood

Bennett Valley Rd.

12

12

S O N O M A

9

12

Glen Elle

M T S.

11

Arrowood Vineyards
& Winery, **10**

Bartholomew Park Winery, **7**

Benziger Family Winery, **11**

Buena Vista
Carneros Winery, **5**

Chateau St. Jean, **16**

Family Wineries, **13**

Gundlach Bundschu, **8**

Jack London State
Historic Park, **9**

Kenwood Vineyards, **15**

Kunde Estate Winery &
Vineyards, **14**

Lachryma Montis, **3**

Landmark Vineyards, **17**

Ledson Winery &
Vineyards, **19**

Matanzas Creek Winery, **12**

Mission San Francisco
Solano, **2**

Ravenswood, **6**

Sonoma Plaza, **1**

St. Francis Winery, **18**

Sebastiani Vineyards, **4**

VALLEY OF
THE MOON

S o n o m a
C o u n t y

Washington

116

Stage Gulch Rd.

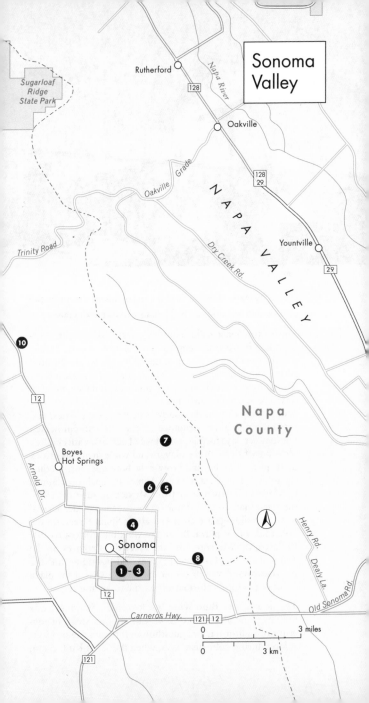

Mission San Francisco Salano

purposely made identical so that none of the merchants on the plaza would feel that city hall had turned its back to them.

The central **Sonoma Plaza** dates from the Mission era; surrounding it are 19th-century adobes, atmospheric hotels, and the swooping marquee of the 1930s Sebastiani Theatre. Although Sonoma has more than its share of historic adobes from the city's Mexican period, this is not a musty museum town. Nor is the plaza a museum piece—it's a place where people hang out on the shady benches, have picnics, and listen to musical performances at the small amphitheater. On summer days the plaza is a hive of activity, with children blowing off steam in the playground while their folks stock up on picnic supplies and browse the boutiques surrounding the square. The plaza is where American rebels proclaimed California's independence from Mexico on June 14, 1846, the event marked by a statue on the northeast side. Several historic buildings are clustered along Spain Street, on the north side of the plaza. Be sure to walk into the courtyards **El Paseo**, the **Mercato**, and the **Place des Pyrenées** on the east side of the plaza, where cafés and boutiques line the passageways. A visitor center on the east side of the plaza doles out helpful information on the town and region.

The now-empty **Blue Wing Inn** (⊠ *133 E. Spain St.*) was built by General Mariano G. Vallejo, the last Mexican governor of California, as a guesthouse. It became a notorious saloon during gold-rush days, when the scout Kit Carson, the bandit Joaquin Murietta (an inspiration for Zorro), and the army officer Ulysses S. Grant were patrons.

The **Toscano Hotel** (⊠ *20 East Spain St.*) dates from the 1850s; step inside the front door to see a musty-smelling re-creation of the hotel's lobby and bar. The building has also served as a warehouse, a general store, and a library during its long history.

On one corner of the Sonoma Plaza the **Mission San Francisco Solano,** whose chapel and school were used to bring Christianity to the Native Americans, is now a museum with a fine collection of watercolors of California missions painted around 1905. ⊠ *114 E. Spain St.* ☎ *707/938–9560* ☞ *$3, includes Sonoma Barracks on central plaza and Lachryma Montis* ☉ *Fri.–Wed. 10–5.*

A tree-lined driveway leads to **Lachryma Montis,** which General Mariano G. Vallejo, the last Mexican governor of California, built for his large family in 1852. The Victorian Gothic house, insulated with adobe, represents a blend of Mexican and American cultures. Opulent furnishings, including white-marble fireplaces and a French rosewood piano, are particularly noteworthy. Free tours are occasionally conducted by docents on the weekend. ⊠ *W. Spain St., near 3rd St. W* ☎ *707/938–9559* ☞ *$3, tour free* ☉ *Fri.–Wed. 10–5.*

VINEYARDS AROUND SONOMA

Originally planted by Franciscans of the Sonoma Mission in 1825, the **Sebastiani Vineyards** were bought by Samuele Sebastiani in 1904. Although the winery is best known for its red wines, including a rich Russian River pinot noir and an approachable cabernet sauvignon, you can also find some unusual whites here, such as a white pinot noir. A regularly scheduled half-hour tour focuses on the history of the winery. The large gift shop is chockablock with porcelain dinnerware, bath products, and other housewares and gift items. ⊠ *389 4th St. E* ☎ *707/933–3230* ⊕ *www.sebastiani.com* ☞ *Tasting $10, tour free* ☉ *Daily 10–5; tour daily at 11, 1, and 3.*

Buena Vista Carneros Winery is the oldest continually operating winery in California. It was here, in 1857, that Count Agoston Haraszthy de Mokcsa laid the basis for modern California wine making, bucking the conventional wisdom that vines should be planted on well-watered ground by

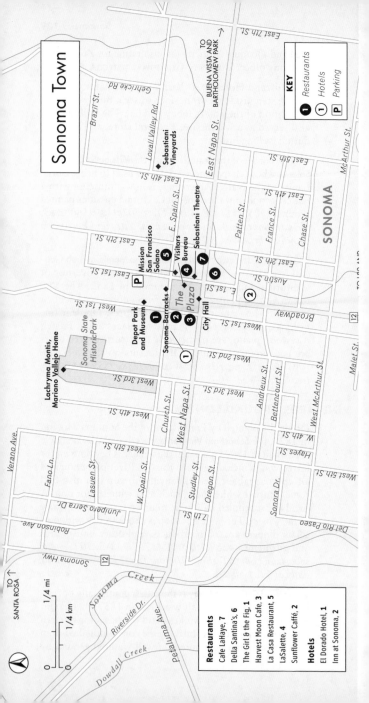

Sonoma Town

Restaurants
Cafe LaHaye, 7
Della Santina's, 6
The Girl & the Fig, 1
Harvest Moon Cafe, 3
La Casa Restaurant, 5
LaSalette, 4
Sunflower Caffé, 2

Hotels
El Dorado Hotel, 1
Inn at Sonoma, 2

KEY
1 Restaurants
① Hotels
P Parking

TO SANTA ROSA
TO BUENA VISTA AND BARTHOLOMEW PARK

Lachryma Montis, Mariano Vallejo Home
Sonoma State Historic Park
Depot Park and Museum
Sonoma Barracks
The Plaza
City Hall
Mission San Francisco Solano
Visitors Bureau
Sebastiani Theatre
Sebastiani Vineyards

SONOMA

Sonoma Creek
Petaluma Ave.
Dowdall Creek
Riverside Dr.

Crush Camp

Are your winery visits making you eager to pitch in and get your hands dirty? Are you starting to look longingly at the pruning shears and rows of vines? Consider signing up for one of the short, hands-on wine-making programs offered by a few wineries, usually in September and October. You'll see the inner workings of the harvest and even blend your own bottle. Below are top options for these "crush camps."

■ **Camp Schramsberg.** Three-day sessions, one in the fall and another in the spring, at Schramsberg focus on making sparkling wines. In the fall campers pick grapes in the vineyards and follow them to the crusher. Winemakers explain and teach traditional methods such as riddling—and as a dramatic finish, the art of sabrage—opening a bottle of bubbly by slicing off its neck with a saber. An additional camp in spring focuses on the art of assemblage, or blending

sparkling wine. ☎ 800/877–3623 ⊕ www.schramsberg.com.
Diageo Crush Camp. Campers can get their hands dirty sorting grape clusters and helping punch down the grape skins at the top of a fermentation tank at this two-day, two-night experience that takes place at various wineries owned by Diageo, including Sterling Vineyards, Beaulieu Vineyard, and Provenance Vineyards. The schedule is also full of winemaker dinners and educational luncheons where you can learn about wine making from those who do it best. ☎ 800/617–7582 ⊕ www.myworldmywine.com.

■ **Sonoma Grape Camp.** Stints in the vineyard are broken up by food and wine workshops and memorable meals before you learn about blending wine from a local winemaker. Hotel accommodations are included in the pricey three-day package. ☎ 707/522–5860 ⊕ www.sonomagrapecamp.com.

instead planting on well-drained hillsides. Chinese laborers dug tunnels 100 feet into the hillside, and the limestone they extracted was used to build the main house, which is now surrounded by redwood and eucalyptus trees and a picnic area. Their best wines are their chardonnay, pinot noir, syrah, and merlot grown in the Ramal Vineyard in the Carneros District, on a cool, windswept hill overlooking San Francisco Bay. If you're a bit peckish, reserve ahead for a seated tasting of five wines paired with cheeses or other nibbles. ✉ *18000 Old Winery Rd., off Napa Rd.*

Bartholomew Park Winery

☎ 800/678–8504 ⊕ buenavistacarneros.com ✉ Tasting $10–$20 ⊘ Daily 10–5.

Ravenswood, whose tasting room is housed in a stone building covered in climbing vines, has a punchy mission statement: "no wimpy wines." They generally succeed, especially with their signature big, bold zinfandels, which are sometimes blended with petit syrah, carignane, or other varietals. Be sure to taste the syrah, early-harvest gewürztraminer, and lightly sparkling moscato, too. Tours that focus on their viticultural practices ($15), held at 10:30 daily, include a barrel tasting of the wines in progress in the cellar. Another tour, at 11:30 on weekdays from mid-May through September, concludes with wine-and-cheese pairings ($25). Reservations are recommended for the former and required for the latter. ✉ 18701 Gehricke Rd., off E. Spain St. ☎ 707/938–1960 ⊕ www.ravenswood-wine.com ✉ Tasting $10–$15, tours $15–$25 ⊘ Daily 10–4:30, call for tour times.

★ **Fodor's**Choice Although **Bartholomew Park Winery** was founded only in 1994, grapes were grown in some of its vineyards as early as the 1830s. The emphasis here is on handcrafted, single-varietal wines—cabernet, merlot, zinfandel, syrah, and sauvignon blanc. The wines themselves, available only at the winery, make a stop worth it, but another reason to visit is its small museum, with vivid exhibits about the history of the winery and the Sonoma region. Another plus is the beautiful, slightly off-the-beaten-path location in a 375-acre private park about 2 mi from downtown Sonoma. Pack a picnic to enjoy on the woodsy grounds, or ask in the tasting room for a map that shows a 3-mi route that climbs about 300 feet to provide lovely views over the valley. ⊠ *1000 Vineyard La.* ☎ *707/939–3026* ⊕ *www.bartpark. com* 🍷 *Tasting $5* ⊘ *Daily 11–4:30.*

Gundlach-Bundschu may look like a grim bunker at first glance, but it's a lot of fun to visit. They let their hair down here, with pop or rock playing on the tasting room's sound system instead of the typical soft classical music, but they're serious about wine, and craft some outstanding ones (including chardonnay, gewürztraminer, cabernet sauvignon, tempranillo, merlot, and zinfandel), all grown in the Rhinefarm Vineyard on the estate. One-hour tours include a visit to their wine cave, and the two-hour tour, offered during the growing season only, includes a ride through the vineyards; both culminate in a tasting. Climb up the hill from the tasting room and you can find a breathtaking valley view (and a perfect picnic spot). In summer, check their Web site for information about the musical and theatrical performances that take place on an outdoor stage. ⊠ *2000 Denmark St.* ☎ *707/939–3015* ⊕ *www.gunbun. com* 🍷 *Tasting $5–$10, tours $20–$40* ⊘ *Daily 11–4:30, tours by reservation.*

WHERE TO EAT

★ **Fodor's**Choice ✕ **Cafe La Haye.** In a postage stamp–size open
$$ kitchen, skillful chefs turn out about half-a-dozen main courses that star on a small but worthwhile seasonal menu emphasizing local ingredients. Chicken, beef, pasta, and fish get deluxe treatment without fuss or fanfare. The chicken roasted with rosemary, for instance, and the daily risotto special are always good. Butterscotch pudding is a homey signature dessert. The dining room is also compact, but the friendly owner, who is often there to greet diners, gives it a particularly welcoming vibe. ⊠ *140 E. Napa St.* ☎ *707/935–5994* ⊕ *cafelahaye.com* ▭ *MC, V* ⊘ *Closed Sun. and Mon. No lunch.*

$ ✕ **Della Santina's.** This longtime favorite, with a charming heated brick patio out back, serves the most authentic Italian food in town. (The Della Santina family, which has been running the restaurant since 1990, hails from Lucca, Italy.) Daily fish and veal specials join classic northern Italian pastas such as linguine with pesto and lasagna Bolognese.

Of special note are the roasted meat dishes and, when available, petrale sole and sand dabs (both types of flounder). ✉ *133 E. Napa St.* ☎ *707/935–0576* ⊕ *www.dellasantinas. com* ▤ *AE, D, MC, V.*

$$ × **The Girl & the Fig.** Chef Sondra Bernstein has turned the historic barroom of the Sonoma Hotel into a hot spot for inventive French cooking. You can always find something with the signature figs in it here, whether it's a fig-and-arugula salad or an aperitif of sparkling wine with a fig liqueur. Also look for duck confit with French lentils, a burger with matchstick fries, or wild boar braised in red wine. The wine list is notable for its emphasis on Rhône varietals, and the *salon de fromage*—a counter in the bar area—sells artisanal cheese platters for eating here as well as cheese by the pound to go. Sunday brunch brings rib-sticking dishes such as steak and eggs and a Basque frittata with potatoes, onions, and tomatoes. ✉ *Sonoma Hotel, Sonoma Plaza, 110 W. Spain St.* ⊕ *www.thegirlandthefig. com* ☎ *707/938–3634* ▤ *D, MC, V.*

$$ × **Harvest Moon Cafe.** It's easy to feel like one of the family at this little restaurant with an odd, zigzagging layout. Diners seated at one of the two tiny bars chat with the servers like old friends, but the husband-and-wife team in the kitchen is serious about the food, much of which relies on local produce. The daily menu sticks to homey dishes like half a grilled chicken served with polenta and tapenade, rib-eye steak with a red wine sauce, and a marinated beet-and-leek salad. Everything is so perfectly executed and the vibe is so genuinely warm that a visit here is deeply satisfying. In fair weather a spacious back patio, with seats arranged around a fountain, more than doubles the number of seats. ✉ *487 W. 1st St.* ☎ *707/933–8160* ⊕ *www.harvestmooncafesonoma. com* ▤ *AE, D, MC, V* ⊘ *No lunch Mon.–Sat.*

$ × **La Casa.** Terra-cotta–colored tile floors and ceramics on the walls evoke Old Mexico at this spot that has been at the edge of Sonoma's plaza for more than four decades. There's bar seating, a patio, and a large menu of traditional Mexican favorites, such as enchiladas suizas (chicken enchiladas with a tomatillo salsa), burritos, and fish tacos. Though the food is fairly standard, the casual, festive atmosphere and margaritas sold by the glass or pitcher make it a popular stop, especially during happy hour (weekdays 4–7). ✉ *121 E. Spain St.* ☎ *707/996–3406* ⊕ *www.lacasarestaurant.com* ▤ *AE, D, DC, MC, V.*

$$ × **LaSalette.** Chef–owner Manuel Azevedo, born in the Azores and raised in Sonoma, serves dishes inspired by

Santé, the restaurant at the Fairmont Sonoma Mission Inn

his native Portugal in this warmly decorated spot, where the best seats are on the patio, along a pedestrian alleyway off of Sonoma's plaza. Boldly flavored dishes such as *pork tenderloin recheado*, stuffed with olives and almonds and topped with a port sauce, or one of the daily seafood specials might be followed by a dish of rice pudding with Madeira-braised figs or a port from the varied list. ⊠ *452 E. 1st St.* ☎ *707/938–1927* ⊕ *www.lasalette-restaurant. com* ⊟ *AE, MC, V.*

★ **Fodor's Choice** ✕ **Santé.** Under the leadership of chef de cuisine
$$$$ Andrew Cain, this elegant dining room in the Sonoma Mission Inn has gained a reputation as a destination restaurant through its focus on seasonal and locally sourced ingredients. The room is understated, with high-backed banquettes and matching drapes in rich earth tones and softly lighted chandeliers, but the food is anything but. Dishes on the frequently changing menu, such as a roasted Sonoma duck breast with braised Swiss chard and duck confit, are complex without being fussy, whereas some dishes, like the butter-poached Maine lobster with flageolet beans and lardons, are pure decadence. ⊠ *Fairmont Sonoma Mission Inn & Spa, 100 Boyes Blvd./Rte. 12, at Boyes Blvd., 2 mi north of Sonoma, Boyes Hot Springs* ☎ *707/939–2415* ⊟ *AE, D, DC, MC, V* ⊗ *No lunch.*

$ ✕ **Sunflower Caffé.** Although you wouldn't realize it as you walk by, this casual breakfast- and lunch-only café has one of Sonoma's prettiest patios. Equipped with both heating lamps and plenty of shade, it's comfortable in all but the most inclement weather. The menu, composed mostly of salads and sandwiches (as well as omelets and waffles for breakfast), is simple but satisfying, and it relies largely on local ingredients. It's also a comfortable spot to take a quick break with an excellent coffee drink or something from the well-stocked outdoor wine bar. ⊠ *421 W. 1st St.* ☎ *707/996–6645* ⊕ *www.sonomasunflower.com* ⚹ *Reservations not accepted* ⊜ *AE, MC, V* ⊗ *No dinner.*

WHERE TO STAY

¢ 🖫 **El Dorado Hotel.** Rooms in this remodeled 1843 building strike a spare, modern pose, with rectilinear four-poster beds and pristine white bedding, but the Mexican-tile floors hint at Sonoma's Mission-era past. Rooms are small, but high-tech features such as flat-panel TVs and iPod alarm clocks are a nice touch, and each has a small balcony that overlooks the street, the courtyard, or El Dorado Kitchen. Though its position (right on Sonoma's plaza and on top of a bustling restaurant and bar) is considered a boon by some, earplugs are advised for all but the hardiest sleepers. **Pros:** stylish for the price; hip restaurant downstairs; central location. **Cons:** rooms could use better lighting; noisy. ⊠ *405 1st St. W* ☎ *707/996–3030* ⊕ *www.eldoradosonoma. com* ⇆ *27 rooms* ⚹ *In-room: a/c, refrigerator, DVD, Wi-Fi. In-hotel: restaurant, bar, pool* ⊜ *AE, MC, V.*

$$$–$$$$ 🖫 **The Fairmont Sonoma Mission Inn & Spa.** The real draw at this Mission-style resort is the extensive, swanky spa, easily the biggest in Sonoma. There's a vast array of massages and treatments, some using locally sourced grape and lavender products. The indoor and outdoor thermal soaking pools draw on the property's own mineral water sources. (It's a coed spa, and there are several treatments designed for couples.) The focus on fitness and rejuvenation extends to a 7,087-yard golf course winding through trees and vineyards, a changing schedule of fitness classes, and guided hiking and biking excursions each morning. The guest rooms aren't terribly large but are supremely comfortable; some have fireplaces and patios or balconies. The staff stays on top of every detail. **Pros:** enormous spa; excellent restaurant on-site; free shuttle to downtown. **Cons:** not as intimate as some similarly priced places. ⊠ *100 Boyes Blvd./Rte. 12, 2 mi north of Sonoma, Boyes Hot Springs* ☎ *707/938–9000* ⊕ *www.fairmont.com/sonoma* ⇆ *168 rooms, 60 suites* ⚹ *In-room: a/c, safe, refrigerator, Internet, Wi-Fi. In-hotel: 2 restaurants, room service, bars,*

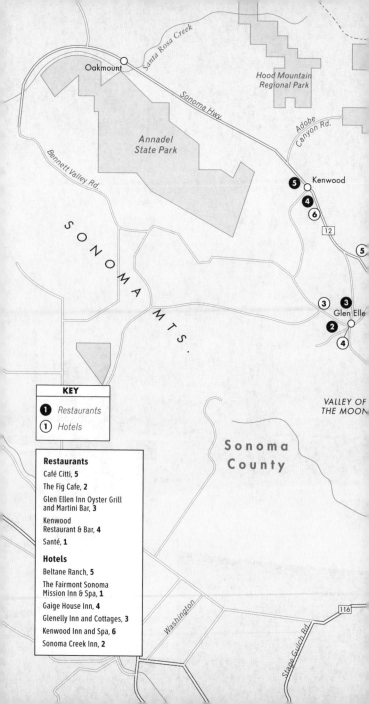

KEY

1 *Restaurants*

① *Hotels*

Restaurants

Café Citti, **5**

The Fig Cafe, **2**

Glen Ellen Inn Oyster Grill
and Martini Bar, **3**

Kenwood
Restaurant & Bar, **4**

Santé, **1**

Hotels

Beltane Ranch, **5**

The Fairmont Sonoma
Mission Inn & Spa, **1**

Gaige House Inn, **4**

Glenelly Inn and Cottages, **3**

Kenwood Inn and Spa, **6**

Sonoma Creek Inn, **2**

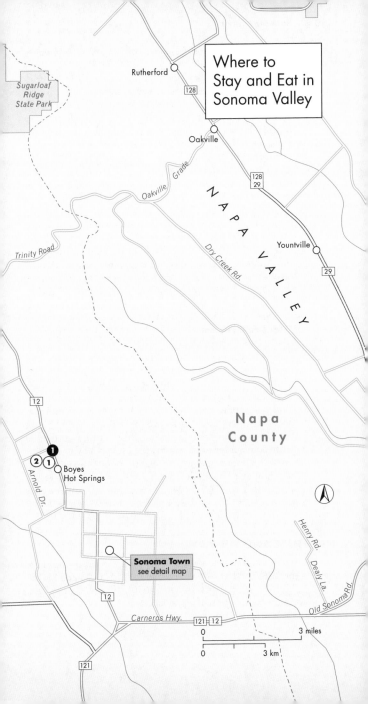

Where to
Stay and Eat in
Sonoma Valley

Rutherford

128

Sugarloaf
Ridge
State Park

Oakville

Oakville Grade

128
29

N A P A   V A L L E Y

Trinity Road

Dry Creek Rd.

Yountville

29

Napa
County

12

Arnold Dr.

2 1

1

Boyes
Hot Springs

Sonoma Town
see detail map

12

Henry Rd.

Dealy La.

Old Sonoma Rd.

Carneros Hwy.

121 12

121

0   3 miles

0   3 km

*golf course, tennis courts, pools, gym, spa, bicycles, laundry
service, some pets allowed (fee)* ⊟ *AE, D, DC, MC, V.*

$–$$ ⊡ **Inn at Sonoma.** They don't skimp on the little luxuries
here: wine and cheese is served every evening in the lobby,
and the cheerfully painted rooms are equipped with Wi-Fi
and warmed by gas fireplaces. In the closets are fluffy terry
robes, which come in handy for trips to the hot tub on the
inn's upper level. A teddy bear perched on each feather
comforter–topped bed holds a remote control to a small
TV. Though the inn is just off heavily trafficked Broadway, good soundproofing makes it quieter than many of
the hotels on Sonoma Plaza. (The town square is a five-
minute walk away.) Though rooms are not particularly
large, you'd be hard pressed to find this much charm for
the price elsewhere in town. **Pros:** last-minute specials are
a great deal; free soda available in the lobby; lovely hot
tub. **Cons:** staff is friendly but seems inexperienced; on a
busy street rather than right on the plaza. ⊠ *630 Broadway*
☎ *707/939–1340* ⊕ *www.innatsonoma.com* ⇥ *19 rooms*
⌂ *In-room: a/c, refrigerator (some), DVD, Wi-Fi. In-hotel:*
bicycles ⊟ *AE, D, DC, MC, V* ⊺⊙⌐*CP.*

¢ ⊡ **Sonoma Creek Inn.** The small but cheerful rooms at this
roadside inn with a sunny yellow exterior are individually
decorated with painted wooden armoires, cozy quilts, and
brightly colored contemporary artwork, elevating this bargain option well above your average motel. Most rooms
even have vaulted ceilings, and many have small patios with
a little fountain. Free rollaway beds for kids and an inde-
pendently owned diner attached to the property make it an
especially family-friendly option. **Pros:** clean, well-lighted
bathrooms; a lot of charm for the low price. **Cons:** office
not staffed 24 hours a day; slightly out-of-the-way location (about a 10-minute drive from Sonoma's plaza). ⊠ *239*
Boyes Blvd. ☎ *707/939–9463* ⊕ *www.sonomacreekinn.com*
⇥ *16 rooms* ⌂ *In-room: a/c, refrigerator, Wi-Fi. In-hotel:*
restaurant, some pets allowed (fee) ⊟ *AE, D, MC, V.*

NIGHTLIFE AND THE ARTS

For specialty cocktails and fairly pricey wines by the glass,
head to the bar at the sleek and stylish **El Dorado Kitchen**
(⊠ *405 1st St. W* ☎ *707/996–3030*). If you're lucky, you
might be able to nab a poolside seat.

Opened in 2007, the **Harmony Lounge** (⌂ *480 1st St. E* ☎ *707/996–9779*) has a full bar, a light menu of snacks, and occasional performances by local and touring jazz musicians.

The **Sebastiani Theatre** (⌂ *476 1st St. E* ☎ *707/996–2020*), built on Sonoma's plaza in 1934 by Italian immigrant and entrepreneur Samuele Sebastiani, schedules first-run films, as well as the occasional musical or theatrical performance.

Hit the bar at the **Swiss Hotel** (⌂ *18 W. Spain St.* ☎ *707/938–2884*) to sip a Glariffee, a cold and potent cousin to Irish coffee that's unique to this 19th-century spot.

SHOPPING

Sonoma Plaza is the town's main shopping magnet, with tempting boutiques, tasting rooms, and specialty food purveyors facing the square or just a block or two away. You could easily spend a few hours taking a spin around the plaza and making a few detours down the side streets to see everything that's on offer.

FARMERS' MARKET. The **Sonoma Farmers' Market** overflows with locally farmed produce, artisanal cheeses, and baked goods. It's held year-round at Depot Park, just north of the Sonoma Plaza, on Friday from 9 AM to noon. From April through October, it gets extra play on Tuesday evening from 5:30 PM to dusk at Sonoma Plaza.

Half-Pint (⌂ *Sonoma Plaza, 450 1st St. E* ☎ *707/938–1722*) carries fashionable clothing and accessories for infants and children, such as party dresses and too-cute knitted hats.

Sign of the Bear (⌂ *Sonoma Plaza, 435 1st St. W* ☎ *707/996–3722*) sells the latest and greatest in kitchenware and cookware, as well as a few Wine Country–themed items, such as lazy Susans made from wine barrels.

The **Sonoma Cheese Factory and Deli** (⌂ *Sonoma Plaza, 2 Spain St.* ☎ *707/996–1931*), run by the same family for four generations, makes Sonoma Jack cheese and the tangy Sonoma Teleme. It has everything you need for a picnic.

A block east of Sonoma Plaza, the **Vella Cheese Company** (⌂ *315 2nd St. E* ☎ *707/938–3232*) has been making superb

Benziger Family Winery

cheeses, such as raw-milk cheddars and several varieties of jack, since 1931.

GLEN ELLEN

7 mi north of Sonoma on Rte. 12.

Craggy Glen Ellen epitomizes the difference between the Napa and Sonoma valleys. Whereas small Napa towns such as St. Helena get their charm from upscale boutiques and restaurants lined up along well-groomed sidewalks, in Glen Ellen the crooked streets are shaded with stands of old oak trees and occasionally bisected by the Sonoma and Calabasas creeks. Tucked among the trees of a narrow canyon, where Sonoma Mountain and the Mayacamas pinch in the valley floor, Glen Ellen looks more like a town of the Sierra foothills gold country than a Wine Country village.

Wine has been part of Glen Ellen since the 1840s, when a French immigrant, Joshua Chauvet, planted grapes and built a winery and the valley's first distillery. The winery machinery was powered by steam, and the boilers were fueled with wood from local oak trees. In 1881 Chauvet built a stone winery to house his operations. Other valley farmers followed Chauvet's example, and grape growing took off. Wine was even made during Prohibition, when the locals took a liberal view of the 200 gallons each family was allowed to produce for personal consumption. There are still dozens of wineries in the area that beg to be visited, but sometimes it's hard not to succumb to Glen Ellen's slow pace and simply lounge poolside at your lodgings or linger over a leisurely picnic. The renowned cook and food writer M.F.K. Fisher, who lived and worked in Glen Ellen for 22 years until her death in 1992, would surely have approved.

Glen Ellen's most famous resident, however, was Jack London, who epitomized the town's rugged spirit.

In the hills above Glen Ellen—known as the Valley of the Moon—lies **Jack London State Historic Park**, where you could easily spend the afternoon hiking along the edge of vineyards and through stands of oak trees. Several of the author's manuscripts and a handful of personal effects are on view at the House of Happy Walls museum, once the home of London's widow. A short hike away from Happy Walls are the ruins of Wolf House. Designed by London, it mysteriously burned down just before he was to move in. Also open to the public are a few restored farm outbuildings. London is buried on the property. ✉ *2400 London Ranch Rd.* ☎ *707/938–5216* 🖃 *Parking $8, admission to buildings free* ☉ *Park Sat.–Wed. 10–5; museum weekends 10–5, Mon.–Wed. 10–4.*

VINEYARDS NEAR GLEN ELLEN

Arrowood Vineyards & Winery is neither as old nor as famous as some of its neighbors (they made their first wines in 1986), but winemakers and critics are quite familiar with the wines produced here by Richard Arrowood, especially the chardonnays, syrahs, and age-worthy cabernets. A wraparound porch with wicker chairs invites you to linger outside the tasting room, built to resemble a New England farmhouse. A stone fireplace inside makes this an especially enticing destination in winter. Tours, offered twice daily by appointment, conclude with a seated tasting. An unusually kid-friendly destination, the winery has a small toy box in the tasting room and will offer a tasting of nonalcoholic drinks on their tour if you give them advance notice. ■TIP→ **If you're doing a reserve tasting on a weekend, and you're interested in discovering what Arrowood wines taste like after several years in the bottle, ask if they happen to have any library wines open they can pour.** ✉ *14347 Sonoma Hwy./ Rte. 12* ☎ *707/935–2600* ⊕ *www.arrowoodvineyards.com*

Matanzas Creek Winery

☎ *Tasting $5–$10, tour $25* ⊘ *Daily 10–4:30, tour by appointment.*

One of the best-known local wineries is **Benziger Family Winery,** on a sprawling estate in a bowl with 360-degree sun exposure. Among the first wineries to identify certain vineyard blocks for particularly desirable flavors, Benziger is noted for its merlot, cabernet sauvignon, chardonnay, and sauvignon blanc. The tram tours here are especially interesting (they're first come, first served). On a ride through the vineyards, guides explain the regional microclimates and geography and give you a glimpse of the extensive cave system. Tours depart several times a day, weather permitting, but are sometimes fully booked during the high season. Reservations are needed for smaller tours that conclude with a seated tasting ($40). ■ TIP→ **Arrive before lunch for the best shot at joining a tour—and bring a picnic, since the grounds here are lovely.** ⊠ *1883 London Ranch Rd.* ☏ *707/935–3000* ⊕ *www.benziger.com* ☎ *Tasting $10–$15, tours $15–$40* ⊘ *Daily 10–5.*

★ **Fodors** Choice The visitor center at beautiful **Matanzas Creek Winery** sets itself apart with an understated Japanese aesthetic, with a tranquil fountain and a koi pond. Best of all, huge windows overlook a vast field of lavender plants. ■ TIP→ **The ideal time to visit is in May and June, when the lavender blooms and perfumes the air.** The winery specializes in sauvignon blanc, merlot, and chardonnay, although they

Jack London Country

Rugged, rakish author and adventurer Jack London is perhaps best known for his travels to Alaska and his exploits in the South Pacific, which he immortalized in tales such as *Call of the Wild, White Fang,* and *South Sea Tales.* But he loved no place so well as the hills of eastern Sonoma County, where he spent most of his thirties and where he died, in 1916, at the age of 40.

In 1913 London rhapsodized about his beloved ranch near Glen Ellen, writing, "The grapes on a score of rolling hills are red with autumn flame. Across Sonoma Mountain wisps of sea fog are stealing. The afternoon sun smolders in the drowsy sky. I have everything to make me glad I am alive. I am filled with dreams and mysteries."

Between 1905 and 1916 London bought seven parcels of land totaling 1,400 acres, which he dubbed Beauty Ranch. When he wasn't off traveling, he dedicated most of his time to cultivating the land and raising livestock here. He also maintained a few acres of wine grapes for his personal use.

Much of Beauty Ranch is now preserved as the Jack London State Historic Park, worth visiting not only for its museum and other glimpses into London's life but also for the trails that skirt vineyards and meander through a forest of Douglas fir, coastal redwoods, oak, and madrones. Here, London and his wife spent two years constructing their dream house, Wolf House, before it burned down one hot August night in 1913, just days before they were scheduled to move in.

A look at the remaining stone walls and fireplaces gives you a sense of the building's grand scale. Within, a fireproof basement vault was to hold London's manuscripts. Elsewhere in the park stands the unusually posh pigsty that London's neighbors called the Pig Palace.

Outside the park, London-related attractions are relatively few. Downhill from the park entrance, the Jack London Saloon, which first opened in 1905, has walls covered with photographs and other London memorabilia.

Parts of Beauty Ranch are still owned by London's descendants, who grow cabernet sauvignon, zinfandel, and merlot on a portion of the property. For a taste of the wines made from these grapes, head a few miles north to Kenwood Vineyards, which uses them to produce Jack London Vineyard reserve wines.

5

A grilled sirloin burger at the Fig Café

also produce a popular dry rosé as well as some syrah, pinot noir, and cabernet. After you taste the wines, ask for the self-guided garden-tour book before taking a stroll. Guided tours range from an hour-long intro to the Bennett Valley, the tiny AVA where the winery is located, to a more expensive one that concludes with a taste of limited-production and library wines paired with artisanal cheeses. ⊠ 6097 Bennett Valley Rd. ☎ 707/528–6464 or 800/590–6464 ⊕ www.matanzascreek.com ⌕ Tasting $5–$10, tour $10–$35 ⊙ Daily 10–4:30, tours by appointment.

WHERE TO EAT

★ **Fodor's** Choice ✕ **The Fig Cafe.** Pale sage walls, a high, sloping
$$ ceiling, and casual but very warm service set a sunny mood in this little bistro that's run by the same team behind Sonoma's The Girl & the Fig. The restaurant's eponymous fruit shows up in all sorts of places—not only in salads and desserts, but also on thin-crusted pizzas piled high with arugula. The small menu focuses on California and French comfort food, such as steamed mussels served with terrific crispy fries, and a braised pot roast served with seasonal vegetables. Don't forget to look on the chalkboard for frequently changing desserts, such as butterscotch pots de crème. ■TIP→ **The unusual no-corkage-fee policy makes it a great place to drink the wine you just discovered down the road.** ⊠ 13690 Arnold Dr. ☎ 707/938–2130 ⊕ www.thegir-

landthefig.com ⊟ *D, MC, V* ⚒ *Reservations not accepted*
⊗ *No lunch weekdays.*

$$ ✕**Glen Ellen Inn Oyster Grill & Martini Bar.** This cozy restaurant
in a creek-side 1940s cottage exudes romance, especially if
you snag a seat in the shady garden or on the patio strung
with tiny lights. After taking the edge off your hunger
with some oysters on the half shell and an ice-cold martini
(or one of their 25 or so variations on the theme), order
from the eclectic, frequently changing menu that plucks
elements from California, French, and occasionally Asian
cuisines. For instance, you might try Dungeness crab pot
stickers or a filet mignon with cambozola cheese and wild
mushrooms. Desserts tend toward the indulgent; witness
the warm pecan bread pudding with a chocolate center
that sits in a puddle of brandy sauce. ⊠ *13670 Arnold Dr.*
☎ *707/996–6409* ⊕ *www.glenelleninn.com* ⊟ *AE, MC, V*
⊗ *No lunch Wed. and Thurs.*

WHERE TO STAY

¢–$ ☖**Beltane Ranch.** On a slope of the Mayacamas range a
few miles from Glen Ellen, this 1892 ranch house stands
in the shade of magnificent oak trees. The charmingly
old-fashioned rooms, each individually decorated with
antiques and thick old-fashioned bedcovers, have exterior
entrances, and some open onto a wraparound balcony
ideal for whiling away lazy afternoons. A detached cottage,
once the gardener's quarters, has a small sitting room and
a gas-burning stove. A bountiful breakfast, included in the
price, incorporates produce from the gardens here, when
it's in season, as well as eggs from their chickens. **Pros:**
casual, friendly atmosphere; reasonably priced; beautiful
grounds with ancient oak trees. **Cons:** downstairs rooms get
some noise from upstairs rooms; cooled with ceiling fans
instead of air-conditioning. ⊠ *11775 Sonoma Hwy./Rte.
12* ☎ *707/996–6501* ⊕ *www.beltaneranch.com* ⟲ *3 rooms,
3 suites* ⚒ *In-room: no phone, no TV, Wi-Fi. In-hotel: ten-
nis court* ⊟ *MC, V* ⍟ *BP.*

★ Fodor'sChoice ☖**Gaige House.** Gorgeous Asian objets d'art and
$$$–$$$$ leather club chairs cozied up to the fireplace in the lobby
are just a few of the graceful touches in this luxurious but
understated bed-and-breakfast. Rooms in the main house,
an 1890 Queen Anne, are mostly done in pale colors, and
each has its advantages. One upstairs room has wrap-
around windows to let in floods of light, for instance, and
the lavish creek-side cottages feel Japanese, with massive

DID YOU KNOW?

Guests staying at Beltane Ranch can take advantage of the loop hiking trail that winds through the olive orchards and vineyards.

granite soaking tubs overlooking private atriums. Magnolia trees shade the backyard, where there's a small but idyllic swimming pool and hot tub. Though the staffers are helpful, service never seems fussy, and there's a bottomless jar of cookies in the common area. A continental breakfast is included, but you can pay a bit more for a full breakfast. **Pros:** beautiful lounge areas; cottages are very private. **Cons:** sound carries in the main house; the least expensive rooms are on the small side. ⊠ *13540 Arnold Dr.* ☎ *707/935–0237 or 800/935–0237* ⊕ *www.gaige.com* ⤴ *10 rooms, 13 suites* ⚲ *In-room: a/c, safe, refrigerator (some), DVD, Wi-Fi. In-hotel: pool, spa, no kids under 12* ▤ *AE, D, DC, MC, V.*

¢ ⌕ **Glenelly Inn and Cottages.** On a quiet side street a few blocks from the town center, this sunny little establishment has a long history as a getaway. It was built as an inn in 1916, and the rooms, each individually decorated, tend toward a simple country style. Many have four-poster beds and touches such as a wood-burning stove or antique oak dresser; some have whirlpool tubs. All have puffy down comforters. Breakfast is served in front of the common room's fireplace, as are cookies or other snacks in the afternoon. ∎TIP→ **Innkeeper Kristi Hallamore Jeppesen has two children of her own, so this is an unusually kid-friendly inn. Pros:** children are welcome; quiet location; hot tub in a pretty garden. **Cons:** some may not appreciate the presence of children; less expensive rooms are on the small side. ⊠ *5131 Warm Springs Rd.* ☎ *707/996–6720* ⊕ *www.glenellyinn. com* ⤴ *8 rooms, 2 suites* ⚲ *In-room: a/c (some), no phone (some), refrigerator (some), DVD, Wi-Fi. In-hotel: laundry facilities, some pets allowed* ▤ *AE, D, MC, V* ⊚*BP.*

NIGHTLIFE

Built in 1905, the **Jack London Saloon** (⊠ *13740 Arnold Dr.* ☎ *707/996–3100* ⊕ *www.jacklondonlodge.com*) is decorated with photos of London and other London memorabilia.

SHOPPING

In the Jack London Village complex, **Figone's Olive Oil Co.** (⊠ *14301 Arnold Dr.* ☎ *707/938–3164*) not only carries many local olive oils, serving bowls, books, and dining accessories but also presses olives for a number of local growers, usually in the late fall. You can taste a selection of olive oils that have surprisingly different flavors.

KENWOOD

3 mi north of Glen Ellen on Rte. 12.

Blink, and you might miss tiny Kenwood, which consists of little more than a few restaurants and shops, a couple of tasting rooms, and a historic train depot, now used for private events. But hidden in this pretty landscape of meadows and woods at the north end of Sonoma Valley are several good wineries, most just off the Sonoma Highway. A hodgepodge of varietals tend to be grown here at the foot of the Sugarloaf Mountains, including sauvignon blanc, chardonnay, zinfandel, and cabernet.

Many wineries around the Kenwood area are small, so tiny that they don't have tasting rooms of their own. At **Family Wineries** you can sample the output of several such spots. Though the lineup of participating wineries occasionally changes, look for sweet flavored sparklers produced by SL Cellars and still wines from Sonoma producers such as David Noyes and Collier Falls. ⊠ *9380 Sonoma Hwy.* ☎ *888/433–6555* ⊕ *www.familywines.com* 🍷 *Tasting $5* ⊗ *Daily 10:30–5.*

VINEYARDS AROUND KENWOOD

On your way into **Kunde Estate Winery & Vineyards** you pass a terrace flanked with fountains, virtually coaxing you to stay for a picnic with views over the vineyard. The tour of the grounds includes its extensive caves, some of which stretch 175 feet below a syrah vineyard. Kunde is perhaps best known for its toasty chardonnays, although tastings might include sauvignon blanc, cabernet sauvignon, and zinfandel as well. If you skip the tour, take a few minutes to wander around the demonstration vineyard outside the tasting room. In the months before crush (usually in September), you can taste the different grapes on the vines and see if you can taste the similarities between the grapes and the wines you just tasted. If there's a crowd at the bar, the reserve tasting ($20), served while you're seated comfortably on couches in the tasting room, is a good option. ⊠ *9825 Sonoma Hwy./Rte. 12* ☎ *707/833–5501* ⊕ *www. kunde.com* 🍷 *Tasting $10–$20, tour free* ⊗ *Daily 10:30– 4:30; tours weekdays at 11, weekends on the hr 11–3.*

Kenwood Vineyards makes some good value-priced red and white wines, as well as some showier cabernet sauvignons, zinfandels, and merlots, many of which are poured in the

Best Tasting Room Snacks

CLOSE UP

Wine is meant to be drunk with food, many vintners would argue, so why is it that you have to taste wines all by themselves at most tasting rooms? Many wineries, in an attempt to show off their wines to best effect, have recently started hiring chefs to create complex wine-and-food pairings. We're not talking about a plate of cheese and crackers here (although some wineries will serve that, too), but elegantly prepared small plates that come hot out of the kitchen.

Many wineries organize occasional food-and-wine pairings on an irregular basis (check their Web sites for information), whereas others have made it a part of their regular wine-tasting program. Expect to pay about $25 to $50 for these pairings, which can range from a few rich bites to a light meal. Though the experience isn't exactly cheap, these tastings can often serve as a light lunch, especially on those days when you need some digestive downtime between a big B&B breakfast and your dinner reservations. The following wineries have a strong emphasis on food-and-wine pairings and regularly serve delicious hot dishes.

■ **J Vineyards and Winery.** Set aside about two hours to taste at least six wines (two white, two red, and two sparkling) paired with elaborate fare in J Vineyards' Bubble Room ($60), where reservations are required. ⊠ 11447 Old Redwood Hwy., Healdsburg ☎ 707/431–3646 ⊕ www.jwine. com.

■ **Mayo Family Winery Reserve Tasting Room.** This cozy spot in Kenwood looks more like a small restaurant than a tasting room, with five or so tables in addition to the bar. For a fee of $35, seven single-varietal wines are paired with a rotating menu of seven morsels of food, like cabernet sauvignon with a duck stuffing with foie gras and brioche, or zinfandel port paired with a chocolate truffle. ⊠ 9200 Sonoma Hwy. ☎ 707/833–5504 ⊕ www. mayofamilywinery.com.

■ **St. Francis Winery.** Generous food-and-wine pairings ($30) here are one of the better deals in the valley. From June through October, cheese and charcuterie are served with wines on a patio overlooking a syrah vineyard. November through May, heartier bites, such as soy-glazed pork riblets, might be served with the wines in the Mission-style dining room. ⊠ 100 Pythian Rd. ☎ 800/543–7713 ⊕ www. stfranciswinery.com.

tasting room housed in one of the original barns on the property. The best of these come from Jack London's old vineyard, in the Sonoma Mountain appellation, above the fog belt of the Sonoma Valley (Kenwood has an exclusive lease). But the crisp sauvignon blanc is what keeps wine connoisseurs coming back for more. ✉ *9592 Sonoma Hwy./ Rte. 12* ☎ *707/833–5891* ⊕ *www.kenwoodvineyards.com* ☞ *Tasting $5* ☉ *Daily 10–4:30.*

At the foot of the Mayacamas Mountains stretch the impeccably groomed grounds of **Chateau St. Jean,** an old-country estate once owned by a family of midwestern industrialists. Pick up a map as you enter: it will identify many of the flowers, trees, and hedges lining the neat pathways in the formal gardens. After a spin around the grounds, whose style harmonizes with the sprawling Mediterranean-style villa, go inside for a tasting of their fine chardonnay, fumé blanc, and reds that include a pinot noir, cabernet sauvignon, merlot, and syrah. The unusually large gift shop sells clothing and housewares, such as a fully equipped picnic backpack, in addition to the usual wine-themed souvenirs. Daily tours (weather permitting) focus on the garden. ✉ *8555 Sonoma Hwy.* ☎ *707/833–4134* ⊕ *www.chateaustjean.com* ☞ *Tasting $10–$15, tour free* ☉ *Daily 10–5 (reserve room daily 10–4:30), tours daily at 11 and 2.*

Landmark Vineyards was founded by the descendants of John Deere, of tractor fame. Evidence of the family affiliation can be seen in the green tractor parked in front of the tasting room, and in the names of some of their wines, such as the Steel Plow Syrah. Rich, round chardonnay used to be Landmark's claim to fame, but in recent years critics have been taking note of its pinot noir and syrah as well. Stop here to taste the wines, but also take a close look at the building, which is a faithful reconstruction of a Mission-period rancho—right on up to the shingle roof. Ask to borrow their boccie balls if you want to take advantage of the court in the picnic area. ■ TIP→ **If you'll be visiting on a summer Saturday, call in advance to reserve a spot on the short horse-drawn wagon tour of the vineyard.** ✉ *101 Adobe Canyon Rd.* ☎ *707/833–0053* ⊕ *www.landmarkwine.com* ☞ *Tasting $5–$15* ☉ *Daily 10–4:30.*

Named for Saint Francis of Assisi, founder of the Franciscan order, which established missions and vineyards throughout California, **St. Francis Winery** has one of the most scenic locations in Sonoma, nestled at the foot of Mount

St. Francis Winery

Hood. The visitor center beautifully replicates the California Mission style, with its red tile roof and dramatic bell tower (a plaque explains that the bell was actually blessed in the Basilica of St. Francis in Assisi, Italy). Out back, a slate patio overlooks vineyards, lavender gardens, and hummingbirds flitting about the flower beds. The charm of the surroundings is matched by the wines, most of them red. Consider paying a bit more ($30) to taste wines paired with artisanal cheeses and charcuterie, served either on the patio or seated in the dining room. ✉ *100 Pythian Rd.* ☎ *800/543-7713* ⊕ *www.stfranciswinery.com* ☞ *Tasting $10–$15* ⊙ *Daily 10–5.*

The outrageously ornate French Normandy castle visible from Route 12 might attract you even before you know that the **Ledson Winery & Vineyards** produces lovely wines, all of which are available only at the winery and a small number of restaurants (including their wine bar in downtown Sonoma). Although they produce only 30,000 cases a year, they make a huge variety of largely single-varietal wines, everything from California standbys such as zinfandel to Rhône varietals such as syrah and mourvèdre. The castle, intended as the Ledson family's opulent home when its construction began in 1989, is now a warren of tasting rooms, special-event spaces, and a small market selling a good selection of cheeses and other picnic supplies. ✉ *7335*

A Great Drive in Sonoma Valley

It's easy to zip through the Sonoma Valley in a day—the drive from Sonoma at the south end to Kenwood to the north can be done in about 25 minutes—but once you start stopping at Sonoma's historic sites and the valley's wineries, your visit could easily be spread over two days. For a day trip of the highlights, start in the town of Sonoma. Do a lap around the historic plaza, and then pick up picnic supplies at the Sonoma Cheese Factory. From the south side of the plaza, drive east on East Napa Street. Turn right on East 8th Street and left onto Denmark Street, where you'll see the Gundlach-Bundschu winery sign. After a tasting, hike up the GunBun hill for your picnic.

Back in the car, head back to Sonoma Plaza and continue along West Napa Street (also Highway 12), following the signs pointing north on High-

way 12. About 20 minutes later, you'll pass the tiny town of Kenwood. Just north of Kenwood, on the right side of Highway 12, is St. Francis Winery, a very photogenic spot and a must for red wine fans. Returning south on Highway 12, look for Kunde Estate just south of Kenwood, just a few minutes down the road. If you've managed to wrap up your wine tasting before 3 PM, continue south on Highway 12 and take the Arnold Drive exit into the picturesque town of Glen Ellen. From Arnold Drive turn right on London Ranch Road. After winding your way uphill for a few minutes you'll reach Jack London State Historic Park. Take a short stroll through the grounds and a gander at some of the historic buildings near the parking area before the park closes at 4 PM (5 PM on weekends). Return to Highway 12 and continue south to the town of Sonoma for dinner.

Sonoma Hwy./Rte. 12 ☎ *707/537–3810* ⊕ *www.ledson.com* ☞ *Tasting $10–$20* ☉ *Daily 10–5.*

WHERE TO STAY AND EAT

$ ✕ **Café Citti.** Opera tunes in the background and a friendly staff (as well as a roaring fire when the weather's cold) keep this no-frills roadside café from feeling too spartan. Order dishes such as roast chicken and slabs of tiramisu from the counter and they're delivered to your table, a few of which are on an outdoor patio. An ample array of prepared salads and sandwiches means they do a brisk business in takeout for picnic packers, but you can also choose pasta made to order, mixing and matching linguine, penne, and other pastas with sauces such as pesto or marinara. ✉ *9049 Sonoma Hwy./Rte. 12* ☎ *707/833–2690* ⊕ *www.cafecitti. com* ▭ *MC, V.*

$$ ✕ **Kenwood Restaurant and Bar.** The small town of Kenwood is short on great restaurants, considering its location in such a culinary hot spot as the Wine Country. But at this airy spot with a sloping wood-beamed ceiling, you'll find a variety of French-inspired contemporary cooking, including a tender beef bourguignonne, hearty hamburgers, and oysters on the half shell. The restaurant's at its best on warm afternoons and evenings, when you can enjoy the view of the vineyards from the patio, but the Sugarloaf Mountains can be glimpsed through the French doors from the dining room as well. The wine list is very good, especially when it comes to local bottlings, and you can also order cocktails from the full bar. ✉ *9900 Sonoma Hwy.* ☎ *707/833–6326* ▭ *AE, MC, V* ⊘ *Closed Mon. and Tues.*

$$$$ ☷ **Kenwood Inn and Spa.** Buildings resembling graceful old haciendas and mature fruit trees shading the courtyards make it seem like this inn has been here for more than a century (it was actually built in 1990). French doors opening onto terraces or balconies, fluffy featherbeds, and wood-burning fireplaces give the uncommonly spacious guest rooms, many with tile floors, a particularly romantic air. A swimming pool, Jacuzzis, and saunas pepper three atmospheric courtyards, and you could easily spend an afternoon padding from one to another in your robe and slippers. The spa is intimate but well equipped. **Pros:** large rooms; lavish furnishings; extremely romantic. **Cons:** Wi-Fi can be spotty in some areas; the expensive restaurant isn't quite up to the level of the inn. ✉ *10400 Sonoma Hwy.* ☎ *707/833–1293* ⊕ *www.kenwoodinn.com* ⤺ *29 rooms* ⚬ *In-room: a/c, no TV, Internet, Wi-Fi. In-hotel: restaurant, bar, pool, spa, laundry service, no kids under 18* ▭ *AE, MC, V.*

Northern Sonoma County

WORD OF MOUTH

"There are 13 small-case producers within walking distance of each other . . . in Healdsburg. . . . The town also has some great wine-and-food pairing adventures at wineries all within the town itself and most of them small producers."

—NinaLa

URBAN SANTA ROSA IS NORTHERN Sonoma's work-horse: It has a population of more than 150,000 residents but precious few visitors—not surprising, since there are far more office parks than wineries within its city limits. Fifteen miles north, on the other hand, ritzy Healdsburg buzzes with luxe hotels, fashionable boutiques, and some of the Wine Country's hottest restaurants. Just outside these towns, however, it's all rolling hills, with only the occasional horse ranch, orchard, or stand of oak trees interrupting the vineyards.

Lovely little Healdsburg is the most convenient home base for exploring most of this region. Not only does it have an easily walkable town center, swank hotels, and a remark-able restaurant scene, but it's smack-dab at the confluence of the Russian River, Dry Creek, and Alexander valleys, three of northern Sonoma's blockbuster appellations. These produce some of the country's best pinot noir, cabernet sauvignon, zinfandel, and sauvignon blanc.

The western stretches of Sonoma County, which reach all the way to the Pacific Ocean, are sparsely populated in comparison with the above destinations, with only the occasional vineyard popping up between isolated ranches. Guerneville, a popular destination for weekending San Fran-ciscans who come to canoe down the Russian River, isn't a big wine destination itself, but it's a convenient place for picking up River Road, then Westside Road, which passes through pinot noir paradise on its way to Healdsburg.

Although each of northern Sonoma's regions claims its own microclimate, soil types, and most-favored varietals, they do have something in common: peace and quiet. Northern Sonoma is far less crowded than Napa Valley and the larger tasting rooms in southern Sonoma. Though Healdsburg in particular is hardly a stranger to overnight visitors, it's rare to bump into more than a few others in most of northern Sonoma's tasting rooms.

GETTING AROUND NORTHERN SONOMA COUNTY

The quickest route to northern Sonoma from San Francisco is straight up U.S. 101 to Healdsburg, but the back roads offer the best rewards. Highway 116 (also called the Gra-venstein Highway), west of 101, leads through the little towns of Forestville and Graton (both with a handful of great restaurants), before depositing you along the Russian

River near Guerneville. Traffic can be slow on U.S. 101, especially around Santa Rosa at rush hour.

NORTHERN SONOMA COUNTY APPELLATIONS

The sprawling Northern Sonoma AVA covers about 329,000 acres, but is divided into about a dozen smaller subappellations. Three of the most important of these sub-appellations meet at Healdsburg: the Russian River Valley AVA, which runs southwest along the lower course of the river; the Dry Creek Valley AVA, which heads northwest from town; and the Alexander Valley AVA, which is east and north of Healdsburg.

The cool climate of the low-lying **Russian River Valley AVA** is perfect for fog-loving pinot noir grapes as well as chardonnay. Although 20 years ago this was a little-known appellation, with as much pastureland and redwood stands as vineyards, in recent years it has exploded with vineyards, and it's now one of Sonoma's most-recognized appellations.

Although it's a small region—only about 16 mi long and 2 mi wide—zin lovers know all about the **Dry Creek Valley AVA,** where coastal hills temper the cooling influence of the Pacific Ocean. But even more acres are planted with cabernet sauvignon, and you'll find a smattering of merlot, chardonnay, sauvignon blanc, syrah, and several other varietals growing in the diverse soils and climate (it's warmer in the north and cooler in the south).

The **Alexander Valley AVA** is an up-and-comer, still in the process of being planted with vines (you're apt to see orchards and pasture between vineyards). Winemakers continue to experiment to determine the varietals that grow best in the relatively warm climate and diverse soils here, but so far chardonnay, sauvignon blanc, zinfandel, and cabernet sauvignon seem to do well.

Also in this area are the Knights Valley, Chalk Hill, Green Valley, and Sonoma Coast AVAs.

SANTA ROSA

8 mi northwest of Kenwood on Rte. 12.

Santa Rosa, the Wine Country's largest city, isn't likely to charm you with its office buildings, department stores, and frequent snarls of traffic along U.S. 101. It is, how-

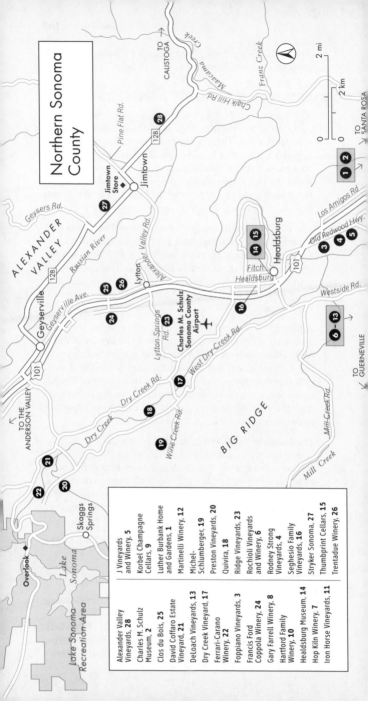

Northern Sonoma County

Alexander Valley
Vineyards, **28**
Charles M. Schulz
Museum, **2**
Clos du Bois, **25**
David Coffaro Estate
Vineyard, **21**
DeLoach Vineyards, **13**
Dry Creek Vineyard, **17**
Ferrari-Carano
Winery, **22**
Foppiano Vineyards, **3**
Francis Ford
Coppola Winery, **24**
Gary Farrell Winery, **8**
Hartford Family
Winery, **10**
Healdsburg Museum, **14**
Hop Kiln Winery, **7**
Iron Horse Vineyards, **11**

J Vineyards
and Winery, **5**
Korbel Champagne
Cellars, **9**
Luther Burbank Home
and Gardens, **1**
Martinelli Winery, **12**
Michel-
Schlumberger, **19**
Preston Vineyards, **20**
Quivira, **18**
Ridge Vineyards, **23**
Rochioli Vineyards
and Winery, **6**
Rodney Strong
Vineyards, **4**
Seghesio Family
Vineyards, **16**
Stryker Sonoma, **27**
Thumbprint Cellars, **15**
Trentadue Winery, **26**

Luther Burbank Home and Gardens

ever, home to a couple of interesting cultural offerings. Its chain motels and hotels are also handy if you're finding that everything else is booked up, especially since Santa Rosa is roughly equidistant from Sonoma, Healdsburg, and the Russian River Valley, three of the most popular wine-tasting destinations.

The **Luther Burbank Home and Gardens** commemorates the great botanist who lived and worked on these grounds and single-handedly developed the modern techniques of hybridization. The 1.6-acre garden and a greenhouse show the results of some of Burbank's experiments to develop spineless cacti, fruit trees, and flowers such as the Shasta daisy. In the music room of his house, a modified Greek Revival structure that was Burbank's home from 1884 to 1906, a dictionary lies open to a page on which the verb "burbank" is defined as "to modify and improve plant life." (To see the house, you'll need to join one of the docent-led tours, which leave from the gift shop every half hour.) ⊠ *Santa Rosa and Sonoma Aves.* ☎ *707/524–5445* ⊕ *www. lutherburbank.org* ⊉ *Gardens free, tours \$7* ⊙ *Gardens daily 8–dusk; museum and gift shop Apr.–Oct., Tues.–Sun. 10–4.*

Fans of Snoopy and Charlie Brown should head to the **Charles M. Schulz Museum,** dedicated to the cartoonist who lived in Santa Rosa for the last 30 years of his life, until his death in 2000. Permanent installations such as a re-creation

Charles M. Schulz Museum

of the artist's studio share the space with temporary exhibits, which often focus on a particular theme in Schulz's work. Both children and adults can try their hand at creating cartoons in the Education Room or wander through the labyrinth in the form of Snoopy's head. Check the Web site or call for information about occasional kid-friendly workshops and events. ⊠ *2301 Hardies Ln.* ☎ *707/579–4452* ⊕ *www.schulzmuseum.org* ⊠ *$10* ⊙ *Labor Day–Memorial Day, Wed.–Fri. and Mon. 11–5, weekends 10–5; Memorial Day–Labor Day, weekdays 11–5, weekends 10–5.*

WHERE TO EAT

$$$$ ✕ **Stark's Steakhouse.** The traditional steak house gets a slightly modern update at this restaurant that opened in Santa Rosa's Railroad Square area in early 2008. Low lighting, well-spaced tables, and a gas fireplace create a congenial setting for generous slabs of steak, like the in-house dry-aged rib eye and grass-fed, bacon-wrapped filet mignon. The nonsteak options, such as the tamarind barbecue prawns, are a cut above those at your average temple to beef, and the pastas are made on the premises. The bill can be hefty, and the densely flavored side dishes, like the truffled french fries and creamed spinach, must be ordered à la carte. Still, when the hankering for beef (and an ice-cold Manhattan or one of their other specialty cocktails) strikes, it's a satisfying choice. The full menu can be ordered

Beer Country

All over California, winemakers happily admit that "it takes a lot of beer to make fine wine." Lucky for them, there's no shortage of good local beer in the Wine Country.

The 1976 opening of the New Albion Brewery in Sonoma was one of the first signs of what became the renaissance of American craft brewing. With California in the forefront, microbreweries took off.

Many of California's brewers now take their inspiration from old British or European styles, tweaking them to sometimes extreme levels of intensity (and alcohol content!). You'll find monstrously malty porters, deep-golden lagers, and hefty wheat beers, plus lots of generously hopped—even triple-hopped—pale ales that finish with a distinctive kick.

Many breweries operate tasting rooms and tours, just as the wineries do. Look for brewpubs and local beer festivals to try more of the state's finest. Below are some of the best California breweries to visit.

Anderson Valley Brewing Company. Go for brewery tours, a tasting room, and an 18-hole disc golf course at the home of Boont Extra Special Beer, Boont Amber Ale, and other consistent medal winners. ⊠ *17700 Hwy. 253, Boonville* ☎ *707/895–2337* ⊕ *www.avbc. com.*

Bear Republic Brewing Company. Hops rule the Racer 5 IPA, XP Pale Ale, and specialty draft brews at this brewpub. ⊠ *345 Healdsburg Ave. Healdsburg* ☎ *707/433–2337* ⊕ *www. bearrepublic.com.*

Mendocino Brewing Company. The beer, such as the amber Red Tail Ale, is made in Ukiah, but you can taste it at the original brewery. ⊠ *13351 S. Hwy. 101, Hopland* ☎ *707/744–1361* ⊕ *www.mendobrew.com.*

Russian River Brewing Company. It's all about the double IPA and Belgian-style ales in this brewery's large pub. ⊠ *725 4th St., Santa Rosa* ☎ *707/545–2337* ⊕ *www.russianriverbrewing.com.*

Silverado Brewing Company. From a crisp blonde ale to a heartier oatmeal stout, the beers go well with the homey American food served at this St. Helena brewery. ⊠ *3020 St. Helena Hwy., St. Helena* ☎ *707/967–9876* ⊕ *www.silveradobrewingcompany.com.*

6

in the large adjoining lounge, where live jazz is performed on Friday. ⊠ *521 Adams St.* ☎ *707/546–5100* ⊟ *AE, D, MC, V* ⊗ *No lunch weekends.*

$$$ ✕ **Willi's Wine Bar.** Don't let the name fool you: instead of a sedate spot serving flights of bubbly with delicate nibbles, you'll find a cozy warren of rooms where boisterous crowds snap up small plates from the globe-trotting menu. Dishes such as the pork-belly pot stickers with shiitake mushrooms represent the East, and Moroccan-style lamb chops and roasted flatbread with caramelized onions and feta are some of the Mediterranean-inspired foods from the West. Oysters baked with caramelized onions and bacon are made with local ingredients. Wines are available in 2-ounce pours, making it easier to pair each of your little plates with a different type. ■ TIP→ **The din inside can be deafening on busy nights. For a slightly quieter experience, ask for a table on the covered patio.** ✉ *4404 Old Redwood Hwy.* ☎ *707/526–3096* ▬ *AE, D, MC, V* ☉ *Closed Tues. No lunch Sun. and Mon.*

★ Fodor'sChoice ✕ **Zazu.** A low wooden ceiling, rustic copper
$$$ tables, and rock music on the stereo create a casual vibe at this roadhouse. It's a few miles from downtown Santa Rosa, but the hearty, soulful cooking of owners Duskie Estes and John Stewart brings passionate fans from all over the Wine Country. Some of the produce for the salads comes from their own garden, and the meats are house-cured, so the antipasto plate or a pizza with house-made pepperoni are both excellent choices. The small seasonal menu—a mix of Italian-influenced dishes and updated American classics—tends toward rich flavors, with items such as rabbit braised in red wine and served with a mushroom risotto. ✉ *3535 Guerneville Rd.* ☎ *707/523–4814* ⊕ *www.zazurestaurant. com* ▬ *MC, V.*

NIGHTLIFE AND THE ARTS

For symphony, ballet, and other live theater performances throughout the year, visit the **Spreckels Performing Arts Center** (✉ *5409 Snyder La.* ☎ *707/588–3400*) in Rohnert Park, a short drive from downtown Santa Rosa.

The **Wells Fargo Center for the Arts** (✉ *50 Mark West Springs Rd.* ☎ *707/546–3600*) presents concerts, plays, and other performances by locally and internationally known artists, including Dolly Parton and the Jazz at Lincoln Center Orchestra.

The rolling hills of the Russian River Valley

RUSSIAN RIVER VALLEY

10 mi northwest of Santa Rosa.

As the Russian River winds its way from Mendocino to the Pacific Ocean, it carves out a valley that's a near-perfect environment for growing certain grape varietals. Because of its low elevation, sea fogs push far inland to cool the land, yet in summer they burn off, giving the grapes enough sun to ripen properly. Fog-loving pinot noir and chardonnay grapes are king and queen here. The namesake river does its part by slowly carving its way downward through many layers of rock, depositing a deep layer of gravel that in parts of the valley measures 60 or 70 feet. This gravel forces the roots of grape vines to go deep in search of water and nutrients. In the process, the plants absorb a multitude of trace minerals that add complexity to the flavor of the grapes.

Visiting wineries in this rich viticultural region is a leisurely affair. Tall redwoods shade many of the two-lane roads that cross this mostly rural area. Westside Road, on which there's another winery visible at almost every bend, roughly follows the curves of the Russian River from Healdsburg to Guerneville, wandering through vineyards, woods, and meadows along the way. Some visitors set up base camp in Guerneville, a popular destination for gay and lesbian travelers who stay in the rustic resorts and sunbathe on the bank of the river. But those on a mission to explore the area's food and wine usually choose to stay in Healdsburg (⇨ *below*), where there are many top restaurants and in-town tasting rooms, and there's easy access to most Russian River wineries.

VINEYARDS IN THE RUSSIAN RIVER VALLEY

Just far enough off the beaten track to feel like a real find, **DeLoach Vineyards** produces a variety of Russian River Valley old-vine zinfandels, chardonnays, and handful of other varietals, but it is best for known for its pinot noir, some of which is made using open-top wood fermentation vats that are uncommon in Sonoma but have been used in France for centuries. (Some think that they intensify a wine's flavor.) Tours focus on the estate vineyards outside the tasting room door, where you can learn about the labor-intensive biodynamic and organic farming methods used here, and take you through their culinary garden. ⊠ *1791 Olivet Rd., Santa Rosa* ☎ *707/526–9111* ⊕ *www.deloachvineyards. com* ▨ *Tasting $10, tour free* ☼ *Daily 10–5, tours daily by appointment.*

Established in 1896, **Foppiano Vineyards** primarily made bulk wine until 1970—visitors used to bring their own jugs to fill. It still has a casual tasting room, where rock music is likely to be playing in the background. Be sure to taste Foppiano's flagship wine, a hearty petite sirah, and the Lot 96, a good, modestly priced Italian table wine that just begs for a pizza or plate of pasta. Pick up a brochure to take a self-guided tour through the vineyard, where you can see the differences between different types of grapes. ⊠ *12707 Old Redwood Hwy., Healdsburg* ☎ *707/433–7272* ⊕ *www. foppiano.com* ▨ *Tasting free* ☼ *Daily 10–4:30.*

Pass through an impressive metal gate and wind your way up a steep hill to reach **Gary Farrell Winery,** a spot with knockout views over the rolling hills and vineyards below. Although the winery has changed hands a few times since Farrell sold it in 2004, it has managed to continue producing well-regarded bottles under Susan Reed, who worked alongside him. Though their earthy, full-bodied zinfandels are winners, the winery has built its reputation on its pinot noirs. They also make a fine sauvignon blanc and chardonnay. ⊠ *10701 Westside Rd. Healdsburg* ☎ *707/473–2900* ⊕ *www.garyfarrellwines.com* ▨ *Tasting $10–$15, tour $20* ☼ *Daily 10:30–4:30, tours by appointment.*

Driving down a meandering country road in Forestville, where small vineyards are interspersed with rustic old barns, you might be surprised to see a large, opulent building, home to the **Hartford Family Winery**. Fans of pinot in particular will want to make a detour here, where grapes from the cooler areas of the Russian River Valley, Sonoma Coast, and other regions are turned into crisp chardonnays, old-vine zinfandels, and a wide variety of pinots, many of which are single-vineyard wines. ⊠ *8075 Martinelli Rd. Forestville* ☎ *707/887–1756* ⊕ *www.hartfordwines.com* 🍷 *Tasting $5–$15* ⊗ *Daily 10–4:30.*

As you wind along Westside Road it's hard to miss the odd-looking **Hop Kiln Winery,** where three towers rise from a stone building that was originally built for the production of America's *other* favorite beverage—beer. Built in 1905, the structure once housed kilns for drying hops. Today wine is stored in those old kilns, whose thick stone walls help keep the wine cool. Poke around the tasting room and you'll see old photos of the property. The picnic tables next to the duck pond are a good place to sip a bottle of their aptly named Big Red or the popular Thousand Flowers, a white blend. Also available are picnic fixings, and they lend items such as knives and cutting boards to picnickers. ⊠ *6050 Westside Rd., Healdsburg* ☎ *707/433–6491* ⊕ *www.hopkilnwinery.com* 🍷 *Tasting $5–$7* ⊗ *Daily 10–5.*

★ Fodor's Choice **Iron Horse Vineyards** makes a wide variety of sparkling wines, from the bright and austere to the rich and toasty, as well as estate chardonnays and pinot noirs. Three hundred acres of rolling, vine-covered hills, barnlike winery buildings, and a beautifully rustic outdoor tasting area with a view of Mt. St. Helena set it apart from stuffier spots. (Instead of providing buckets for you to dump out the wine you don't want to finish, they ask you to toss it into the grass behind you.) Tours are available by appointment on weekdays at 10 AM. ⊠ *9786 Ross Station Rd., Sebastopol* ☎ *707/887–1507* ⊕ *www.ironhorsevineyards.com* 🍷 *Tasting $10, tour free* ⊗ *Daily 10–3:30, tour weekdays at 10 by appointment.*

At the **J Vineyards and Winery,** behind the bar in the tasting room is a dramatic steel sculpture studded with illuminated chunks of glass that suggests a bottle of bubbly. It's a big clue to what's most important here. The dry sparkling wines, made from pinot noir and chardonnay grapes planted in Russian River vineyards, have wonderfully com-

6

Iron Horse Vineyards

plex fruit and floral aromas and good acidity. Still best known for its sparklers, J has also begun to make a larger number of fine still wines, often from pinot and chardonnay grapes but also from pinot gris, viognier, and zinfandel. Although you can sample wines on their own at the tasting bar, for a truly indulgent experience make a reservation for the Bubble Room, where you should set aside a couple of hours for a selection of top-end still and sparkling wines served with different foods. Tours are offered twice daily by appointment. ✉ *11447 Old Redwood Hwy. Healdsburg* ☎ *707/431–3646* 🍷 *Tasting $20–$60* ⊕ *www.jwine.com* ☉ *Daily 11–5, Bubble Room hrs vary.*

Korbel Champagne Cellars produces several tasty, reasonably priced bubblies and still wines, as well as its own brandy. The wine tour clearly explains the process of making sparkling wine and takes you through the winery's ivy-covered 19th-century buildings. If you've already had the process of wine making explained to you one too many times, a tour of the rose garden, where there are more than 250 varieties of roses, may be a welcome break. Garden tours are given a few times daily Tuesday through Sunday, mid-April through mid-October. ✉ *13250 River Rd., Guerneville* ☎ *707/824–7000* ⊕ *www.korbel.com* 🍷 *Tasting and tour free* ☉ *Daily 10–4:30, call for tour times.*

Martinelli Winery, housed in a 100-year-old hop barn with the telltale triple towers, has the feel of an old country

Martinelli Winery

store, with a wood-beam ceiling and an antique stove in the corner. The warm welcome you'll get from the tasting room staff might also remind you of another era. The Martinelli family has been growing grapes in the Russian River Valley since the late 1800s. Still, there's nothing old-fashioned about these sophisticated wines. Under the guidance of the acclaimed Helen Turley (currently the consulting winemaker), Bryan Kvamme crafts wines that are typically big, complex, and well balanced. Although they make a variety of excellent pinots and chardonnays (as one expects in the Russian River Valley), as well as a bit of sauvignon blanc and syrah, it's their incredibly rich zinfandels, which are usually quite high in alcohol, that often bring visitors to this back road in Windsor. ✉ 3360 River Rd., Windsor ☎ 707/525–0570 ⊕ www.martinelliwinery.com ✉ Tasting $5 ☉ Daily 10–5.

Rochioli Vineyards and Winery claims one of the prettiest picnic sites in the area, with tables overlooking vineyards, which are also visible from the airy little tasting room hung with modern artwork. Production is small—about 12,000 or 13,000 cases annually—and fans on the winery's mailing list snap up most of the bottles, but the wines are still worth a stop. Because of the cool growing conditions in the Russian River Valley, the flavors of their chardonnay and sauvignon blanc are intense and complex. It's their pinot, though, that is largely responsible for the winery's stellar reputation; it helped cement the Russian River's status as a pinot powerhouse. ■TIP→ **Though Rochioli typically pours only a couple of wines for visitors, it's one of the few wineries of its stature that doesn't charge for a tasting.** ⊠ *6192 Westside Rd., Healdsburg* ☎ *707/433–2305* ⊡ *Tasting free* ⊕ *www. rochioliwinery.com* ⊙ *Thurs.–Mon. 11–4, Tues. and Wed. by appointment; closed mid-Dec.–early Jan.*

Although its founder passed away in 2006, **Rodney Strong Vineyards** continues to produce highly regarded wines, from a crisp sauvignon blanc to merlot, zinfandel, and cabernet sauvignon. The 1970s concrete building doesn't look particularly enticing from the exterior, but inside is an attractive octagonal tasting room ringed by a balcony overlooking the production facilities. An excellent self-guided tour leads along the balcony for a good view of the fermentation tanks and other machinery, but twice-daily guided tours are also available. Back at the bar, you can taste the fruits of the winery's labors. Symmetry, a red Bordeaux-style blend, is one of their most impressive offerings, but also taste the excellent pinot noir. (Strong was one of the first to plant pinot noir in the Russian River Valley.) The winery hosts outdoor jazz and rock concerts on the grounds during summer. ⊠ *11455 Old Redwood Hwy., Healdsburg* ☎ *707/431–1533* ⊕ *www. rodneystrong.com* ⊡ *Tasting free–$10, tour free* ⊙ *Daily 10–5, tour daily at 11 and 3 by reservation.*

WHERE TO EAT AND STAY

★ Fodor's Choice ✕ **The Farmhouse Inn.** From the personable som-
$$$$ melier who arrives at the table to help you pick wines from the excellent list to the servers who lovingly describe the provenance of the black truffles shaved over your pasta stuffed with salt-roasted pears and Parmesan, the staff match the quality of the outstanding French-inspired cuisine. The signature dish, "rabbit, rabbit, rabbit," a rich trio of confit of leg, rabbit loin wrapped in applewood-smoked bacon, and roasted rack of rabbit with a whole-grain mustard sauce, is typical of the dishes that are both rustic and refined, and the starters often include a seared Sonoma foie gras served with an apple cider sauce. ■TIP→ **The inn's a favorite of local foodies in the wine industry, who also know that their head sommelier is one of only about 100 Master Sommeliers working in the United States, so reserve well in advance.** ⊠ *7871 River Rd. Forestville* ☎ *707/887–3300 or 800/464–6642* ⊴ *Reservations essential* ⊟ *AE, D, DC, MC, V* ⊙ *Closed Tues. and Wed. No lunch.*

Dessert at the Farmhouse Inn and Restaurant

$$–$$$ ☎ **Applewood Inn & Restaurant.** On a knoll in the shelter of towering redwoods, this romantic inn has two distinct types of accommodations. The original Belden House, built in 1922, has a river-rock fireplace that encourages loitering in the reception area. Its rooms are smaller than those in the newer buildings, but have charming touches, such as an exposed brick wall in one or a view of a stand of redwood trees from another. Most of the rooms in the newer buildings are larger and airier, decorated in sage-green and terra-cotta tones. Readers rave about the stellar service, soothing atmosphere, and the earthy Cal-Italian cuisine that's served in the restaurant ($$$), built to recall a French barn. In winter, you can up the romance factor by asking for a table near the fireplace. At this writing, new owners have begun redecorating, added a small spa, and planned to begin regional Italian cooking classes, so call ahead or check the Web site for the latest. **Pros:** quiet, secluded location; friendly, homey service. **Cons:** planned improvements may cause some disruption; sounds can carry in the Belden House. ✉ *13555 Rte. 116, Guerneville* ☎ *707/869–9093 or 800/555–8509* ⊕ *www.applewoodinn. com* ➪ *19 rooms* ⚹ *In-room: a/c (some), Wi-Fi. In-hotel: restaurant, pool, spa* ☐ *AE, D, MC, V* ⅋⃝*BP.*

★ Fodor'sChoice ☎ **The Farmhouse Inn.** This pale yellow 1873 farm-
$$$–$$$$ house and adjacent cottages offer individually decorated rooms with comfortable touches such as down comforters and whirlpool tubs. Most of the cottages have wood-

burning fireplaces and even their own private saunas, which make this place especially inviting during the rainy months. The most romantic (and expensive) rooms are those in the newest building, finished in 2009 and built to resemble an old barn that was once on the property. With a chic rustic-farmhouse-meets-modern-loft aesthetic, the spacious rooms have king-size four-poster beds, spa tubs, and patios or balconies overlooking the hillside. It's worth leaving your supremely comfortable bed for the sumptuous breakfasts here. The inn's restaurant is one of the most highly regarded in the Wine Country ($⇨$ *see* above). **Pros:** one of Sonoma's best restaurants is on-site; free snacks, games, and movies available; extremely comfortable beds. **Cons:** rooms closest to the street get a bit of road noise. ✉ *7871 River Rd., Forestville* ☎ *707/887–3300 or 800/464–6642* ⊕ *www.farmhouseinn.com* ⤵ *12 rooms, 6 suites* ♿ *In-room: a/c, refrigerator, DVD, Wi-Fi. In-hotel: restaurant, pool, spa* ▭ *AE, D, DC, MC, V* ⋈ *BP.*

¢ 🏨 **Sebastopol Inn.** Simple but cheerful rooms, freshly painted a sunny yellow and equipped with blue-and-white-striped curtains, have a spare California country style at this reasonably priced inn. Rooms clustered around a pleasant courtyard are also steps away from an old train station that has been converted into a cluster of cafés and shops. Some rooms have microwaves, some have small balconies or patios, and the uncommonly spacious suites (which also have jetted tubs) offer plenty of room for families. **Pros:** friendly staff; just steps from a café, wine bar, and spa. **Cons:** at least a 30-minute drive from most Russian River wineries; some will find the beds too firm. ✉ *6751 Sebastopol Ave., Sebastopol* ☎ *707/829–2500* ⊕ *www.sebastopolinn.com* ⤵ *29 rooms, 2 suites* ♿ *In-room: refrigerator, Wi-Fi. In-hotel: restaurant, pool, laundry facilities* ▭ *AE, D, DC, MC, V.*

SPORTS AND THE OUTDOORS

At **Burke's Canoe Trips** (✉ *River Rd. and Mirabel Rd., 1 mi north of Forestville* ☎ *707/887–1222*) you can rent a canoe for a leisurely paddle 10 mi downstream to Guerneville. A shuttle bus will return you to your car at the end of the day. Late May through mid-October is the best time for boating.

HEALDSBURG

17 mi north of Santa Rosa on U.S. 101.

Just when it seems that the buzz about Healdsburg couldn't get any bigger, there's another article published in a glossy food or wine magazine about posh properties such as the restaurant Cyrus and the ultra-luxe Hotel Les Mars. But you don't have to be a tycoon to stay here and enjoy the town. For every ritzy restaurant there's a great bakery or relatively modest bed-and-breakfast. A whitewashed bandstand on Healdsburg's plaza hosts free summer concerts, where you might hear anything from bluegrass to Sousa marches. Add to that the fragrant magnolia trees shading the square and the bright flower beds, and the whole thing is as pretty as a Norman Rockwell painting.

The countryside around Healdsburg is the sort you dream about when you're planning a Wine Country vacation, with orderly rows of vines alternating with beautifully overgrown hillsides. Alongside the relatively untrafficked roads country stores offer just-plucked fruits and vine-ripened tomatoes. The wineries here are barely visible, since they're tucked behind groves of eucalyptus or hidden high on fog-shrouded hills.

Most visitors use Healdsburg as a base for visiting wineries in the surrounding hillsides and river valleys—it's ideally located at the confluence of the Dry Creek, Alexander, and Russian River valleys—but you could easily while away the day without setting foot outside of town. Around the old-fashioned plaza you'll find fashionable boutiques, art galleries, spas, hip tasting rooms, and some of the best restaurants in the Wine Country, so don't forget to save some time to savor Healdsburg's particular pleasures.

In addition to several wineries on the outskirts of town, more than a dozen tasting rooms reside in the blocks surrounding the plaza, enabling you to sample wine all day without even getting in your car.

To take a short break from wine tasting, you can visit the **Healdsburg Museum,** which displays a collection of local historical objects, including baskets and artifacts from native tribes. Other exhibits cover the Mexican Rancho period, the founding and growth of Healdsburg in the 1850s, and the history of local agriculture. ⊠ *221 Matheson St.* ☎ *707/431–3325* ⊕ *www.healdsburgmuseum.org* ⊠ *Free* ☉ *Wed.–Sun. 11–4.*

The most stylish of the tasting rooms is **Thumbprint Cellars Tasting Lounge.** With exposed brick walls, sleek leather chairs, brown silk curtains, and rotating artwork on the walls, it could be a very hip friend's San Francisco living room. The provocatively named wines (including Arousal, Four Play, and Three Some) come primarily from Russian River and Dry Creek grapes. ✉ *102 Matheson St.* ☎ *707/433–2393* ⊕ *www.thumbprintcellars.com* ☉ *Sun.–Thurs. 11–6, Fri. and Sat. 11–7.*

VINEYARDS AROUND HEALDSBURG

Italian immigrant Edoardo Seghesio and his wife Angela planted zinfandel vineyards here in 1895, and added a winery in 1902. For years they and their descendants sold wine in bulk to other wineries, but they finally began bottling wines under their own name in the 1980s at **Seghesio Family Vineyards.** The majority of the grapes used by Seghesio are estate grown, in vineyards in the Alexander, Dry Creek, and Russian River valleys. Even though winemaker Ted Seghesio prefers his wines to be immediately drinkable, they have surprising depth and aging potential. Be sure to try the zinfandel and the sangiovese, as well as their super-Tuscan blend called Omaggio, a blend of cabernet sauvignon and sangiovese. To make an afternoon of it, bring a picnic lunch and challenge your friends to a boccie game in the shade of the property's cork tree. Though the tables and court are free of charge to walk-ins when they're available, call ahead to reserve (for a fee) if you have your heart set on using them (both are $25 an hour when they are reserved). ✉ *14730 Grove St.* ☎ *707/433–3579* ⊕ *www.seghesio.com* ▭ *Tasting $5* ☉ *Daily 10–5.*

WHERE TO EAT

$$$ ✕ **Barndiva.** This hip joint abandons the homey vibe of so many Wine Country spots for a younger, more urban feel. Electronic music plays quietly in the background while hipster servers ferry inventive seasonal cocktails. The food is as stylish as the well-dressed couples cozying up next to each other on the banquette seats. Make a light meal out of starters such as goat-cheese croquettes or "The Works," a bountiful plate of cheeses and charcuterie, or settle in for the evening with crispy lamb cheeks or risotto with seasonal vegetables. During warm weather the beautiful patio is the place to be. ✉ *231 Center St.* ☎ *707/431–0100* ⊕ *www.barndiva.com* ▭ *AE, MC, V* ☉ *Closed Mon. and Tues.*

$ ✕**Bear Republic Brewing Company.** This wide-open hall of a brewpub on Healdsburg Plaza is a local favorite for a casual lunch or dinner of burgers, chicken wings, or pasta. Although the food is nothing out of the ordinary, the beers are good (if you like hoppy brews, try their flagship, the Racer 5 IPA) and the service is fast. In warm weather there's often a wait for the seats outdoors, but there's usually room in the spacious interior. This pub is for people who like to socialize, and can be a welcome relief from the serious demeanor of some other local spots. ⊠ *345 Healdsburg Ave.* ☎ *707/433–2337* ⊕ *www.bearrepublic.com* ⌚ *Reservations not accepted* ⊟ *AE, MC, V.*

$ ✕**Bovolo.** Husband-and-wife team John Stewart and Duskie Estes serve what they call "slow food . . . fast." Though you might pop into this casual café at the back of Copperfield's Books for half an hour, the staff will have spent hours curing the meats that star in the menu of salads, pizzas, pastas, and sandwiches. For instance, the Salumist's Salad mixes a variety of cured meats with greens, white beans, and a tangy vinaigrette; and a thin-crusted pizza might come topped with house-made Italian pork sausage and roasted peppers. House-made gelato served with a dark chocolate sauce or zeppole (Italian doughnuts) are a simply perfect ending to a meal. Although there's no dinner service Sunday through Thursday, breakfast is served and there is continual service until 6, until 8 on Friday and Saturday. ⊠ *106 Matheson St.* ☎ *707/431–2962* ⊕ *www.bovolorestaurant.com* ⌚ *Reservations not accepted* ⊟ *MC, V* ⊗ *No dinner Sun.–Thurs. 9–6.*

★ Fodor's Choice ✕**Cyrus.** Hailed as the best thing to hit the Wine
$$$$ Country since French Laundry, Cyrus has collected lots of awards and many raves from guests. From the moment you're seated to the minute your dessert plates are whisked away, you'll be carefully tended by gracious servers and an expert sommelier. The formal dining room, with its vaulted Venetian-plaster ceiling, is a suitably plush setting for chef Douglas Keane's creative, subtle cuisine. Keane has a notably free hand with costly ingredients such as truffles, lobster, and wagyu beef. Each night diners have their choice of four set menus: five- and eight-course extravaganzas ($102 and $130) for both omnivores and vegetarians. Set aside three hours to work your way from savory starters like the terrine of foie gras with curried apple compote, through fragrant dishes like the truffled wine risotto with Parmesan broth, to desserts such as the hazelnut dacquoise. If you've failed to make reservations, you can order à la carte at the bar, which

also has the best collection of cocktails and spirits in all of the Wine Country. ⊠ *29 North St.*☎ *707/433–3311* ⊕ *www. cyrusrestaurant.com* ⚲ *Reservations essential* ▭ *AE, DC, MC, V* ⊘ *Closed Tues. and Wed. in winter. No lunch.*

$$ ✕ **Healdsburg Charcuterie.** This cozy restaurant with a slightly Provençal feel serves a hodgepodge of cuisines, from an all-American chicken-salad sandwich and an excellent house-cured pork tenderloin sandwich to Italian favorites like a chicken *piccata* and fusilli pasta with a basil cream sauce. Some of the standout dishes are French through and through, such as the escargots in garlicky butter and a generous charcuterie plate that includes pâté, duck rillettes, salami, and cornichons. An extensive menu of homey desserts might include a lemon pot de crème or pecan pie à la mode. The vibe is casual rather than refined, but reasonable prices and ample portions makes it one of Healdsburg's better values for a sit-down meal. ■TIP→ **If you're planning a picnic, they'll pack up their food to go for you.** ⊠ *335 Healdsburg Ave.* ☎ *707/431–7213* ▭ *AE, DC, MC, V.*

$$ ✕ **Scopa.** Scopa is a card game played in much of Italy, but at this tiny Healdsburg eatery the food is very serious business. Chef Ari Rosen cooks up rustic Italian specialties such as house-made ravioli stuffed with ricotta cheese, braised chicken with greens and polenta, and polpette Calabrese (spicy meatballs served with smoked mozzarella in a tomato sauce). Simple thin-crust pizzas are worth ordering, too. Locals love the restaurant for its lack of pretension: wine is served in juice glasses, and the friendly hostess visits guests frequently to make sure all are satisfied. You'll be packed in elbow-to-elbow with your fellow diners, but for a convivial evening over a bottle of nebbiolo, there's no better choice. ⊠ *109A Plaza St.* ☎ *707/433–5282* ⊕ *www.scopahealdsburg. com* ▭ *AE, MC, V* ⊘ *Closed Mon. No lunch.*

$$–$$$ ✕ **Willi's Seafood & Raw Bar.** Open for lunch and dinner daily, Willi's seems perpetually packed with a festive crowd that likes to have one of their specialty cocktails at the full bar before sitting down to a dinner of small seafood plates. A few dishes, such as the warm Maine lobster roll with fennel, conjure a New England fish shack, and others, like the scallops served with a cilantro-and-pumpkin-seed pesto, have a Latin American accent; the ceviches are a standout, too. Reservations aren't taken for Friday or weekends, but if you call ahead, they'll put your name on the waiting list. ■TIP→ **In summer the most appealing seats are on the patio, but in the winter ask for one of the small booths in the back, which**

The Honor Mansion

have the most privacy. ⊠ *403 Healdsburg Ave.* ☎ *707/433–9191* ⊕ *www.starkrestaurants.com* ⊟ *AE, D, MC, V.*

$$$–$$$$ ✕ **Zin Restaurant and Wine Bar.** Concrete walls and floors and large canvases on the walls make the restaurant casual, industrial, and slightly artsy. The American cuisine—such as smoked pork chop with homemade applesauce or the lamb sirloin with mint jelly—is hearty and highly seasoned. Portions are large, so consider sharing if you hope to save room for desserts such as the brownie sundae with Kahlua chocolate sauce. As you might have guessed, zinfandel is the drink of choice here: the varietal makes up roughly half of the 100 or so bottles on the wine list. ⊠ *344 Center St.* ☎ *707/473–0946* ⊟ *AE, MC, V* ⊗ *No lunch weekends.*

WHERE TO STAY

¢–$ ▥ **Camellia Inn.** In a well-preserved Victorian constructed in 1869, this colorful B&B is on a quiet residential street a block from the town's main square. The parlors downstairs are chockablock with ceramics and other decorative items, and rooms are individually decorated with antiques that include an impressive mid-19th-century tiger-maple bed from Scotland (one of the owners used to work as an antiques dealer). Each room has its own charms, such as a canopy bed, a claw-foot tub, or a whirlpool bath. ■TIP→ Those on a budget should ask about the cozy (and popular) budget room with a full-size bed and large private bath across the hall. **Pros:** reasonable rates for the neighborhood; a rare family-friendly inn; within easy walking distance of dozens of restaurants. **Cons:** a few rooms have a shower but no bath; the only TV on the property is in the common sunroom. ☒ *211 North St.* ☎ *707/433–8182 or 800/727–8182* ⊕ *www.camelliainn.com* ↘ *8 rooms, 1 suite* ⬧ *In-room: no phone, a/c, no TV, Wi-Fi. In-hotel: pool, some pets allowed* ⊟ *AE, D, MC, V* ⌸|*BP.*

$$$ ⊡ **The Honor Mansion.** Each room is unique at this photogenic 1883 Italianate Victorian. Rooms in the main house preserve a sense of the building's heritage, and the larger suites are comparatively understated. Luxurious touches such as antiques and decanters of sherry are found in every room, and suites have the advantage of a deck; some even have private outdoor hot tubs. The spacious grounds even include a boccie court and putting green. Fodors.com readers rave about the attentive staff, who "think of things you don't even know you want." **Pros:** beautiful grounds with boccie and tennis courts, a putting green, and half-court for basketball!; homemade sweets available at all hours; spa pavilions by pool available for massages in fair weather. **Cons:** almost a mile from Healdsburg's plaza; on a moderately busy street. ☒ *14891 Grove St.* ☎ *707/433–4277 or 800/554–4667* ⊕ *www.honormansion.com* ↘ *5 rooms, 8 suites* ⬧ *In-room: a/c, safe (some), refrigerator (some), DVD (some), Wi-Fi. In-hotel: tennis court, pool, Internet terminal* ⊟ *AE, MC, V* ⊘ *Closed 1 wk around Christmas* ⌸|*BP.*

$$$–$$$$ ⊡ **Hotel Healdsburg.** Across the street from Healdsburg's tidy town plaza, this spare, sophisticated hotel caters to travelers with an urban sensibility. Unadorned olive-green walls, dark hardwood floors, and clean-lined furniture define the guest rooms; the beds are some of the most comfortable you can find. Spacious bathrooms continue the sleek style with monochromatic tiles and deep soaking tubs that are all right angles. The attached restaurant, Dry Creek Kitchen ($$$$), is one of the best in Healdsburg. Celebrity chef Charlie Palmer is the man behind seasonal dishes that largely rely on local ingredients, such as a spice-crusted Sonoma duck breast or seared Sonoma foie gras, plus a wine list covering the best Sonoma vintners. **Pros:** several rooms overlook the town plaza; free valet parking; extremely comfortable beds. **Cons:** least expensive rooms are small; exterior rooms get some street noise. ☒ *25 Matheson St.* ☎ *707/431–2800 or 800/889–7188* ⊕ *www. hotelhealdsburg.com* ↘ *45 rooms, 10 suites* ⬧ *In-room: a/c, safe, refrigerator, DVD, Internet, Wi-Fi. In-hotel: restau-*

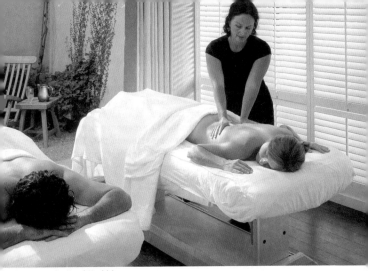

The spa at the Hotel Healdsburg

rant, room service, bar, pool, gym, spa, laundry service, some pets allowed ⊟ AE, MC, V ⵔⵔ CP.

$$$$ ⵔ **Hôtel Les Mars.** In 2005, posh Healdsburg got even more chichi with the opening of this opulent Relais & Châteaux hotel. Guest rooms are spacious and elegant enough for French nobility, with 18th- and 19th-century antiques and reproductions, canopied beds, and gas-burning fireplaces. Most of the gleaming, white-marble bathrooms have spa tubs in addition to enormous showers. Rooms on the third floor have soaring 20-foot ceilings that make them feel particularly large, whereas the second-floor rooms have a slightly more understated style. Wine and cheese are served every evening in the library, which is sumptuously paneled with hand-carved black walnut, and a continental breakfast is delivered to your room each morning. **Pros:** large rooms; just off Healdsburg's plaza; impeccable service; Bulgari bath products. **Cons:** very expensive. ⊠ 27 North St. ☎ 707/433–4211 ⊕ www.lesmarshotel.com ⌁ 16 rooms ⌂ In-room: a/c, safe, DVD, Internet, Wi-Fi. In-hotel: restaurant, bar, pool, gym, laundry service ⊟ AE, MC, V ⵔⵔ CP.

$$$–$$$$ ⵔ **Madrona Manor.** The oldest continuously operating inn in the area, this 1881 Victorian mansion, surrounded by 8 acres of wooded and landscaped grounds, is straight out of a storybook. Rooms in the three-story mansion, the carriage house, and the three separate cottages are splendidly ornate, with mirrors in gilt frames and paintings covering every wall. Much of the furniture is even original to the

19th-century house. Candlelight dinners are served in the formal dining rooms nightly except Monday and Tuesday. Chef Jesse Mallgren has earned much praise for his elaborate three-, four-, and five-course menus ($$$$), where luxuries such as a Périgord truffle risotto might precede a bacon-wrapped rabbit loin and a warm chocolate soufflé. ■TIP→ For a ridiculously romantic experience, ask for Room 203 or 204. The most requested rooms at the inn, they both have huge balconies that overlook the hotel grounds and beyond. Pros: old-fashioned and romantic; pretty veranda perfect for a cocktail. Cons: pool heated May through October only; decor might be too fussy for some. ⊠ *1001 Westside Rd., central Healdsburg exit off U.S. 101, then left on Mill St.,* ☎ *707/433–4231 or 800/258–4003* ⊕ *www.madronamanor. com* ⚭ *17 rooms, 5 suites* ⚸ *In-room: a/c, no TV, Wi-Fi. In-hotel: restaurant, bar, pool* ⊟ *AE, MC, V* ⊚*BP.*

NIGHTLIFE AND THE ARTS

Even if you think it's virtually sacrilegious to drink anything other than wine in this neck of the woods, the bartenders at **Cyrus** (⊠ *29 North St.* ☎ *707/433–3311*) will change your mind. At the bar of Healdsburg's hottest restaurant, they mix superb, inventive drinks with house-made infused syrups and seasonal ingredients such as local Meyer lemons.

As in many Wine Country towns, nightlife in Healdsburg tends to consist of lingering over a glass of dessert wine after a decadent dinner. There is a modest arts scene, though, and you can catch the occasional live music or theater performance at the **Raven Performing Arts Theater** (⊠ *115 North St.* ☎ *707/433–6335* ⊕ *www.raventheater.org*).

SHOPPING

Healdsburg is the most pleasant spot in Sonoma for an afternoon of window-shopping, with dozens of boutiques, food markets, and tasting rooms clustered within easy walking distance around the bucolic main plaza. Healdsburg's food fetish extends from the restaurants to the specialty grocers and markets, but there are plenty of stores selling nonedibles, too.

To truly catch the Healdsburg spirit, go to the plaza early in the morning and order a fragrant sticky bun and a cup of coffee at the **Downtown Bakery & Creamery** (⊠ *308A Center St.* ☎ *707/431–2719*), a local cult favorite. The bakery uses local dairy products and fruit in their breads and pastries.

Chandeliers light the opulent **La Farmacista** (⊠ *115 Plaza St.* ☎ *707/473–0382*) a fragrant shop selling perfumes, skin-care products, and an enormous selection of candles scented with everything from the usual choices to ginger and currants and caramel.

Oakville Grocery (⊠ *124 Matheson St.* ☎ *707/433–3200*) has a bustling Healdsburg branch filled with wine, condiments, and deli items. A terrace with ample seating makes a good place for an impromptu picnic, but you might want to lunch early or late to avoid the worst crowds.

A block off the plaza, the **Plaza Arts Center** (⊠ *130 Plaza St.* ☎ *707/431–1970*) displays work by local artists who also staff the gallery. In addition to the larger-scale paintings and photography, look for suitcase-friendly fine crafts, such as jewelry.

You'll find not only wine-related gadgets and gifts but also a wide selection of kitchenware and serving pieces at **Plaza Gourmet** (⊠ *108 Matheson St.* ☎ *707/433–7116*).

Spirits in Stone (⊠ *401 Healdsburg Ave.* ☎ *707/723–1723*) is known for its popular Zimbabwe Shona sculpture; it also has a collection of African baskets, paintings, jewelry, and other art.

You'll have to get in your car to head north on Healdsburg Avenue to **Tip Top Liquor Warehouse** (⊠ *90 Dry Creek Rd.* ☎ *707/431–0841*), a nondescript spot that stocks an interesting selection of wines and spirits at fair prices. Though it's strongest in bottles from Sonoma, you'll also find a few Napa wines, including some rare cult cabernets.

FARMER'S MARKETS. During two weekly **Healdsburg farmers' markets** you can buy locally made goat cheese, fragrant lavender, and olive oil in addition to the usual produce. On Saturday from May through November the market takes place one block west of the town plaza, at the corner of North and Vine streets, from 9 AM to noon. The Tuesday market, which runs from June through October, takes place on the plaza itself from 4 to 6:30 PM.

SPORTS AND THE OUTDOORS

In summer, head for **Memorial Beach** (✉ *13839 Old Redwood Hwy.* ☏ *707/433–1625*) on the Russian River, where you can swim in the pool created behind a seasonal dam. Parking costs $6 from Memorial Day weekend through Labor Day weekend; it's $5 during the rest of the year. Lifeguards are generally on duty in the summer.

SOAR/Russian River Adventures (✉ *20 Healdsburg Ave.* ☏ *707/433–5599* ⊕ *www.soar1.com*) rents inflatable canoes for leisurely trips down the Russian River. The $49-per-person fee includes a shuttle back to the starting point at the end of the day.

DRY CREEK VALLEY

Starting about 17 mi north of Santa Rosa on U.S. 101.

If you follow Healdsburg Avenue from downtown Healdsburg to Dry Creek Road and turn northwest, you'll soon feel like you've slipped back in time. Healdsburg looks totally urban in comparison with the pure, unspoiled countryside of Dry Creek Valley. Although the valley has become renowned for its wines, it preserves a rural simplicity rarely found in California's Wine Country today.

Dry Creek Road and the parallel West Dry Creek Road, brightened by wildflower-strewn shoulders in spring and early summer, offer tantalizing vineyard views as they skirt the hillside on the east side of the narrow valley. The winding roads can be quite narrow in places, forcing you to slow down—a good thing for the many bicyclists who navigate this route.

The valley's well-drained, gravelly floor is planted with chardonnay grapes to the south, where an occasional sea fog creeping in from the Russian River cools the vineyards. Sauvignon blanc is planted in the north, where the vineyards are warmer. The red decomposed soils of the benchlands bring out the best in zinfandel—the grape for which Dry Creek has become famous—but they also produce great cabernet sauvignon. And these soils seem well suited to Rhône varieties such as cinsault, mourvèdre, and marsanne, which need heat to ripen properly.

The Dry Creek Valley is so picture-perfect it would be a shame to pass up the opportunity to picnic at one of the wineries. For sandwiches, bread, terrific cheeses, and other

Michel-Schlumberger

picnic supplies, stop by the **Dry Creek General Store** (✉ *3495 Dry Creek Rd.* ☎ *707/433–4171*), established in 1881 and still a popular spot for locals to hang out on the porch.

VINEYARDS IN THE DRY CREEK VALLEY

David Coffaro himself tends to every aspect of the wine-making process at **David Coffaro Estate Vineyard,** where Coffaro's beloved Raiders memorabilia lines the wall behind the bar. (And on game days, you might find a few staffers watching sports on a large screen tucked between the barrels.) Despite the relaxed attitude, they produce some serious wines here. Although they make a handful of single-varietal wines, Coffaro specializes in crafting unique blends, mixing up, for example, cabernet, petite sirah, petite verdot, and tannat, a varietal that's popular in Europe's Basque region but rarely grown in the United States. ■TIP→ **If you're interested in learning more about the unusual varietals they grow (which include the little-seen tinto cão, peloursin, and lagrein), ask if you can taste some straight from the barrels.** ✉ *7485 Dry Creek Rd., Geyserville* ☎ *707/433–9715* ⊕ *www.coffaro. com* ▦ *Tasting $5, tour free* ⊗ *Daily 11–4, tour Friday at 11 and 1 by appointment.*

At **Dry Creek Vineyard,** fumé blanc is king. In 1972 the founder was the first in the area to plant sauvignon blanc, the grapes used to make it. Dry Creek also makes well-regarded zinfandels, a zesty dry chenin blanc, a pinot noir,

and a handful of cabernet sauvignon blends. Since many of their high-quality wines go for less than $20 or $30 a bottle, it's a popular stop for those who want to stock their cellars for a reasonable price. After picking up a bottle you might want to picnic on the lawn, next to the flowering magnolia tree. Conveniently, a general store and deli with plenty of picnic fixings is just steps down the road. ⊠ *3770 Lambert Bridge Rd.* ☎ *707/433–1000* ⊕ *www.drycreekvineyard.com* ☞ *Tasting $5–$10* ⊗ *Daily 10:30–4:30.*

Known for its Disney-esque Italian villa, which has as many critics as it does fervent fans for its huge size, sprawling gift shop, and general over-the-topness, **Ferrari-Carano Winery** produces mostly chardonnays, fumé blancs, zinfandels, and cabernet sauvignons. Though whites have traditionally been the specialty here, the reds are now garnering more attention. Tours cover not only the wine-making facilities and underground cellar but also the manicured gardens, where you can see a cork oak tree and learn about how cork is harvested. For a more relaxed experience, head downstairs to the reserve tasting room. ⊠ *8761 Dry Creek Rd., Healdsburg* ☎ *707/433–6700* ⊕ *www.ferrari-carano. com* ☞ *Tasting $5–$15, tour free* ⊗ *Daily 10–5; reserve room daily 10–4:30; tour by appointment.*

★ Fodor's Choice Down a narrow road at the westernmost edge of the Dry Creek Valley, **Michel-Schlumberger** is one of Sonoma's finest producers of cabernet sauvignon, aptly described by the winery's tour guide as a "full, rich big mouthful of wine." The tour is unusually casual and friendly. Weather permitting, you'll wander up a hill on a gravel pathway to the edge of their lovely terraced vineyards before swinging through the barrel room in the California Mission–style building that once served as the home of the winery's founder, Jean-Jacques Michel. To taste older vintages of their cabernet and learn what their wines will taste like after 10 or so years in the bottle, reserve in advance for a vertical tasting. ⊠ *4155 Wine Creek Rd.* ☎ *707/433–7427 or 800/447–3060* ⊕ *www.michelschlumberger.com* ☞ *Tasting $25, tour $15* ⊗ *Tours at 11 and 2, by appointment; tasting by appointment.*

★ Fodor's Choice Once you wind your way down **Preston Vineyards'** long driveway, flanked by vineyards and punctuated by the occasional olive tree, you'll be welcomed by the sight of a few farmhouses encircling a shady yard prowled by several friendly cats. In summer a small selection of

A Great Drive in Northern Sonoma County

Healdsburg is the area's hub, so plan on starting a day's drive here, nabbing an early breakfast in the town plaza. From downtown Healdsburg, take Healdsburg Avenue to Dry Creek Road and turn west. Almost as soon as you pass under the U.S. 101 freeway bridge, you'll feel like you're in the true countryside, free of urban sprawl. Turn left on Lambert Bridge Road, then right on West Dry Creek Road, taking your time on this scenic track. Drive past the NO OUTLET sign and veer right on the narrow lane alongside Peña Creek until you see an old barn on your left and the Preston Vineyard sign on the right. After visiting Preston, return the way you came until you reach Yoakim Bridge Road. Turn left there, then right on Dry Creek Road and left on Canyon Road. Just after Canyon Road crosses U.S. 101, turn right on Highway 128, which will lead you through Geyserville to Jimtown. Pick up picnic fixings at the Jimtown Store, then backtrack along Highway 128 less than a mile to the dramatic tasting room at Stryker Sonoma, where you can taste their wines and enjoy your picnic.

Backtrack southeast on Highway 128; at the Jimtown Store, turn left on Alexander Valley Road. Veer left at Healdsburg Avenue to return to downtown Healdsburg, where you can taste wine at one of its many tasting rooms before dinner.

If you're lucky enough to have a second day, stock up on sandwiches at the Oakville Grocery before leaving Healdsburg. Drive south on Healdsburg Avenue and turn right on Mill Street. After it crosses U.S. 101, it turns into Westside Road. Wind along Westside Road—looking out for the many cyclists along this route—for about 20 minutes to Gary Farrell, where you can see much of the Russian River Valley below you from the tasting room. Return to Healdsburg by winding back the way you came along Westside Road, stopping to taste at whichever of the many tasting rooms appeals to you: Rochioli pours pinots that have their ardent admirers, and Hop Kiln is housed in an unusual historic building.

organic produce grown in their gardens is sold from an impromptu stand on the front porch, and house-made bread and olive oil are available year-round. Their down-home style is particularly in evidence on Sunday, the only day of the week that tasting-room staffers sell a 3-liter

Ridge Vineyards

bottle of Guadagni Red, a primarily zinfandel blend filled from the barrel right in front of you. Owners Lou and Susan Preston are committed to organic growing techniques and use only estate-grown grapes in their wines, which include a viognier, a rousanne, a cinsault, and syrah–petite sirah blend, among several others. ✉ *9282 West Dry Creek Rd.* ☎ *707/433-3372* ⊕ *www.prestonvineyards.com* ✉ *$5* ⊙ *Daily 11–4:30.*

An unassuming winery in a modern wooden barn topped by solar panels, **Quivira** produces some of the most interesting wines in Dry Creek Valley. It's known for its dangerously drinkable reds, including a petite sirah, and a few hearty zinfandel blends. The dry rosé made from grenache grapes and the crisp sauvignon blanc, which spends all its time in stainless-steel tanks rather than oak barrels, are also worth checking out. The excellent tour provides information about their biodynamic farming practices and also offers a glimpse of the chickens and goats kept on the property. Redwood and olive trees shade the picnic area. ✉ *4900 W. Dry Creek Rd.* ☎ *707/431-8333* ⊕ *www.quivirawine.com* ✉ *Tasting $5, tour $15* ⊙ *Daily 11–5, tours by appointment.*

★ **Fodor's** Choice Visitors receive an unusually warm welcome in the spare but spacious tasting room at **Ridge Vineyards,** one of the more highly regarded wineries in all of California, and not only because one of its 1971 cabernets snagged first place in a 2006 re-creation of the 1976 Judgment of Paris. Although their grapes comes from several locations in Northern California—including here in the Dry Creek Valley as well Sonoma Valley, Napa Valley, and Paso Robles—they focus on making single-vineyard wines of unusual depth and complexity. They are best known for cabernet sauvignon, zinfandel, and chardonnay, but you'll also find a few blends of Rhône varietals. Plan a visit for the weekend if you want a chance to taste some of their very best selections, such as their exceptional Monte Bello cabernet blend grown in the Santa Cruz Mountains. The lovely view of the undulating vineyards, visible from the expanse of windows in the tasting rooms, can be enjoyed at greater length from the picnic tables just outside. ⌧ *650 Lytton Springs Rd., Healdsburg* ☎ *707/433–7721* ⊕ *www. ridgewine.com* ⌺ *Free–$20* ⊙ *Nov.–Mar., daily 11–4; Apr.– Oct., Mon.–Thurs. 11–4, Fri.–Sun. 11–5.*

WHERE TO STAY

★ Fodor'sChoice ⏣ **Best Western Dry Creek Inn.** The lackluster loca-
¢–$$ tion of this Spanish Mission–style motel near U.S. 101 nevertheless means quick access to downtown Healdsburg and other Wine Country hot spots. Deluxe rooms are slightly more spacious than the standard rooms, but both types are spotless. The more expensive rooms in the Tuscan building, which opened in 2007, are considerably more upscale, with amenities such as flat-panel TVs, gas fireplaces, spa tubs, and patios. A casual family restaurant is next door. **Pros:** free Wi-Fi and laundry facilities; frequent discounts available on their Web site. **Cons:** thin walls; basic furnishings in standard rooms. ⌧ *198 Dry Creek Rd., Healdsburg* ☎ *707/433–0300 or 800/222–5784* ⊕ *www.drycreekinn. com* � *163 rooms* ⌂ *In-room: refrigerator, DVD (some), Internet (some), Wi-Fi. In-hotel: restaurant, pool, gym, laundry facilities, some pets allowed (fee)* ⊟ *AE, D, DC, MC, V* ⊺⊙⊺ *CP.*

ALEXANDER VALLEY AND ANDERSON VALLEY

Starting about 17 mi north of Santa Rosa on U.S. 101.

The lovely Alexander Valley, which extends northeast of Healdsburg to the Mendocino County line north of Cloverdale, is one of Sonoma's least-visited regions. Driving through the rolling hills along Highway 128, you're more likely to have to slow down for tandem bicyclists than for other drivers. And you might find you're the only visitor in the tasting room at some of the small, family-owned wineries. Though most Californians couldn't find the Alexander Valley on a map if pressed, this appellation got a boost in 2006, when film- and winemaker Francis Ford Coppola bought the old Chateau Souverain here and opened a tasting room. Some combination of distance from San Francisco (a drive here takes about 2½ hours on a good day) and hairpin switchback roads seems to have preserved the unpretentious, rustic nature of this region. Restaurants and B&Bs are relatively few and far between. And although the increasing attention to Anderson Valley, grown northwest of the Alexander Valley, wines has brought an uptick in tourism, this is still the spot to enjoy life in the slow lane.

There are a wide variety of soils and microclimates in this neck of the woods. It is warmer than the Russian River appellation, and its small side valleys become very hot in summer. Sea fogs only occasionally drift in from the Santa Rosa Plain, and though they cool the land, they burn off more quickly than on the lower river. As recently as the 1980s the valley was mostly planted in walnuts, pears, prunes, and bulk grapes, so one might argue that experimentation here has hardly begun. So far, chardonnay, sauvignon blanc, zinfandel, and cabernet sauvignon seem to do well in places. Italian grapes such as sangiovese or the Rhône varieties, which do so well in the Dry Creek Valley, may make great wines in the warmer parts of the Alexander Valley. Stay posted for a decade or two. This valley is sure to be full of surprises.

At the western end of the valley, known to locals as the Deep End, cool fog and rainfall create ideal conditions for growing certain northern European varietals such as chardonnay, riesling, gewürztraminer, and the Anderson Valley AVA's star, pinot noir. Farther inland, where summer temperatures can be up to 15 degrees warmer than those of the Deep End, chardonnay and sauvignon blanc are the favored varietals.

GEYSERVILLE

Geyserville is about 8 mi north of Healdsburg on U.S. 101.

Though most visitors to the Alexander Valley establish their home base in Healdsburg, you might end up passing through the town of **Geyserville.** Not long ago, it was a dusty farm town with little to offer wine tourists besides a grocery store. Though Geyserville is still little more than a crossroads with a few small markets and a good restaurant, the storefront tasting room **Locals** (✉ *21023A Geyserville Ave.* ☎ *707/857–4900*) is definitely worth a stop for serious wine tasters. Local winemakers and tourists come here to taste wines produced by around 10 small wineries that do not have tasting rooms of their own, such as Hawley, Eric Ross, Ramazzotti, and others. There's no fee for tasting (a great deal for wines of this quality), and the extremely knowledgeable staff is happy to pour you a flight of several wines so you can compare, say, several different cabernet sauvignons.

The Alexander Valley's best picnic-packing stop is the **Jimtown Store** (✉ *6706 Hwy. 128, Healdsburg ✣ 5 mi northeast of Healdsburg* ☎ *707/433–1212* ⊕ *www.jimtown.com*), which has great espresso and a good selection of deli items, including their signature Brie-and-chopped-olive sandwich. While you're here, take a few minutes to browse through their gifts, which include both housewares and old-fashioned toys such as sock monkeys.

BOONVILLE

Boonville is about 47 mi northwest of Healdsburg on U.S. 101 and Hwy. 128.

Navigating the Anderson Valley is a cinch, since almost all the wineries are just off Highway 128, which heads northwest from U.S. 101. About 30 mi and 45 minutes after leaving U.S. 101 you'll roll through Boonville, the valley's biggest town, where you might want to get out, stretch your legs, and get lunch or stock up on picnic supplies before continuing west. This small farming town was once so isolated that its residents invented a lingo all their own, known as Boontling, or Boont, for short. Few traces of this unique language survive, though you'll still find Boontling dictionaries sold in local shops.

Boonville is also a good option for spending the night. You'll find fairly basic but attractive rooms with little touches such as fresh wildflowers and down comforters at the **Boonville Hotel** (✉ *Hwy. 128 at Lambert La.* ☎ *707/895–2210* ⊕ *www.boonvillehotel.com*). The hotel is also the site of the Anderson Valley's most exciting restaurant, which focuses on organic ingredients and local produce.

Continuing northwest from Boonville, you'll pass through the towns of **Philo** and **Navarro,** little more than wide spots in the road. If you're visiting in summer or fall, stock up at one of the many fruit stands you'll see along the highway. Just past Navarro—2 mi before you would hit Highway 1—stand the magnificent giant trees of **Navarro River Redwoods State Park,** a lovely spot for a shady stroll.

VINEYARDS IN THE ALEXANDER AND ANDERSON VALLEYS

Off Highway 128 is the 1841 homestead of Cyrus Alexander, for whom the valley is named, now the site of **Alexander Valley Vineyards.** The Wetzel family bought the land from Alexander's heirs in 1963 and restored the historic adobe to serve as their family home. But the Wetzels also planted vineyards, and in 1975 they built a winery with adobe blocks and weathered wood. Today when you visit, the yellow Labrador belonging to Hank Wetzel, who oversees the winery operations, is likely to lope up to meet you. Head into the tasting room to taste the popular Sin Zin, which is fairly low in alcohol for a California zinfandel and full of ripe cherry flavor, as well as their round, rich chardonnay. After tasting, you can wander up a grassy hill behind the winery to the cemetery of the Alexander family or grab a bottle and head for the picnic tables. ⊠ *8644 Hwy. 128, Healdsburg* ☎ *707/433–7209* ⊕ *www.avvwine.com* ☜ *Tasting free–$10* ☉ *Daily 10–5, tour by appointment.*

Despite the name, there's no Gallic connection to **Clos du Bois:** the name was suggested by the first owner's children, who thought the ho-hum name "Woods Vineyard" would sound better in French. Although the large, airy, modern tasting room and gift shop here aren't particularly atmospheric, the winery is worth a stop for its in-depth tour (offered spring through fall) that takes you through a demonstration vineyard and usually includes a barrel tasting in the cellar. Though you may be familiar with their inexpensive, approachable Classic wines, also look for their more intense Proprietary Series. ■TIP→ **Their shop sells half bottles—a good choice for picnickers who want to pick up some cheese from the deli case and take a seat under the gazebos outside.** ⊠ *19410 Geyserville Ave., Geyserville* ☎ *707/857–1651* ⊕ *www.closdubois.com* ☜ *Tasting $10, tour $15* ☉ *Daily 10–4:30; tour Apr.–Nov., daily at 11 and 2 by appointment.*

In 2006, filmmaker-winemaker-publisher-hotelier Francis Ford Coppola snapped up a majestic French-style château, formerly Chateau Souverain and now called **Francis Ford Coppola Winery,** to showcase his less expensive wines. (His Napa winery, Rubicon Estate, focuses on the high-end vintages.) It's still very much a work in progress: at this writing, the property was in full renovation mode, and wines were being poured in a makeshift tasting room. After all the dust settles, however, the winery intends to have a full-service restaurant, a café, and an area for viewing Coppola memorabilia (the desk from *The Godfather* and costumes from *Bram Stoker's Dracula,* for example) that were once housed at Rubicon. Fans of Coppola's wines or movies should check the Web site or call ahead for the latest. ⊠ *400 Souverain Rd.* ☎ *707/433–8282* ⊕ *www.franciscoppolawinery.com* ⧓ *Tasting free–$8* ☉ *Daily 11–5.*

Goldeneye Winery. The owners of the Napa Valley's well-respected Duckhorn Vineyards have been making pinot noir here from local grapes with very satisfying results. Leisurely tastings take place in either a restored farmhouse with Arts and Crafts–style furnishings or on the lovely back patio, which overlooks a vineyard. ⊠ *9200 Hwy. 128, Philo* ☎ *707/895–3203* ⊕ *www.goldeneyewinery.com.*

Handley Cellars. The winery produces a splendid chardonnay from Anderson Valley grapes, a delicately blushing pinot gris, an exotically fruity gewürztraminer, a variety of pinots, and some very good sparkling wines. The tasting room is decorated with international folk art collected by winemaker Milla Handley. ⊠ *3151 Hwy. 128, Philo* ☎ *707/895–3876* ⊕ *www.handleycellars.com.*

Husch Vineyards. The setting here—a converted late-19th-century barn, with a rusted '32 Plymouth in the yard and picnic tables spread out under the trees—makes a tasting feel particularly "down home." Established in 1971, this is the oldest winery in the Anderson Valley. ⊠ *4400 Hwy. 128, Philo* ☎ *707/895–3216* ⊕ *www.huschvineyards.com.*

Navarro Vineyards. This winery produces an unusually diverse array of wines for the region, including cabernet sauvignon and a dry rosé. But not surprisingly, considering their location, they produce the greatest quantity of pinot noir and chardonnay. The unusual Alsatian-style gewürztraminers, though, are the winery's most impressive offering. The cheeses and smoked salmon for sale inspire more than a few picnics at the tables overlooking

The tasting room at Stryker Sonoma

the vineyards. ✉ *5601 Hwy. 128, Philo* ☎ *707/895–3686* ⊕ *www.navarrowine.com.*

Roederer Estate. From the looks of this unassuming tasting room, it would be hard to guess that this is an outpost of a renowned French Champagne maker. Only Anderson Valley grapes go into the sparkling wines, which are generally considered among the very best sparklers made in the United States. They share characteristics of the finest Champagne, with a creamy, full-bodied character and fine, tiny bubbles. ✉ *4501 Hwy. 128, Philo* ☎ *707/895–2288* ⊕ *www.roedererestate.com.*

★ Inside the tasting room at **Stryker Sonoma,** vaulted ceilings and seemingly endless walls of windows onto the vineyards suggest you've entered a cathedral to wine. The wines are almost as impressive as the architecture: most of their bottles are single varietals, such as chardonnay, merlot, zinfandel, and cabernet sauvignon. An exception, however, are a few Bordeaux-style blends, including the powerful E1K, which, unfortunately, is not usually poured in the tasting room (though it never hurts to ask whether they have a bottle open). The picnic tables are a particularly lovely way to enjoy the quiet countryside of the Alexander Valley. ✉ *5110 Hwy. 28, Geyserville* ☎ *707/433–1944* ⊕ *www. strykersonoma.com* ◫ *Tasting free–$10* ☉ *Daily 10:30–5.*

When Leo and Evelyn Trentadue decided to move to a rural location in 1959, they found their new home in a neglected Alexander Valley prune and pear orchard. True to their Tuscan heritage, the family planted classic Italian grape varietals at **Trentadue Winery.** They still produce wines that are 100% sangiovese and carignane, something of a rarity in the area, but their diverse lineup includes everything from a sparkling wine made from chardonnay grapes to wines made from viognier, merlot, tempranillo, cabernet sauvignon, petite sirah, zinfandel, and more. When visiting their ivy-covered Tuscan-style villa, be sure to taste their most celebrated wine, the La Storia Meritage, a blend of Bordeaux varietals. ⊠ *19170 Geyserville Ave., Geyserville* ☎ *707/433-3104* ⊕ *www.trentadue.com* ☜ *Tasting $5, tours $5–$10* ☉ *Daily 10–5, tours by appointment.*

WHERE TO EAT

$$ ✕ **Diavola Pizzeria and Salumeria.** A cozy dining room with hardwood floors, a pressed-tin ceiling, and exposed brick walls seems a fitting setting for the rustic cuisine at this Geyserville charmer. Chef Dino Bugica studied with several artisans in Italy before opening this spot, which specializes in pizzas pulled from a wood-burning oven and several types of house-cured meats. A small selection of salads and meaty main courses round out the menu. If you're impressed by the antipasto plate, stop by the deli case on your way out and pick up some smoked pork belly, pancetta, or spicy Calabrese sausage to take home. ⊠ *21021 Geyserville Ave., Geyserville* ☎ *707/814–0111* ⊕ *www.diavolapizzeria.com* ⚭ *No reservations* ⊟ *AE, MC, V.*

Winespeak

WORD OF MOUTH

"It was our third visit [to California's Wine Country] and we can't wait for our fourth. My husband said that he felt like a kid in a candy shop—so much to sample!"

—MarieF

WINE-TASTING GLOSSARY

Wine snobs might toss around terms like "Brett effect" and "*barrique*," but don't let that turn you off. Like any activity, wine making and wine tasting have specialized vocabularies. Some words are merely show-off jargon, but some are specific and helpful. Here's a handful of core terms to know—and things you can say with a straight face. (⇨ *See also chapter 1.*)

Acidity. The tartness of a wine, derived from the fruit acids of the grape. Acids stabilize a wine (i.e., preserve its character), balance its sweetness, and bring out its flavors. Too little or too much acid spoils a wine's taste. Tartaric acid is the major acid in wine, but malic, lactic, and citric acids also occur.

Aging. The process by which some wines improve over time, becoming smoother and more complex and developing a pleasing bouquet. Wine is most commonly aged in oak vats or barrels, slowly interacting with the air through the pores in the wood. Sometimes wine is cellared for bottle aging. Today many wines are not made for aging and are drunk relatively young, as little as a few months after bottling. Age can diminish a wine's fruitiness and also dull its color: whites turn brownish, rosés orange, reds brown.

Alcohol. Ethyl alcohol is a colorless, volatile, pungent spirit that not only gives wine its stimulating effect and some of its flavor but also acts as a preservative, stabilizing the wine and allowing it to age. A wine's alcohol content must be stated on the label, expressed as a percentage of volume, except when a wine is designated table wine (⇨ *below*).

American Viticultural Area (AVA). More commonly termed an "appellation." A region with unique soil, climate, and other grape-growing conditions can be designated an AVA by the Alcohol and Tobacco Tax and Trade Bureau. When a label lists an appellation—Napa Valley or Mount Veeder, for example—at least 75% of the grapes used to make the wine must come from that region.

Appellation. See *American Viticultural Area.*

Aroma. The scent of young wine derived directly from the fresh fruit. It diminishes with fermentation and is replaced by a more complex bouquet as the wine ages. The term may also be used to describe special fruity odors in a wine, such as black cherry, green olive, ripe raspberry, or apple.

Astringent. The puckery sensation produced in the mouth by the tannins in wine.

AVA. See *American Viticultural Area.*

Balance. A quality of wine in which all desirable elements (fruit, acid, tannin) are present in the proper proportion. Well-balanced wine has a pleasing nose, flavor, and mouth feel.

Barrel fermenting. The fermenting of wine in small oak barrels instead of large tanks or vats. This method allows the winemaker to keep grape lots separate before blending the wine. The cost of oak barrels makes this method expensive.

Barrique. An oak barrel used for aging wines.

Biodynamic. An approach to agriculture that focuses on regarding the land as a living thing; it generally incorporates organic farming techniques and the use of the astronomic calendar in hopes of cultivating a healthy balance in the vineyard ecosystem.

Blanc de blancs. Sparkling or still white wine made solely from white grapes.

Blanc de noirs. White wine made with red grapes by removing the skins during crush. Some sparkling whites, for example, are made with red pinot noir grapes.

Blending. The mixing of several wines to create one of greater complexity or appeal, as when a heavy wine is blended with a lighter one to make a more approachable medium-bodied wine.

Body. The wine's heft or density as experienced by the palate. A full body makes the mouth literally feel full. It is considered an advantage in the case of some reds, a disadvantage in many lighter whites. *See also Mouth feel.*

Bordeaux blend. A red wine blended from varietals native to France's Bordeaux region—cabernet sauvignon, cabernet franc, malbec, merlot, and petit verdot.

Botrytis. *Botrytis cinerea*, a beneficial fungus that can perforate a ripe grape's skin. This dehydrates the grape and concentrates the remaining juice while preserving its acids. Botrytis grapes make a sweet but not cloying wine, often with complex flavors of honey or apricot.

Bouquet. The odors a mature wine gives off when opened. They should be pleasantly complex and should give an indication of the wine's grape variety, origin, age, and quality.

Brettanomyces. Also called Brett. A strain of yeast that gives wine a funky, off flavor. Winemakers try to keep Brett away from their wines, but some drinkers enjoy a mild "Brett effect."

Brix. A method of telling whether grapes are ready for picking by measuring their sugars. Multiplying a grape's Brix number by .55 approximates the potential alcohol content of the wine.

Brut. French term for the driest category of sparkling wine. *(See also Demi-sec, Sec.)*

Case. A carton of 12 750-ml bottles of wine. A magnum case contains six 1.5-liter magnum bottles. Most wineries will offer a discount if you purchase wine by the case (or sometimes a half case).

Cask. A synonym for barrel. More generally, any size or shape wine container made from wood staves.

7

Cellaring. Storage of wine in bottles for aging. The bottles are laid on their sides to keep the corks moist and prevent air leakage that would spoil the wine.

Champagne. The northernmost wine district of France, where sparkling wine originated and where the world's only genuine Champagne is made. The term is often used loosely in America to denote sparkling wines in general.

Cloudiness. The presence of particles that do not settle out of a wine, causing it to look and taste dusty or even muddy. If settling and decanting *(see Decant)* do not correct cloudiness, the wine has been badly made or is spoiled.

Complexity. The qualities of good wine that provide a multilayered sensory experience to the drinker. Balanced flavors, harmonious aromas or bouquet, and a long finish are components of complexity.

Corked. Describes wine that is flawed by the musty, wet-cardboard flavor imparted by cork mold, technically known as TCA, or 2,4,6-Trichloroanisole.

Crush. American term for the harvest season, or vintage. Also refers to the year's crop of grapes crushed for wine.

Cuvée. Generally a sparkling wine, but sometimes a still wine, that is a blend of different wines and sometimes different vintages. Most sparkling wines are cuvées.

Decant. To pour a wine from its bottle into another container either to expose it to air or to eliminate sediment. Decanting for sediment pours out the clear wine and leaves the residue behind in the original bottle.

Demi-sec. French term that translates as "half-dry." It is applied to sweet wines that contain 3.5%–5% sugar.

Dessert wines. Sweet wines that are big in flavor and aroma. Some are quite low in alcohol; others, such as port-style wines, are fortified with brandy or another spirit and may be 17%–21% alcohol.

Dry. Having very little sweetness or residual sugar. Most wines are dry, although some whites, such as rieslings, are made to be "off-dry," which is on the sweet side.

Estate bottled. A wine entirely made by one winery at a single facility. The grapes must come from the winery's own vineyards within the same appellation (which must be printed on the label).

Fermentation. The biochemical process by which grape juice becomes wine. Enzymes generated by yeast cells convert grape sugars into alcohol and carbon dioxide. Fermentation stops when either the sugar is depleted and the yeast starves, or when high alcohol levels kill the yeast.

Fermenter. Any vessel (such as a barrel, tank, or vat) in which wine is fermented.

Filtering, Filtration. A purification process in which wine is pumped through filters to rid it of suspended particles.

Fining. A method of clarifying wine by adding egg whites, bentonite (a type of clay), or other natural substances to a barrel. As these solids settle to the bottom, they take various dissolved compounds with them. Most wine meant for everyday drinking is fined; however, better wines are fined less often.

Finish. Also aftertaste. The flavors that remain in the mouth after swallowing wine. A good wine has a long finish with complex flavor and aroma.

Flight. A few wines—usually three to five—specially selected for tasting together.

Fortification. A process by which brandy or another spirit is added to a wine to stop fermentation and to increase its level of alcohol, as in the case of port-style dessert wines.

Fruity. Having aromatic nuances of fresh fruit, such as fig, raspberry, or apple. Fruitiness, a sign of quality in young wines, is replaced by bouquet in aged wines.

Fumé blanc. A nonspecific term for wine made with sauvignon blanc. Robert Mondavi coined the term originally to describe his dry, crisp, oak-aged sauvignon blanc.

Green. Said of a wine made from unripe grapes, with a pronounced leafy flavor and a raw edge.

Horizontal tasting. A tasting of several different wines of the same vintage.

Late harvest. Wine made from grapes harvested later in the fall than the main lot, and thus higher in sugar levels. Many dessert wines are late harvest.

Lees. The spent yeast, grape solids, and tartrates that drop to the bottom of the barrel or tank as wine ages. Wine, particularly white wine, gains complexity when it is left on the lees for a time.

Library wine. An older vintage that the winery has put aside to sell at a later date.

Malolactic fermentation. A secondary fermentation in the tank or barrel that changes harsh malic acid into softer lactic acid and carbon dioxide. Wine is sometimes inoculated with lactic bacteria, or placed in wood containers that harbor the bacteria, to enhance this process. Often referred to as ML or malo. Too much malo can make a wine too heavy.

Meritage. A trademarked name for American (mostly California) Bordeaux blends that meet certain wine-making and marketing requirements and are made by member wineries of the Meritage Association.

Méthode champenoise. The traditional, time-consuming method of making sparkling wines by fermenting them in individual bottles.

Mouth feel. Literally, the way wine feels in the mouth. Mouth feel, such as smoothness or astringency, is detected by the sense of touch rather than of smell or taste.

Must. The slushy mix of crushed grapes—juice, pulp, skin, seeds, and bits of stem—produced by the crusher–de-stemmer at the beginning of the wine-making process.

Neutral oak. The wood of older barrels or vats that no longer pass much flavor or tannin to the wine stored within.

New oak. The wood of a fresh barrel or vat that has not previously been used to ferment or age wine. It can impart desirable flavors and enhance a wine's complexity, but if used to excess it can overpower a wine's true character.

Noble rot. See Botrytis.

Nonvintage. A blend of wines from different years. Nonvintage wines have no date on their label. Wine may be blended from different vintages to showcase strong points that complement each other, or to make a certain wine taste the same from one year to the next.

Nose. The overall fragrance (aroma or bouquet) given off by a wine; the better part of its flavor.

Oaky. A vanilla-woody flavor that develops when wine is aged in oak barrels. Leave a wine too long in a new oak barrel and that oaky taste overpowers the other flavors.

Organic viticulture. The technique of growing grapes without the use of chemical fertilizers, pesticides, or fungicides. *See also the "Organic Wines" box in chapter 4.*

Oxidation. Undesirable flavor and color changes to juice or wine caused by too much contact with the air, either during processing or because of a leaky barrel or cork. Most often occurs with white wine, especially if it's over the hill.

pH. Technical term for a measure of a wine's acidity. It is a reverse measure: the lower the pH level, the higher the acidity. Most wines range in pH from 2.9 to 4.2, with the most desirable level at 3.2 and 3.5. Higher pHs make wine flabby and dull, whereas lower pHs make it tart.

Phylloxera. A disease caused by the root louse *Phylloxera vastatrix*, which attacks and ultimately destroys grape-vine roots. The pest is native to the United States; it traveled to France with American grape vines in the 19th century and devastated nonresistant vineyards there.

Pomace. Spent grape skins and solids left over after the juice has been pressed, commonly returned to the fields as fertilizer.

Racking. Moving wine from one tank or barrel to another to leave unwanted deposits behind; the wine may or may not be fined or filtered in the process.

Reserve wine. Fuzzy term applied by vintners to indicate that a wine is better in some way (through aging, source of the grapes, etc.) than others from their winery.

Residual sugar. The natural sugar left in a wine after fermentation, which converts sugar into alcohol. If the fermentation was interrupted or if the must has very high sugar levels, some residual sugar will remain, making a sweeter wine.

Rhône blend. A wine made from grapes hailing from France's Rhône Valley, such as marsanne, roussanne, syrah, cinsault, mourvèdre, or viognier.

Rosé. Pink wine, usually made from red-wine grapes. The juice is left on the skins only long enough to give it a tinge of color. Rosés can be made from any variety of red-wine grape. After decades in the shadows, they're getting serious attention again.

Rounded. Said of a well-balanced wine in which fruity flavor is nicely offset by acidity—a good wine, though not necessarily a distinctive or great one.

Sec. French for "dry." The term is generally applied within the sparkling or sweet categories, indicating the wine has 1.7%–3.5% residual sugar. Sec is drier than demi-sec but not as dry as brut.

Sediment. Dissolved or suspended solids that drop out of most red wines as they age in the bottle, thus clarifying their appearance, flavors, and aromas. Sediment is not a defect in an old wine or in a new wine that has been bottled unfiltered.

Sparkling wines. Wines in which carbon dioxide is dissolved, making them bubbly. Examples are French Champagne, Italian Prosecco, and Spanish *cava*.

Sugar. Source of grapes' natural sweetness. When yeast feeds on sugar, it produces alcohol and carbon dioxide. The higher the sugar content of the grape, the higher the potential alcohol level or sweetness of the wine.

Sulfites. Compounds of sulfur dioxide that are almost always added before fermentation during wine making to prevent oxidation and to kill bacteria and wild yeasts that can cause off flavors. Sulfites are sometimes blamed as the culprit in headaches caused by red wine, but the connection has not been proven.

Sustainable viticulture. A viticultural method that aims to bring the vineyard into harmony with the environment. Organic and other techniques are used to minimize agricultural impact and to promote biodiversity.

Table wine. Any wine that has at least 7% but not more than 14% alcohol by volume. The term doesn't necessarily imply anything about the wine's quality or price— both super-premium and jug wines can be labeled as table wine.

Tannins. You can tell when they're there, but their origins are still a mystery. These natural grape compounds produce a sensation of drying or astringency in the mouth and throat. Tannins settle out as wine ages; they're a big player in many red wines.

Tartaric acid, Tartrates. The principal acid of wine. Crystalline tartrates form on the insides of vats or barrels and sometimes come out of solution in the bottle or on the cork. They look like tiny shards of glass but are not harmful.

Terroir. French for "soil." Typically used to describe the soil and climate conditions that influence

Unsurprisingly, wine bars are very popular in Napa and Sonoma.

the quality and characteristics of grapes and wine.

Varietal. A wine that takes its name from the grape variety from which it is predominantly made. California wines that qualify are almost always labeled with the variety of the source grape. According to U.S. law, at least 75% of a wine must come from a particular grape to be labeled with its variety name.

Vat. A large container of stainless steel, wood, or concrete, often open at the top, in which wine is fermented or blended. The term is sometimes used interchangeably with "tank."

Vertical tasting. A tasting of several wines of different vintages.

Vinification. Wine making, the process by which grapes are made into wine.

Vintage. The grape harvest of a given year, and the year in which the grapes are harvested. A vintage date on a bottle indicates the year in which the grapes were harvested rather than the year in which the wine was bottled.

Viticulture. The cultivation of grapes.

Woody. Describes excessively musty wood aromas and flavors picked up by wine that has been stored in a wood barrel or cask for too long. Unlike "oaky," the term "woody" is always a negative.

Yeast. A minute, single-celled fungus that germinates and multiplies rapidly as it feeds on sugar with the help of enzymes, creating alcohol and releasing carbon dioxide in the process of fermentation.

WHO'S WHO IN THE GRAPE WORLD

Well over 50 different varieties of grapes are grown in the California Wine Country, from the Mr. Popularities like chardonnay and cabernet sauvignon to less familiar types such as tannat. Although you don't need to be on a first-name basis with them all, you'll see the following varietals again and again as you visit the wineries.

WHITE

Chardonnay

Now as firmly associated with California wine making as it is with Burgundy, where it's used extensively. California chardonnays spent many years chasing big, buttery flavor, but the current trend is toward more restrained wines that let the grape's taste shine through. Because of the area's warmer, longer growing seasons, California chardonnay will always be bolder than Burgundian.

Chenin Blanc

Although a lot of it goes into mediocre mass-market wines, this Loire Valley native can produce a smooth, pleasingly acidic California wine. It gets short shrift with a lot of wine reviewers because of its relative simplicity and light body, but many drinkers appreciate the style.

Gewürztraminer

Cooler California climes such as the Russian River Valley are great for growing this German-Alsatian grape, which is turned into a boldly perfumed, fruity wine.

Marsanne

A white-wine grape of France's northern Rhône Valley that can produce a full-bodied, overly heavy wine unless handled with care. Becoming more popular in California in these Rhône-blend-crazy times.

Pinot Gris

The same grape as Italy's pinot grigio. This varietal yields a more deeply colored wine in California. It's not highly acidic, and has a medium to full body.

Roussanne

This grape from the Rhône Valley makes an especially fragrant California wine that can achieve a lovely balance of fruitiness and acidity.

Riesling

Also called Johannisberg Riesling or White Riesling, this cool-climate German grape has a sweet reputation in America. When made in a dry style, though, as it more and more often is, it can be crisply refreshing, with lush aromas.

Sauvignon Blanc

Hailing from Bordeaux and France's Loire Valley, this white grape does very well almost anywhere in California. Wines made from this grape display a wide range of personalities, from herbaceous to tropical-fruity.

7

Sémillon

A white Bordeaux grape that, blended with sauvignon blanc, has made some of the best sweet wines in the world. Like the riesling grape, it can benefit from *Botrytis cinerea*, the noble rot, which intensifies its flavors and aromas.

Viognier

Until the early 1990s this was rarely planted outside France's Rhône Valley, but today it's one of the hottest white-wine varietals in California. Usually made in a dry style, the best viogniers have an intense fruity or floral bouquet.

RED

Barbera

Prevalent in California thanks to 19th-century Italian immigrants, barbera yields easy-drinking, low-tannin wine that's got big fruit and high acid.

Cabernet Franc

Most often used in blends, often to add complexity to cabernet sauvignon, this French grape can produce aromatic, soft, and subtle wine. An often earthy, or even stinky, aroma that can repel some drinkers makes avid fans of others.

Cabernet Sauvignon

The king of California reds, this Bordeaux grape grows best in austere, well-drained soils. At its best, the California version is dark, bold, and tannic, with black currant notes. On its own, it can need a long aging period to become enjoyable, so it's often blended with cabernet franc, merlot, and other red varieties to soften the resulting wine and make it ready for earlier drinking.

Gamay

Also called gamay beaujolais, this vigorous French grape variety is widely planted in California. It produces pleasant reds and rosés that should be drunk young.

Grenache

This Spanish grape, which makes some of the southern Rhône Valley's most distinguished wine, ripens best in hot, dry conditions. Done right, grenache is dark and concentrated, improved with age. Although it has limited plantings in California, it has gotten more popular along with other Rhône-style California wines.

Merlot

This blue-black Bordeaux variety makes soft, full-bodied wine when grown in California. It is often fruity, and can be quite complex even when young. The easy quaffer was well on its way to conquering cabernet sauvignon as the most popular red until anti-merlot jokes (popularized in the hit movie *Sideways*) damaged its rep . . . for now.

Mourvèdre

This red-wine grape makes wine that is deeply colored, very dense, high in alcohol, and at first harsh, but it mellows with several years of aging. It is a native of France's Rhône Valley and is increasingly popular in California.

Nebbiolo

The great red-wine grape of Italy's Piedmont region is now widely planted in California. It produces full-bodied, sturdy wines that are fairly high in alcohol and age splendidly.

Drying trays at Stony Hill Vineyard

Petite Sirah

Unrelated to the Rhône grape syrah, petite sirah may be a hybrid created in the mid-19th-century California vineyard—no one is sure. It produces a hearty wine that is often used in blends.

Pinot Noir

The darling of grape growers in cooler parts of Napa and Sonoma, such as the Carneros region and the Russian River Valley, pinot noir is also called the "heartbreak grape" since it's hard to cultivate. At its best it has a subtle but addictive earthy quality.

Sangiovese

The main red grape of Italy's Chianti district and of much of central Italy. Depending on how it is grown and vinified, it can be made into vibrant, light- to medium-bodied wines, as well as into long-lived, very complex reds. Increasingly planted in California.

Syrah

Another big California red, this grape comes from the Rhône Valley. With good tannins it can become a full-bodied, almost smoky beauty, but without them it can be flabby and forgettable. Once very limited in California, syrah plantings increased rapidly after the mid-1990s, thanks in part to the soaring popularity of Rhône-style wines in general, and in part to the popularity of syrah from Australia, where it is called shiraz.

Zinfandel

Celebrated as California's own (though it has distant, hazy old-world origins), zinfandel is a rich and spicy wine. Its tannins can make it complex, well suited for aging, but too often it is made in an overly jammy, almost syrupy, style. Typically grown to extreme ripeness, the sugary grape can produce high alcohol levels in wine.

BEST BOOKS AND FILMS

BOOKS

California's Napa Valley: One Hundred Sixty Years of Wine Making (1999), by William F. Heintz. Beautifully illustrated volume chronicles the Napa Valley's rise to prominence in the wine world.

A Companion to California Wine: An Encyclopedia of Wine and Winemaking from the Mission Period to the Present (1998), by Charles Sullivan. Straightforward coverage of the California wine story up to 1997 includes entries on most wineries, grape growing, vinification, varietals, regions, vintages, and history.

The Emperor of Wine: The Rise of Robert M. Parker, Jr. and the Reign of American Taste (2005), by Elin McCoy. Examination of the American critic's enormous influence considers the sources and worldwide impact of his wine rating system's dominance.

The Far Side of Eden: The Ongoing Saga of Napa Valley (2002), by James Conaway. Conaway's second book on the Wine Country picks up where the first, *Napa* (⇨ *below)*, left off.

Grapes & Wines (2003), by Oz Clarke and Margaret Rand. Highly readable reference describes grape varietals and the wines made from them.

Harvests of Joy: How the Good Life Became Great Business (1999), by Robert Mondavi and Paul Chutkow. Wine tycoon Robert Mondavi tells his story.

The House of Mondavi: The Rise and Fall of an American Wine Dynasty (2007), by Julia Flynn Siler. The author ruffled a lot of feathers in Napa when she published this tell-all book about the much-loved Mondavi family.

Jancis Robinson's Concise Wine Companion (2001), by Jancis Robinson. Handy paperback distillation of the second edition of Robinson's *The Oxford Companion to Wine* (⇨ *below)*.

Judgment of Paris: California vs. France and the Historic 1976 Paris Tasting That Revolutionized Wine (2005), by George M. Taber. Journalist who originally broke the story of the pivotal event analyzes its history and repercussions.

Matt Kramer's New California Wine: Making Sense of Napa Valley, Sonoma, Central Coast & Beyond (2004), by Matt Kramer. *Wine Spectator* columnist explains in entertaining detail the development of California wine and the wine industry.

Murder Uncorked (2005), *Murder by the Glass: A Wine-Lover's Mystery* (2006), and *Silenced by Syrah* (2007), by Michele Scott. Vineyard manager Nikki Sands is the protagonist of this light and humorous mystery series that unfolds in the Napa Valley.

Napa (1992), by James Conaway. The Wine Country lifestyle and local politics undergo intense scrutiny in this behind-the-scenes exposé.

Napa Valley: The Land, the Wine, the People (2001), by Charles O'Rear. A former *National Geographic* photographer portrays the valley in this lush book.

The Oxford Companion to Wine, 3rd edition (2006), by Jancis Robinson. Authoritative, comprehensive encyclopedia by one of the world's leading experts illuminates all things wine.

Sniff, Swirl & Slurp (2002), by Max Allen. Compact handbook provides guidelines on maximizing the wine-drinking experience.

When the Rivers Ran Red: An Amazing Story of Courage and Triumph in America's Wine Country (2009), by Vivienne Sosnowski. A thoroughly researched account of the devastating effect of Prohibition on Northern California winemakers.

Wine Spectator's California Wine (1999), by James Laube. *Wine Spectator* editor offers detailed background on California wineries and ratings of their wines.

Wine-Tasting, Wine & Food Matcher, Wine Vintages, and *Wine Finder* (2002), by Oz Clarke. The popular wine writer has created four pocket-size, foldout tip sheets to make buying and drinking wine easier.

Zinfandel: A History of a Grape and Its Wine (2003), by Charles Sullivan. The story of America's unique varietal is the story of California wine country.

FILMS

Bottle Shock (2008). Filmed primarily in the Napa and Sonoma valleys, this lighthearted, fictionalized feature about the 1976 Paris tasting focuses on Calistoga's Chateau Montelena.

Mondovino (2005). Documentary filmmaker Jonathan Nossiter probes the rocky relationship between the wine industries of California and Europe.

Sideways (2004). In this popular film, buddies Jack and Miles take a road trip to Santa Barbara County wine country, where they have hilarious misadventures in tasting, dating, and friendship.

7

DID YOU KNOW?

Wineries may age wine in giant stainless steel vats or wooden vats such as these; wood, particularly oak, has a profound effect on the taste and character of the wine.

Travel Smart Napa and Sonoma

WORD OF MOUTH

"Sacramento Airport (SMF) is an easy, handy airport for the Napa Valley, where we live. It's easy to get the rental car and get in and out. Depending on arrival time, there should not be an issue with traffic. It takes about an hour to make the drive."

—elnap29

GETTING HERE AND AROUND

Most travelers to the California Wine Country will start their trip in San Francisco, which is about 1½ to 2 hours south of Napa and Sonoma. Public transportation between these regions is almost nonexistent, so you'll need a car to travel between them, and to visit the wineries while you're there.

▌ AIR TRAVEL

Nonstop flights from New York to San Francisco take about 5½ hours, and with the three-hour time change, it's possible to leave JFK by 8 AM and be in San Francisco by 10:30 AM. Some flights may require a midway stop, making the total excursion between 8 and 9½ hours.

Of the major carriers, Alaska, American, Continental, Delta, Mexicana, Southwest, and United all fly into San Francisco (SFO), Oakland, and San Jose airports. JetBlue, Primaris, and US Airways service Oakland. Frontier, Hawaiian, Horizon Air (a subsidiary of Alaska Airlines), and Delta fly into SFO and San Jose. Virgin Atlantic and the budget-conscious Midwest Express fly into SFO. Only Horizon Air flies into the Sonoma County Airport (STS) in Santa Rosa.

Airline Contacts Alaska Airlines/ Horizon Air (☎ 800/252–7522 or 206/433–3100 ⊕ www.alaskaair.com). **American Airlines** (☎ 800/433–7300 ⊕ www.aa.com). **Continental Airlines** (☎ 800/523–3273 for U.S. and Mexico reservations, 800/231–0856 for international reservations ⊕ www. continental.com). **Delta Airlines** (☎ 800/221–1212 for U.S. reservations, 800/241–4141 for international reservations ⊕ www.delta.com). **Frontier Airlines** (☎ 800/432–1359 ⊕ www.frontierairlines.com). **jetBlue** (☎ 800/538–2583 ⊕ www.jetblue. com). **Midwest Airlines** (☎ 800/452–2022 ⊕ www.midwestairlines.com). **Southwest Airlines** (☎ 800/435–9792 ⊕ www.southwest.com). **United Airlines** (☎ 800/864–8331 for U.S. reservations, 800/538–2929 for international reservations ⊕ www. united.com).

AIRPORTS

The major gateway to San Francisco is San Francisco International Airport (SFO), 15 mi south of the city. It's off U.S. 101 near Millbrae and San Bruno. Oakland International Airport (OAK) is across the bay, not much farther away from downtown San Francisco (via I–80 east and I–880 south), but rush-hour traffic on the Bay Bridge may lengthen travel times considerably. San Jose International Airport (SJC) is about 40 mi south of San Francisco; travel time depends largely on traffic flow, but plan on an hour and a half with moderate traffic.

Most visitors opt to fly to San Francisco International Airport because it has the greatest number of flights. The airport is about 60 mi from the towns of Napa and Sonoma.

The smaller Oakland airport is slightly closer to Napa (50 mi) than the San Francisco airport and is a good option. If you're headed to Sonoma and want to skip passing through San Francisco, Horizon Air flies nonstop from Los Angeles and Seattle to Charles M. Schulz Sonoma County Airport (STS) in Santa Rosa, which is only 15 mi from Healdsburg in northern Sonoma. You could also fly into Sacramento International Airport (SMF), about an hour from Napa and 1½ hours from Sonoma.

At all three airports security check-in can take 15 to 30 minutes at peak travel times.

Airport Information Charles M. Schulz Sonoma County Airport (*[STS]* ☏ *707/565–7243* ⊕ *www. sonomacountyairport.org*). **Oakland International Airport** (*[OAK]* ☏ *510/563–3300* ⊕ *www.flyoakland. com*). **Sacramento International Airport** (*[SMF]* ☏ *916/929–5411* ⊕ *www.sacairports.org*). **San Francisco International Airport** (*[SFO]* ☏ *800/435–9736* ⊕ *www.flysfo. com*). **San Jose International Airport** (*[SJC]* ☏ *408/277–4759* ⊕ *www.sjc.org*).

GROUND TRANSPORTATION
FROM SAN FRANCISCO INTERNATIONAL AIRPORT

Transportation signage at the airport is color-coded by type and is quite clear. If you are going into San Francisco before heading to Napa or Sonoma, a taxi ride to downtown costs $35 to $45. Airport shuttles are inexpensive and generally efficient and cost $15 to $17. You can also take BART directly to downtown San Francisco; the trip takes about 30 minutes and costs less than $5.50. (There are both manned booths and vending machines for ticket purchases.) Trains leave from the international terminal every 15 minutes on weekdays and every 20 minutes on weekends.

Another inexpensive way to get to San Francisco is via two SamTrans buses: No. 292 (55 minutes, $1.50 from SFO, $3 to SFO) and the KX (35 minutes, $4; only one small carry-on bag permitted). Board the SamTrans buses on the lower level.

To drive to downtown San Francisco from the airport, take U.S. 101 north to the Civic Center/9th Street, 7th Street, or 4th Street/ Downtown exits. If you're headed to the Embarcadero or Fisherman's Wharf, take I–280 north (the exit is to the right, just north of the airport, off U.S. 101) and get off at the 4th Street/King Street exit. King Street becomes the Embarcadero a few blocks east of the exit. The Embarcadero winds around the waterfront to Fisherman's Wharf.

FROM OAKLAND INTERNATIONAL AIRPORT

A taxi to downtown San Francisco costs $35 to $40. By airport regulations, you must make reservations for shuttle service. The best way to get to San Francisco via public transit is to take the AIR BART bus ($3) to the Coliseum/Oakland International Airport BART station (BART fares vary depending on where you're going; the ride to downtown San Francisco from here costs $3.55).

If you're driving from Oakland International Airport, take Hegenberger Road east to I–880 north to I–80 west over the Bay Bridge. This will likely take at least an hour.

FROM SAN JOSE INTERNATIONAL AIRPORT

It's not very practical to use San Jose's airport if you are going into San Francisco first. A taxi to San Francisco runs about $140 to $150, but there are cheaper shuttle services.

To drive to downtown San Jose from the airport, take Airport Boulevard east to Route 87 south. To get to San Francisco from the airport, take Route 87 south to I–280 north. The trip will take roughly two hours.

At $7.25 for a one-way ticket, there is no question that Caltrain provides the most affordable option for traveling between San Francisco and San Jose's airport. However, the Caltrain station in San Francisco at 4th and Townsend streets is not in a conveniently central location. It's on the eastern side of the South of Market (SoMa) neighborhood and not easily accessible by other public transit. You'll need to take a taxi or walk from the nearest bus line. From San Francisco it takes 90 minutes and costs $7.50 to reach the Santa Clara Caltrain station, from which a free shuttle runs every 15 minutes, whisking you to and from the San Jose International Airport in 15 minutes.

▌ CAR TRAVEL

A car is the most logical and convenient way to navigate Napa and Sonoma. Although some thoroughfares can be congested, especially during rush hour and on summer weekends, there are plenty of less trafficked routes to explore. Parking is generally not a problem.

GASOLINE

Gas is readily available on all but the most remote back roads. Be prepared for sticker shock, however, since gas prices in California are among the highest in the United States. Major credit cards are accepted at all gas stations.

PARKING

Finding a place to leave your wheels is rarely a problem in the Wine Country, as wineries and hotels have ample free parking lots. A few towns—notably St. Helena, Sonoma, and Healdsburg—can get a bit congested during the day, but you can always find parking by driving a block or two off the main drag or taking one more lap around the plaza. Do keep an eye out, however, for signs, since many town centers have a two-hour limit until 6 PM or so. If you're going to be parked for longer, simply drive a block or two away from the center of town to find street parking without a time limit. Many towns also have reasonably priced municipal lots near the center of town; signs will generally point you in the right direction.

ROAD CONDITIONS

Roads are good in the Wine Country, whether they are four-lane highways or winding country back roads. That doesn't mean, however, that you won't run into plenty of traffic. The worst jams tend to be in and around San Francisco and on the peninsula between San Francisco and San Jose. If you're headed north from San Francisco, expect plenty of traffic on U.S. 101 around Santa Rosa, and often around San Rafael, too. Weekdays during morning and afternoon rush hours and Sunday evening tend to be the worst, but heading out of San Francisco on a summer Friday afternoon trumps them all. Traffic tends to be equally bad heading north from Oakland to Napa along I–80 north, again, especially during rush hour. For up-to-the-minute traffic info, you can log on to ⊕ www.511.org or tune your radio to KCBS, 740 AM, which broadcasts traffic news every 10 minutes.

Once you've reached the Wine Country, traffic eases up and the roads get more scenic. Still, as you cruise down the winding lanes and highways, drive carefully. You may be on vacation, but the people who live and work here are not, so expect heavier traffic during rush hours (generally between 7 and 9 AM and 4 and 6 PM). Traffic can be especially bad on Friday and Sunday afternoons, when weekenders add to the mix. Highway 29, which runs the length of Napa Valley, can be slow going in summer, especially on weekends, and it can slow to a crawl around the town of St. Helena. Some drivers in the largely rural wine regions, especially workers in a hurry during the harvest and crush season, will cross double yellow lines before blind curves to get past slow drivers. For everyone's sake, pull over at a safe turnout and let them pass.

ROADSIDE EMERGENCIES
Dial 911 to report accidents on the road and to reach police, the highway patrol, or the fire department.

RULES OF THE ROAD
To encourage carpooling during heavy traffic times, some freeways have special lanes for so-called high-occupancy vehicles (HOVs)—cars carrying more than one or two passengers. Look for the white-painted diamond in the middle of the lane. Road signs next to or above the lane indicate the hours that carpooling is in effect. If you're stopped by the police because you don't meet the criteria for travel in these lanes, expect a fine of more than $200.

Don't overindulge when you go wine tasting, and don't drive if you're planning on tasting more than a few sips. Local cops always keep an eye out for drivers who have had one too many, especially on summer weekends. If you can, bring a designated driver; if not, consider spitting when you taste. State law bans drivers from using handheld mobile telephones while operating a vehicle, and the use of seat belts in both front and back seats is required. The speed limit on city streets is 25 mph unless otherwise posted. A right turn on a red light after stopping is legal unless posted otherwise, as is a left on red at the intersection of two one-way streets. Always strap children under 60 pounds or age five into approved child-safety seats.

CAR RENTALS

Since public transportation is patchy, having a car is critical in the Wine Country. If you're flying into the area, it's almost always easiest to pick up a car at the airport (they all have rental-car service), but you'll also find car-rental companies in just about every major Wine Country town. The winding roads and beautiful landscapes of the Wine Country make it a popular place for renting specialty vehicles, especially convertibles. Many major agencies have a few on hand, but your best chance of finding one is from two San Francisco–based agencies: Specialty Rentals and City Rent-a-Car. The former specializes in high-end vehicles and arranges for airport pickup and drop-off. City Rent-a-Car also arranges airport transfers but also delivers cars to Bay Area hotels. Both agencies also rent standard vehicles at prices competitive with those of the majors.

Car-rental costs in the area vary seasonally but generally begin at $50 a day and $250 a week for an economy car with air-conditioning, automatic transmission, and unlimited mileage. This doesn't include tax on car rentals, which is 8.5%. Expect to pay almost double that or more for a sports car, convertible, or other luxury car. ■TIP→ If you're renting a specialty car, be sure to check whether there are any mileage limits: though most standard cars come with unlimited mileage, some higher-end sports cars can stick you with per-mile charges if you drive more than 100 mi a day or so. Most rental companies require you to be at least 20 years old to rent a car, but some agencies won't rent to those under 25; check when you book.

When you reserve a car, ask about cancellation penalties, taxes, drop-off charges (if you're planning to pick up the car in one city and leave it in another), and surcharges (for being under or over a certain age, for additional drivers, or for driving across state or country borders or beyond a specific distance from your point of rental). All these things can add substantially to your costs. Request car seats and extras such as GPS when you book.

Rates are sometimes—but not always—better if you book in advance or reserve through a rental agency's Web site. There are other reasons to book ahead, though: for popular destinations, during busy times of the year, or to ensure that you get certain types of cars (vans, SUVs, exotic sports cars).

Rental agencies in California aren't required to include liability insurance in the price of the rental. If you cause an accident, you may expose your assets to litigation. When in doubt about your own policy's coverage, take the liability coverage that the agency offers. If you plan to take the car out of California, ask if the policy is valid in other states or countries.

Automobile Associations U.S.: American Automobile Asso-

ciation ([AAA] ☎ 415/565-2141 ⊕ www.aaa.com); most contact with the organization is through state and regional members. **National Automobile Club** (☎ 800/622-2136 ⊕ www.thenac.com); membership is open to California residents only.

Local Agencies A-One Rent-a-Car (☎ 415/771-3978). **City Rent-a-Car** (☎ 415/861-1312 or 415/359-1331 ⊕ www.cityrentacar.com). **Specialty Rentals** (☎ 415/701-1600 or 800/400-8412 ⊕ www.specialty-rentals.com). **Super Cheap Car Rental** (☎ 650/777-9993 ⊕ www.supercheapcar.com).

Major Agencies Alamo (☎ 800/462-5266 ⊕ www.alamo.com). **Avis** (☎ 800/331-1212 ⊕ www.avis.com). **Budget** (☎ 800/527-0700 ⊕ www.budget.com). **Hertz** (☎ 800/654-3131 ⊕ www.hertz.com). **National Car Rental** (☎ 800/227-7368 ⊕ www.nationalcar.com).

▌ **TAXI TRAVEL**

Taxis aren't a common sight in the Wine Country—most visitors are driving their own rental car, or, if they're really lucky, riding in a chauffeured vehicle. Still, you might want to take a cab to and from dinner, especially if you want to indulge in a cocktail or a few glasses of vino. (Before you order a taxi, however, be sure to ask your hotel if they might be able to give you a lift to dinner. A few hotels have regularly scheduled shuttle service into the nearest town every evening, and some others might be able to offer you a lift if they happen to have the staff available.)

Cabs must be called rather than hailed. The staff at your hotel can likely provide the telephone number of the local cab company, and will usually call them for you, if asked. All cabs are metered: expect to pay a fairly steep $2.50 to $3 upon pickup and another $2.50 to $3 per mile thereafter, depending on the city you're in. Taxi drivers usually expect a 15%–20% tip for good service.

Taxi Companies Healdsburg Taxi Cab Co. (☎ 707/433-7088 ⊕ www.healdsburgtaxicab.com). **Napa Valley Cab** (☎ 707/257-6444). **Yellow Cab Co. (Sonoma County)** (☎ 707/544-4444).

ESSENTIALS

▮ COMMUNICATIONS

INTERNET

Given the California Wine Country's proximity to Silicon Valley and San Francisco, it's no surprise that it's easy to get connected almost everywhere you go. At hotels in the area, Wi-Fi is the rule rather than the exception. Access is usually free, but some properties charge (usually about $10 a day) to get connected. The rare hotel or bed-and-breakfast that doesn't have Wi-Fi might have an Ethernet cable stashed in the desk drawer: call the reception desk if you don't find it, because staffers are accustomed to dealing with high-tech execs not used to being unplugged.

Most cafés in the Wine Country also offer Wi-Fi service, often for free if you order something.

Contacts Cybercafes (⊕ *www.cybercafes.com*) lists more than 4,000 Internet cafés worldwide.

▮ EATING OUT

There is perhaps no place in the United States where you'll find food that's as consistently excellent as it is in California's Wine Country. In part you can thank the vintners and other folks in the wine industry, who spend years developing their palates—they bring a keen, appreciative attitude to the table. These winemakers know that there is no better way to show off their wines than with creative cooking, so they've encouraged a lively, top-notch food scene.

But we can't give the wine industry all the credit for those organic frisée salads and galettes made with perfectly ripe peaches. California's unique climate nurtures a rich variety of produce year-round, so Wine Country chefs are able to take advantage of ripe, local fruits and vegetables and artisanal products that simply aren't available elsewhere.

The Wine Country's top restaurants tend to serve what is often called "California cuisine," which incorporates elements of French and Italian cooking and emphasizes the use of fresh, local products. If the restaurant scene here has a weakness, it's the absence of a greater variety of cuisines. However, the number of immigrants from Central America who live here ensure that in almost any town you'll find some good, inexpensive spots selling tacos and other Latin American fare.

Vegetarians shouldn't have any trouble finding excellent choices on Wine Country menus. The region's bounty of fresh produce and California's general friendliness toward vegetarians mean that restaurants are usually willing to go out of their way to accommodate you.

The Wine Country's restaurants, though excellent, can really dent your wallet. One way to avoid sticker shock is to try restaurants at lunch, when prices are marginally lower. It also doesn't hurt to ask about a restaurant's corkage policy: some restaurants eliminate their corkage fee one night a week, or even every night, hoping to attract locals in the wine industry who would rather drink bottles from their own cellar than the restaurant's. The sheer number of restaurants means you can always find an empty table somewhere, but it pays to call ahead for a reservation, even if only a day or two before you visit. For the big-name restaurants such as Cyrus, Terra, Martini House, and Farmhouse Inn, calling a few weeks in advance is advised, though you can often get in on short notice if you're willing to eat early or late. (For the famed French Laundry, you must call two months ahead to the day.)

MEALS AND MEALTIMES

Lunch is typically served 11:30 to 3, and dinner service in most restaurants starts at 5 or 5:30 and ends around 9 or 10. The Wine Country is short on late-night dining, so don't put off eating until any later than 10, or you might end up raiding the minibar at your hotel. Most of the hotels and inns listed here offer breakfast service—anything from a basic continental breakfast to a lavish buffet to an individually prepared feast—but if it doesn't, you'll find a good bakery in just about every Wine Country town.

Many, though by no means all, restaurants close for a day or two a week, most often on Tuesday or Wednesday, when the number of visitors is fewest, so be sure to check in advance if you're planning on dinner out midweek. Unless otherwise noted, the restaurants listed in this guide are open daily for lunch and dinner.

PAYING

Almost all restaurants in the Wine Country accept credit cards. On occasion, you might find a bakery or a casual café that takes cash only. *For guidelines on tipping see* ⇨ *Tipping, below.*

RESERVATIONS AND DRESS

Restaurants throughout the Wine Country tend to be fairly casual, especially in Sonoma. This is generally less true in Napa Valley, where you're unlikely to see jeans or shorts at dinner except at the more casual restaurants. Jackets, however, are very rarely required for men. At French Laundry, though, they're necessary for both lunch and dinner. At some top-tier restaurants such as Cyrus and the Farmhouse Inn, they would certainly be appropriate.

Regardless of where you are, it's a good idea to make reservations if you can. We mention them specifically only when reservations are essential (there's no other way you'll ever get a table) or when they are not accepted. For popular restaurants, book as far ahead as you can (often 30 days), and reconfirm as soon as you arrive. (Large parties should always call ahead to check the reservations policy.) We mention dress only when men are required to wear a jacket or a jacket and tie.

Online reservation services make it easy to book a table before you even leave home. Tables at many Wine Country restaurants are available at the OpenTable and DinnerBroker Web sites.

Contacts DinnerBroker (⊕ www. dinnerbroker.com). **Open Table** (⊕ www.opentable.com).

WINES, BEER, AND SPIRITS
It should come as no surprise that wine is ubiquitous in Wine Country restaurants, and nowhere in the United States are you more likely to see someone enjoying a glass or two of wine not only with dinner, but with lunch as well. Only the smallest dives and most casual cafés lack a wine list; lists here are usually strongest in local bottles, with a smattering of French and Italian wines as well.

Many more upscale restaurants have full bars as well. Though it's legal to serve alcohol as late as 2 AM in California, most restaurants close down by 10 PM or so.

▌ FESTIVALS AND EVENTS

WINTER
Winter Wineland. In the Russian River Valley, more than 100 wineries—many of them not generally open to the public—feature seminars, tastings, and entertainment on one weekend in January. ⊕ www.wineroad.com.

Napa Valley Mustard Festival. In February and March, when Napa is at its least crowded, and wild mustard blooms in between the vines, locals celebrate wine, food, and art with exhibitions, auctions, dinners, and cooking competitions at venues throughout the valley. ⊕ www.mustardfestival.org.

SPRING
Russian River Wine Road Barrel Tasting Weekends. For two weekends in March, more than 100 Russian River wineries open their cellars to visitors who want to taste the wine in the barrels, getting a preview of what's to come. ⊕ www. wineroad.com.

Hospice du Rhône. This three-day event in Paso Robles in early May is the largest celebration of Rhône varietals in the world. ⊕ www.hospicedurhone.org.

Paso Robles Wine Festival. Most of the local wineries pour at this event held in Paso's City Park on the third weekend in May. The outdoor tasting—the largest such California event—includes live bands and upscale food vendors. ⊕ www. pasowine.com.

Sonoma Jazz + Festival. Headlining jazz performers play in a 3,800-person tent in downtown Sonoma in late May, while smaller music, food, and wine events take place around town. ☎ 866/468–8355 ⊕ www.sonomajazz.org.

SUMMER
Auction Napa Valley. The world's biggest charity wine auction, in early June, is one of Napa's glitziest nights. Dozens of events hosted by various wineries culminate in an opulent dinner and auction. ⊕ www.napavintners.com.

Santa Cruz Mountains Winegrowers & Vintners Festival. The first two weekends of June bring food, music, art exhibits, winery tours, and barrel tastings. ⊕ www.scmwa.com.

FALL

Sonoma County Harvest Fair. This festival in early October celebrates agriculture in Sonoma County, with wine tastings, cooking demos, livestock shows, crafts, carnival rides, and local entertainers filling the Sonoma County Fairgrounds in Santa Rosa. ⊕ *www.harvestfair.org.*

Paso Robles Harvest Wine Weekend. Winemaker dinners, barrel samples, cooking classes, barbecues, music performances, and winery tours take place at about 130 wineries in the Paso Robles area in mid- to late October. ⊕ *www. pasowine.com.*

Pinot on the River. Those who are passionate about pinot make their way to the Russian River Valley in late October for a weekend of tastings and seminars. ⊕ *www.pinot-festival.com.*

▌ HOURS OF OPERATION

Winery tasting rooms are generally open 10 or 11 AM to 4:30 or 5 PM. Larger wineries are usually open every day, but some of the smaller ones may open only on weekends. Tuesday and Wednesday are the quietest days of the week for wine touring. If you have a particular winery in mind, check their hours before you make the trek: many are open by appointment only.

▌ MONEY

The sweet life costs a pretty penny in most Wine Country areas, where even a basic hotel tends to cost around $200 a night. That said, it is possible to stick to a lower budget if you're willing to stay in a fairly basic motel, eat at some of the less expensive restaurants, and take advantage of the many picnicking opportunities.

ITEM	AVERAGE COST
Cup of Coffee (Not a Latte!)	$2
Glass of Wine	$11
Glass of Beer	$7
Sandwich	$9
One-Mile Taxi Ride	$6
Museum Admission	$5

Prices throughout this guide are given for adults. Substantially reduced fees are almost always available for children, students, and senior citizens.

CREDIT CARDS

Throughout this guide, the following abbreviations are used: **AE,** American Express; **D,** Discover; **DC,** Diners Club; **MC,** MasterCard; and **V,** Visa.

▌ SAFETY

The Wine Country is generally a safe place for travelers who observe all normal precautions. Most visitors will feel safe walking at night in all the smaller towns and in the downtown area of towns like Sonoma. Still, the largest towns, such as Napa and Santa Rosa, have a few rougher areas (typically far removed from where the tourists are), so you should check with a local before you go wandering in unknown neighborhoods. Car break-ins are not particularly common here, although it's always best to remove valuables from your car, or at least keep them out of sight.

The main danger you face traveling in the Wine Country is the threat of drunk drivers. Keep an eye out for drivers who may have had one too many glasses of wine, as well as for bikers who might be hidden around the next bend in the road.

▌ SPECIAL-INTEREST TOURS

CULINARY TOURS

Tours usually include one or more of the following: cooking classes, festive dinners at some of the region's better restaurants, excursions to the Culinary Institute of America or local markets, and the opportunity to meet chefs who make their home here. Tours can last from a few days to a week, and start at around $500 per day, accommodations included. Both Epiculinary and Food & Wine Trails offer itineraries tailored to Napa and Sonoma valleys. Epiculinary's tours have a stronger emphasis on cooking workshops.

Contacts Epiculinary (☎ 847/295–5363 ⊕ www.epiculinary.com). **Food and Wine Trails** (☎ 800/367–5348 ⊕ www.foodandwinetrails.com).

BICYCLING TOURS

Biking tours of the Wine Country range from one-day excursions to weeklong vacations with lavish picnic lunches, leisurely dinners, and stays at some of the region's fanciest inns. For more on companies that rent bikes, see "The Wine Country on Two Wheels" in chapter 3. The following companies focus on multiday excursions and cost about $250 to $500 per day, including

accommodations. Some companies, such as Backroads, provide guides who ride with the group and lay out extravagant picnics, whereas others will set you up with everything you need and transfer your luggage, but otherwise leave you largely on your own.

Contacts Backroads (☎ 800/462–2848 ⊕ www.backroads.com). **Napa Wine Tours** (☎ 888/881–3309 ⊕ www.napawinetours.net). **Wine Country Bikes** (☎ 707/473–0610 ⊕ www.winecountrybikes.com).

BUS, VAN, AND LIMO TOURS

Whether you're content to tour the Wine Country in a full-size bus with dozens of other passengers or you want to spring for your own private limo to take you to your favorite wineries, there are plenty of operators who can accommodate you. The following companies each offer a range of services.

Contacts California Wine Tours (☎ 800/294–6386 ⊕ www.californiawinetours.com). **Napa Wine Tours** (☎ 888/881–3309 ⊕ www.napawinetours.net). **Sonoma Wine Tours** (☎ 888/881–3309 ⊕ www.sonomawinetours.net). **Wine Country Tour Shuttle** (☎ 415/513–5400 ⊕ www.winecountrytourshuttle.com). **Wine & Dine Events and Adventures** (☎ 707/963–8930 ⊕ www.wineanddinetours.com).

▌ TAXES

Sales tax is 8.25% in Monterey and San Luis Obispo counties, 9% in Sonoma County, and 8.75% in Napa County. Nonprepared foods bought in grocery stores are exempt. The tax on hotel rooms is 9% in Sonoma County, 12% in Napa County.

TIME

California is on Pacific Time. Chicago is 2 hours ahead of the West Coast, New York is 3 hours ahead, and, depending on whether daylight saving time is in effect, London is either 8 or 9 hours ahead and Sydney is 17 or 18 hours ahead.

TIPPING

TIPPING GUIDELINES FOR NAPA AND SONOMA	
Bartender	About 15%, starting at $1 a drink at casual places
Bellhop	$1 to $5 per bag, depending on the level of the hotel
Hotel concierge	$5 or more, if he or she performs a service for you
Hotel doorman, room service, or valet	$2–$3
Hotel maid	$2–$3 a day (either daily or at the end of your stay, in cash)
Taxi Driver	15%–20%, but round up the fare to the next dollar amount
Tour Guide	10% of the cost of the tour
Waiter	15%–20%, with 20% being the norm at high-end restaurants; nothing additional if a service charge is added to the bill

VISITOR INFORMATION

Regional Contacts Napa Valley Conference and Visitors Bureau (☎ 707/226–7459 ⊕ www.napavalley.com). **Russian River Wine Road** (☎ 707/433–4335 or 800/723–6336 ⊕ www.wineroad.com). **Sonoma County Tourism Bureau** (☎ 707/522–5800 or 800/576–6662 ⊕ www.sonomacounty.com). **Sonoma Valley Visitors Bureau** (☎ 707/996–1090 or 866/996–1090 ⊕ www.sonomavalley.com).

State Contacts California Travel and Tourism Commission (☎ 916/444–4429 ⊕ www.visitcalifornia.com). **California Welcome Center** (⊕ www.visitcwc.com).

Vintners Associations Carneros Wine Alliance (⊕ www.carneros.com). **Monterey County Vintners & Growers Association** (⊕ www.montereywines.org). **Napa Valley Vintners Association** (⊕ www.napavintners.com). **Paso Robles Wine Country Alliance** (⊕ www.pasowine.com). **San Luis Obispo Vintners & Growers Association** (⊕ www.slowine.com). **Santa Barbara County Vintners' Association** (⊕ www.sbcountywines.com). **Santa Cruz Mountains Winegrowers Association** (⊕ www.scmwa.com). **Sonoma County Vintners** (⊕ www.sonomawine.com).

INDEX

Photo Credits

1-7, Robert Holmes. Chapter 1: Experience Napa and Sonoma : 8-9, Robert Holmes. 10, sddbb, Fodors.com member. 11 (left), Robert Holmes. 11 (right), Vincent Thompson, Fodors.com member. 14 (left), The Hess Collection. 14 (top right), Tori Wilder. 14 (bottom right), Far Niente+Dolce+Nickel & Nickel. 15 (top left), Laurence G. Sterling/Iron Horse Vineyards. 15 (bottom left), Matanzas Creek.15 (top right), Heidi Nigen/Ridge Vineyards. 15 (bottom right), Eric Risberg/Schramsberg Vineyards. 16, Robert Holmes. 17, di Rosa. 18, Robert Holmes. 20, michale/Flickr. Chapter 2: Visiting the Wineries : 21-38, Robert Holmes. 44, Warren H. White. 47, Beltane Ranch. Chapter 3: Napa Valley: 51, 3Neus/Flickr. 53, Robert Holmes. 55, Opus One. 71, Robert Holmes Photography. 72, OPENKITCHENPhotography. 73, Robert Holmes. 75, star5112/Flickr. 76, Robert Holmes. 82, hirohama/Flickr. 83, Far Niente+Dolce+Nickel & Nickel. 85, Olaf Beckman. 86, Terry Joanis/Frog's Leap. 92, John McJunkin. 98-101, Meadowood Napa Valley. 106, Chuck Honek/Schramsberg Vineyard. 114-15, Robert Holmes. Chapter 4: The Carneros District: 119, Robert Holmes. 123, CornerStone Sonoma. 127, Robert Holmes. 128, Robert Holmes. 129, Avis Mandel. 131, Robert Holmes. Chapter 5: Sonoma Valley: 133, Beltane Ranch. 138, Nigel Wilson/Flickr. 142, Robert Holmes. 145-47, Fairmont Hotels & Resorts. 152, Robert Holmes. 154, Matanzas Creek. 155, Robert Holmes. 156, The Fig Cafe. 158-59, Beltane Ranch. 164, jumpyjodes/Flickr. Chapter 6: Northern Sonoma County: 167, Maggie Preston. 171, Jeffrey M. Frank/Shutterstock. 172, Joe Shlabotnik/Flickr. 175, Warren H. White. 178, Laurence G. Sterling/Iron Horse Vineyards. 179, Martinelli Winery. 181, The Farmhouse Inn and Restaurant. 187, The Honor Mansion. 189, Cesar Rubio. 193, Cuvée Corner Wine Blog/Flickr. 194, Maggie Preston. 197, Jamey Thomas/Ridge Vineyards. 203, star5112/Flickr. Chapter 7:Winespeak: 205 and 212, Robert Holmes. 215, Stony Hill Vineyard. 218, Charles O'Rear.

ABOUT OUR WRITER

Sharron Wood escaped from Texas to Northern California to attend graduate school at the University of California at Berkeley. Though she wrapped up her studies many years ago, she hasn't been able to bring herself to leave the land of cult cabernet sauvignons, outstanding restaurants, and perpetually perfect weather. She has contributed to *Compass American Guides:* *California Wine Country, 6th edition* and several editions of Fodor's annual *San Francisco* guide, among other publications. When she's not traveling in the Wine Country, she edits cookbooks and writes about food and entertaining from her home in San Francisco's Mission District, where she spends most of her weekends concocting cocktails for a house full of guests.